Exploring the US Language Flagship Program

NEW PERSPECTIVES ON LANGUAGE AND EDUCATION

Series Editor: **Professor Viv Edwards**, *University of Reading, Reading, UK* and **Professor Phan Le Ha**, *University of Hawaii at Manoa.*

Two decades of research and development in language and literacy education have yielded a broad, multidisciplinary focus. Yet education systems face constant economic and technological change, with attendant issues of identity and power, community and culture. This series will feature critical and interpretive, disciplinary and multidisciplinary perspectives on teaching and learning, language and literacy in new times.

Full details of all the books in this series and of all our other publications can be found on http://www.multilingual-matters.com, or by writing to Multilingual Matters, St Nicholas House, 31-34 High Street, Bristol BS1 2AW, UK.

NEW PERSPECTIVES ON LANGUAGE AND EDUCATION: 50

Exploring the US Language Flagship Program

Professional Competence in a Second Language by Graduation

Edited by

Dianna Murphy and Karen Evans-Romaine

MULTILINGUAL MATTERS
Bristol • Buffalo • Toronto

Library of Congress Cataloging in Publication Data
A catalog record for this book is available from the Library of Congress.
Names: Murphy, Dianna, 1967- editor. | Evans-Romaine, Karen, editor.
Title: Exploring the US Language Flagship Program: Professional Competence
   in a Second Language by Graduation/Edited by Dianna Murphy and Karen
   Evans-Romaine.
Description: Bristol; Buffalo: Multilingual Matters, [2016] | Series: New Perspectives on
   Language and Education: 50 | Includes bibliographical references and index.
Identifiers: LCCN 2016022804| ISBN 9781783096091 (hbk: alk. paper) |
   ISBN 9781783096114 (epub) | ISBN 9781783096121 (kindle)
Subjects: LCSH: Language and languages--Study and teaching--United States. | Second
   language acquisition--United States. | Communicative competence--United States.
Classification: LCC P57.U7 E96 2016 | DDC 418.007073--dc23 LC record available at
   https://lccn.loc.gov/2016022804

British Library Cataloguing in Publication Data
A catalogue entry for this book is available from the British Library.

ISBN-13: 978-1-78309-609-1 (hbk)

Multilingual Matters
UK: St Nicholas House, 31-34 High Street, Bristol BS1 2AW, UK.
USA: UTP, 2250 Military Road, Tonawanda, NY 14150, USA.
Canada: UTP, 5201 Dufferin Street, North York, Ontario M3H 5T8, Canada.

Website: www.multilingual-matters.com
Twitter: Multi_Ling_Mat
Facebook: https://www.facebook.com/multilingualmatters
Blog: www.channelviewpublications.wordpress.com

The policy of Multilingual Matters/Channel View Publications is to use papers that
are natural, renewable and recyclable products, made from wood grown in sustainable
forests. In the manufacturing process of our books, and to further support our policy,
preference is given to printers that have FSC and PEFC Chain of Custody certification.
The FSC and/or PEFC logos will appear on those books where full certification has been
granted to the printer concerned.

Typeset by Deanta Global Publishing Services Limited.
Printed and bound in the UK by the CPI Books Group Ltd.
Printed and bound in the US by Edwards Brothers Malloy, Inc.

Contents

Acknowledgements

This book came about on the initiative of Language Flagship director Samuel Eisen and Professor Mahmoud Al-Batal, founding director of the University of Texas at Austin Arabic Flagship. They approached us with the idea to edit this volume, which we accepted with some trepidation, understanding that no project this ambitious can come to fruition without the work of many; thus, we gratefully acknowledge their work. We were delighted that Multilingual Matters agreed with us that this volume could make an important contribution beyond the Language Flagship, and we are tremendously grateful to Multilingual Matters for their support of this project, and for the prompt and informative responses of Kim Eggleton, Florence McClelland and Sarah Williams to our many questions throughout the editorial process. We thank the copy editors for their meticulous review of the manuscript. We are also very grateful to our anonymous reviewer for comments that helped us improve this volume.

In many ways, as we hope this volume will demonstrate, a successful academic program is based on collegiality and trust, as well as a sense of common goals. We are very fortunate to work with inspiring and generous colleagues. The contributors to this volume were not only stimulating interlocutors, but models of kindness, tact and patience in responding to our comments and requests for further information and clarification. We not only corresponded, as would authors and editors in any scholarly collection, but we also met annually at Language Flagship meetings to discuss the project at every stage. As the volume was coming together, authors read each other's work and provided valuable feedback to each other and to us. We worked very much as a team.

The completion and production of this book would have been if not impossible, then likely the work of at least a dozen years, had we not had the constant and invaluable assistance of two brilliant and conscientious graduate assistants at the University of Wisconsin–Madison: Colleen Hamilton, PhD candidate in the doctoral program in second language acquisition, and Melissa Miller, PhD candidate in the Department of Slavic Languages and Literature. Colleen and Melissa made tremendous editorial contributions to this volume, from the bird's-eye perspective, with eagle-eye focus on details, to the microscopic but no less important. They not only ensured the consistency and editorial cohesiveness of this volume, but provided countless substantive insights as colleagues entering our profession blessed with rich knowledge and experience in the theory and practice of second language learning and teaching, while working outside the Flagship (in Colleen's case), or inside as a graduate teaching assistant and tutor (in Melissa's case). Throughout the editorial stages of this book, they have served as models of professionalism and tireless assistants in a vast array of tasks. As the book neared production, we were extremely fortunate to have the assistance of Sandrine Pell, PhD candidate in the doctoral program in second language acquisition, who helped with the thankless task of creating the index.

The assistance of these graduate students, and our annual gatherings with authors, would not have been possible without the financial support of the Language Flagship, the administration of which was provided by the Institute for International Education (IIE). Both Samuel Eisen and Edward McDermott at the National Security Education Program (NSEP) were very generous in providing us with vital statistical data and information about Language Flagship programs in all their variety. Staff at IIE provided us with prompt and able assistance, as well as the flexibility that allowed us to continue relying on the editorial ministrations provided by Colleen and Melissa. Both NSEP and IIE were careful at every stage, however, to respect the independence without which scholarly work cannot exist, and we are grateful to them for that space as well.

Abbreviations

A-level	Pre-university level in United Kingdom educational system
AAUP	American Association of University Professors
ACTFL	American Council on the Teaching of Foreign Languages
AI	Assistant instructor
AIIS	American Institute for India Studies
ARK	Assessment of Regional Knowledge
AS-units	Analysis of Speech Units
BYU	Brigham Young University
CAL	Center for Applied Linguistics
CALLM	Chinese Academic Language Learning Modules
CBI	Content-based instruction
CED	Committee for Economic Development
CEO	Chief executive officer
CFR	Council on Foreign Relations
CIC	Competence in intercultural communication
CLIL	Content and language integrated learning
DO	[Intercultural] development orientation
ERASMUS	European Region Action Scheme for the Mobility of University Students
ETS	Educational Testing Service
EU	European Union
EX-LL	Experiential language learning
FLMI	Foreign Language Medium Instruction
FL	Foreign language

FLAC	Foreign Language Across the Curriculum
FIPSE	Fund for the Improvement of Postsecondary Education
FLAS	Foreign Language and Area Studies
GRANT	General Regional Aptitude Network Test
HASC	US House of Representatives Armed Services Committee
HLL	Heritage language learner
IC	Intercultural competence
ICFL	Integrated Content and Foreign Language
IDC	Intercultural Development Continuum
IDI	Intercultural Development Inventory
IEP	International Engineering Program
ILI	Individualized Language Instruction
ILR	Interagency Language Roundtable
IT	Information technology
K-12	Kindergarten through 12th Grade in US public school system
L1	First language
L2	Second language, target language of study
LMS	Learning Management System
LOE	Language other than English
LPAC	Language Policy Advisory Committee (University of Texas at Austin)
LRE	Language-related episodes
LSP	Language for specific purposes
LTI	Language Testing International
LUNN	Linguistics University of Nizhnyi Novgorod
LUR	Language Utilization Report
MA	Master of arts
MAPP	Mobile Attrition Prevention Program
MIT	Massachusetts Institute of Technology
MLA	Modern Language Association
NCATE	National Council for Accreditation of Teacher Education

NGO	Non-governmental organization
NFLI	National Flagship Language Initiative
NFLRC	National Foreign Language Resource Center
NSEP	National Security Education Program
NSLI-Y	National Security Language Initiative for Youth
OG	Orientation gap
OPI	Oral Proficiency Interview
OPIc	Oral Proficiency Interview by computer
PLUS	Partners for Languages in the United States
PO	Perceived [intercultural] orientation
post-BA	Post bachelor of arts
RAC	Russian across the Curriculum
RLASP	Russian Language and Areas Studies
ROF	Russian Overseas Flagship
SA	Study abroad
SCH	Student credit hours
SCS	Student Certification System (Flagship)
SLA	Second language acquisition
STEM	Science, technology, engineering and math
TCFL	Teaching Chinese as a foreign language
TIOPI	Truncated Institutional Oral Proficiency Interview
TLC	Texas Language Center
UMD	University of Maryland
UNESP	Universidade Estadual Paulista (State University of São Paulo, Brazil)
UO	University of Oregon
USED	US Department of Education
UT Austin	University of Texas at Austin
UW–Madison	University of Wisconsin–Madison
WPM	Words per minute
YES	[Kennedy Lugar] Youth Exchange and Study Abroad Program
ZAP	Zone of Actual Development
ZPD	Zone of Proximal Development

Contributors

Mahmoud Al-Batal (PhD, University of Michigan) is Professor of Arabic and founding director of the Arabic Flagship at The University of Texas at Austin. He specializes in applied linguistics and teaching Arabic as a foreign language. He is co-author of the *Al-Kitaab* Arabic textbook series published by Georgetown University Press.

Anna Alsufieva (PhD, Herzen State Pedagogical University) is Assistant Professor of Russian and assistant director of the Russian Flagship at Portland State University. She is a specialist in Russian grammar, syntax, stylistics and teaching methodology. She is co-author of *Advanced Russian through History* (Yale, 2007) and author of two other Russian language textbooks. Her current research is in corpus linguistics.

Valerie Anishchenkova (PhD, University of Michigan) is Director of the Arabic Flagship and Associate Professor of Arabic Literature and Culture at the University of Maryland. Her current scholarly interests are identity studies, cultural discourses on war and the relationship between culture and new forms of media. She is the author of *Autobiographical Identities in Contemporary Arab Culture* (Edinburgh University Press, 2014).

Sharon Bain (PhD, Bryn Mawr College) formerly served as Lecturer in Russian and as co-director of the Bryn Mawr Russian Flagship Program at Bryn Mawr College, where she is now Associate Director of Institutional Grants. Her research and teaching interests include second language acquisition, Russian folklore and Russian cultural history.

Dan E. Davidson (PhD, Harvard University) is President of the American Councils for International Education and Professor of Russian and second language acquisition at Bryn Mawr College. He has published extensively in the fields of language, culture and educational development, including a major longitudinal study of adult SLA.

Samuel Eisen (PhD, Stanford University) is Director of the Language Flagship at the National Security Education Program. He has managed international education and exchange programs at the US Department of Education, the US Department of State and the US Information Agency, and taught Russian language, literature and culture at American University.

Karen Evans-Romaine (PhD, University of Michigan) is Professor of Russian and Director of the Russian Flagship at the University of Wisconsin–Madison. She is a co-author of *Golosa: A Basic Course in Russian* and co-editor of the Routledge *Encyclopedia of Contemporary Russian Culture*. Her research is in Russian language pedagogy and 20th-century Russian poetry.

Sandra Freels (PhD, Stanford University) is Professor Emerita of Russian Language and Literature at Portland State University. Specializing in Russian language, literature and cultural history, she served as Head of the Russian Program (1981–2014) and Director of the Russian Flagship Center (2008–2014). She is co-author of *Focus on Russian* and *The Golden Age: Readings in Russian Literature of the Nineteenth Century*, and sole author of *Russian in Use*.

Nadra Garas (MA, American University in Cairo) is Research Director at American Councils for International Education. She manages and conducts research and program evaluation for grants held by the American Councils, as well as research on survey methods. She is the co-author of articles on survey research methodology. Garas is an IDI-qualified administrator and works extensively on related data.

Thomas Jesús Garza (EdD, Harvard University) is Distinguished Teaching Associate Professor of Slavic and Eurasian Studies and Director of the Texas Language Center and Arabic Flagship Program at the University of Texas at Austin. He has written or contributed to several English and Russian language textbooks and has published numerous articles on language pedagogy and contemporary Russian culture. His current research examines the outcomes of intensive language instruction.

Christian Glakas (MA, University of Texas at Austin) is assistant director of the Arabic Flagship Program at the University of Texas at Austin. He previously served as the employment program supervisor at Refugee Services of Texas, where he worked with Iraqi refugees to help them secure employment in Austin.

Peter John Glanville (PhD, University of Texas at Austin) is Associate Director of the Arabic Flagship Program at The University of Maryland.

His pedagogical interests focus on materials design and curriculum development.

Fernanda Guida (PhD, University of Georgia) is Director of the Lauder Portuguese Language and Culture Program at the University of Pennsylvania. Her experience teaching Portuguese encompasses her involvement with the Portuguese Flagship at the University of Georgia in the United States and Brazil. Her research interests include Brazilian literature, film studies and foreign language education.

Victoria Hasko (PhD, Pennsylvania State University) is Associate Professor of TESOL and World Language Education at the University of Georgia. She investigates the dynamics of second language development as it interrelates with students' learning histories and sociocultural milieus, with a particular interest in comparing digitally mediated telecollaborative and face-to-face learning environments.

Mary Elizabeth Hayes (MA, University of Florida) is a PhD student in World Language Education at the University of Georgia, where she served as graduate assistant in the World Language Education and TESOL Endorsement programs within the College of Education. She currently conducts effectiveness and academic research for Open English, a global leader in online EFL education and technology.

Zhuo Jing-Schmidt (PhD, University of Cologne, Germany) is Associate Professor of Chinese Linguistics at the University of Oregon. Her research focuses on the interface of language structure, discourse pragmatics, emotion in language and Chinese second language acquisition. She is on the editorial boards of *Chinese Language and Discourse* and the *Journal of the Chinese Language Teachers Association*.

Olga Kagan (PhD, Pushkin Russian Language Institute, Moscow) is Professor in the Department of Slavic, East European and Eurasian Languages and Cultures and Director of the Russian Flagship and Title VI National Heritage Language Resource Center at UCLA. Her research focuses on proficiency-based teaching for heritage language learners. She is co-author of 12 textbooks for heritage speakers and second language (L2) learners of Russian.

Olesya Kisselev (MA, Portland State University) is a PhD candidate in Applied Linguistics at Pennsylvania State University. As an instructor in the Portland State University Russian Flagship, she developed curricula and materials for Flagship courses. Her research focuses on the development of writing ability in advanced learners of Russian as a heritage language and L2.

Viviane Klen Alves (MA, University of Georgia) is a PhD student in TESOL and World Language Education and graduate assistant for the Portuguese Flagship at the University of Georgia. She has published on reading and writing, second language acquisition and bilingual education and bilingualism.

Maria D. Lekic (PhD, University of Pennsylvania) is Associate Professor of Russian at the University of Maryland and Academic Director of the Russian Overseas Flagship in St. Petersburg, Russia and Almaty, Kazakhstan. She is author and co-author of several research studies and major textbooks.

Cynthia Martin (PhD, University of Pennsylvania) is Associate Professor of Russian at the University of Maryland. Her scholarly interests include second language acquisition and assessment (theory and practice) and contemporary Russian culture and art. She is the author of numerous publications, including the intermediate-level Russian textbook *Welcome Back!* An ACTFL OPI-certified tester and trainer, she is involved in national assessment initiatives for academia, government and business.

Robert Moser (PhD, Brown University) is Associate Professor of Portuguese and Director of the Portuguese Flagship at the University of Georgia. Aside from publications on Luso-Brazilian literature, Moser has been at the forefront of integrating telecollaborative learning into Portuguese curriculum and published a study on the role of student motivation for choosing Portuguese at the university level.

Dianna Murphy (PhD, Ohio State University) is Associate Director of the Language Institute and the Russian Flagship Program at the University of Wisconsin–Madison. In addition to numerous research articles, she is co-author of the MLJ monograph, *The Goals of Collegiate Learners and the Standards for Foreign Language Learning*. Her current research examines the alignment of national and local frameworks for foreign language education with student goals for their learning.

Michael Nugent (PhD, Pennsylvania State University) is Director of the Defense Language National Security Education Office and the National Security Education Program, where he provides guidance on policy and programs related to foreign language, culture and regional expertise. He oversees initiatives designed to attract, recruit and train a federal workforce skilled in languages and culture. He has managed international, language and cultural education programs at the US Department of Education, including Title VI National Resource Centers.

Robert Slater (PhD, American University) is co-director of the American Councils Research Center, co-directing a US government-funded study examining the impact of dual-language immersion programs on K-12 academic performance. As Director of the National Security Education Program (1992–2010), he was the principal architect of the Language Flagship. He has published in major scholarly journals and has edited three books focusing on global transformation, revolution and political change.

Madeline K. Spring (PhD, University of Washington) is Professor of Chinese, Director of the Chinese Language Flagship and co-director of the Language Flagship Technology Innovation Center at the University of Hawai'i at Mānoa. Her research interests are divided between medieval Chinese literature and current issues in teaching Chinese as a foreign language, e.g. curricular design and implementation, content-based instruction and linguistic and cultural literacy.

Introduction

Karen Evans-Romaine and Dianna Murphy

This volume is the first devoted to sharing research, instructional practices and curricular and programmatic models in US undergraduate Language Flagship programs. The Language Flagship[1] is a federally funded initiative, launched in 2002, that provides opportunities for US undergraduate students in any area of specialization to reach a professional level of competence in a targeted second language (L2)[2] by graduation. Students who successfully complete a Language Flagship program achieve an L2 proficiency rating of 3 on the Interagency Language Roundtable (ILR) scale used by the US federal government, or Superior on the scale adapted for academic purposes by the American Council on the Teaching of Foreign Languages (ACTFL) (Appendix A). This level, roughly equivalent to C1 on the scale of the Common European Framework of Reference,[3] is the minimum set by many US federal government agencies for positions that require proficiency in a language other than English, but one rarely achieved by US undergraduates.

The innovative practices that enable US undergraduate students to achieve this goal – even those students with no exposure to the L2 prior to matriculation to the university – is the subject of many of the contributions to this volume. Individual chapters highlight many aspects of Language Flagship programs, such as an emphasis on the articulation of learning outcomes on functional abilities in the L2, in addition to knowledge-based goals; various forms of language study across the curriculum; independent learning; technology to enhance language and cultural learning and proficiency development; an adaptive, inclusive approach that takes into account the needs of students with different language backgrounds (e.g. heritage students as well as students who begin study of the L2 at the college level); the assessment of both language proficiency and intercultural development; professional internships as an integral part of capstone overseas programs; and program evaluation that includes examination of the program's impact on alumni.

Contributors to this book are directors and other scholars affiliated with Language Flagship programs or leaders of the Language Flagship in the US Department of Defense. Their scholarship, presented here, builds on previous research from Language Flagship programs on topics such as curricular and program design (Eisen, 2014; Falsgraf & Bourgerie, 2008;

Falsgraf & Spring, 2007; Spring, 2012, 2015; van Olphen, 2008), heritage learners in Language Flagship programs (Davidson & Lekic, 2013; Kagan & Kudyma, 2012), individualized instruction (Christensen & Bourgerie, 2015) and language gain in overseas Flagship programs (Davidson, 2010, 2015; Davidson & Lekic, 2010); and presented in collections of articles on these and other aspects of Russian and Chinese Flagship Programs, respectively, in special focus issues of the *Russian Language Journal* (Lekic *et al.*, 2012) and the *Journal of Chinese Teaching and Research in the U.S.* (Jiao & Huang, 2012). Perhaps more importantly, this volume contributes more broadly to the growing body of research in the United States devoted to understanding and promoting the development of L2 abilities beyond the ACTFL Advanced (ILR 2) level (see, for example, Leaver & Shekhtman, 2002), especially in the context of US higher education (for example, Brown & Bown, 2015; Byrnes *et al.*, 2010).

The first chapter is co-authored by Michael Nugent and Robert Slater, leaders in the establishment of the Language Flagship and current and former (respectively) directors of the National Security Education Program (NSEP) in the US Department of Defense, whose initiatives include the Language Flagship. Their chapter outlines the rationale for the Language Flagship program and describes its establishment and history. The authors highlight the national need in the United States – a need that, the authors argue, was not being met by US institutions of higher learning – for specialists in a variety of disciplines who have a professional-level command of languages deemed critical to the interests of the US government. The authors envision the Language Flagship as meeting two challenges: to raise expectations regarding language proficiency levels at the post-secondary level and to address structural gaps in the curricula of many US L2 programs. Thus, the proficiency target for students in Language Flagship programs was set at an unprecedented level of ILR 3, or ACTFL Superior. The authors describe how the Language Flagship initiative provided grant funding to universities to establish innovative curricula on US campuses that would enable students with a variety of specializations to meet the high expectations of the program, and to assess students' developing proficiency through the creation and regular administration of proficiency-based assessments in the targeted L2. This funding was (and is) allocated on the conditions of institutional accountability in meeting stated objectives and local institutionalization of new instructional and assessment practices. In addition, Flagship funding has required from the outset that all Flagship programs integrate both domestic and overseas study, including a capstone year of immersion in the language and culture through study in a country where the target language is dominant. Capstone overseas programs must include direct enrollment in courses at the host university, targeted instruction geared toward achievement of proficiency at ILR 3 and a professional internship to provide experience using the language in a workplace setting. Nugent and Slater close their chapter with data on the outcomes of the Flagship to date and a description of how the federal initiative has aimed to develop a collaborative 'community of innovators' committed to the Flagship's goals.

Chapter 2, by the editors of this volume together with two other Flagship program directors, Valerie Anishchenkova and Zhuo Jing-Schmidt, provides a more detailed overview of these shared goals and common characteristics of Flagship programs, focusing on several examples of their implementation in three US Flagship programs: in Arabic at the University of Maryland, Chinese at the University of Oregon and Russian at the University of Wisconsin–Madison. The shared program characteristics described in Chapter 2 include a persistent focus on language development and proficiency-based assessments throughout the student's course of study; options for intensive and accelerated programs of study, as well as advanced coursework on the home campus that prepares students for advanced overseas study; opportunities for disciplinary learning in the L2, connecting the student's L2 development with learning in other subject areas; focused attention and support for individual learners, including individual or small-group tutoring in the L2; extensive co- and extra-curricular programming that provides opportunities for language use outside of traditional classroom environments; and articulated domestic and overseas programs of study, with direct enrollment and professional internships during advanced overseas study on a capstone program that targets ILR 3 proficiency in the L2.

Chapter 3, by the former director and other scholars formerly or currently affiliated with the Portland State University Russian Flagship, Sandra Freels, Olesya Kisselev and Anna Alsufieva, explores the many forms that interdisciplinary language learning takes in Flagship programs. Information for this chapter came from a variety of sources, including a 2011 survey of Flagship programs and a 2014 survey of Flagship directors. What emerges is a kaleidoscope of variations. Examples range from courses in subject areas such as economics, taught in Chinese at a US university and open to both Flagship students studying Chinese and international students from China, to individualized approaches including tutorials in the L2 with a disciplinary specialist, to community-based service learning and internship opportunities in the L2, with various Language Across the Curriculum models in between. As the authors point out, each model presents its own advantages and challenges, from the curricular to the structural and the budgetary.

An approach that emphasizes individual learning is the focus of Chapter 4, by Peter John Glanville, University of Maryland Arabic Flagship. Glanville describes a model for developing learning strategies by training students to notice and document from a written or spoken text language features that are new to them, and then to incorporate those new features into their own discourse. This model incorporates both 'top-down' and 'bottom-up' strategies: students learn to build global comprehension and to hone in on micro-portions of new texts, focusing in their analysis on those elements that are both new and salient to them, making logically supported guesses and checking their conclusions. The model also features pair and small-group activities involving discussion of recorded oral and written assignments, in order to foster further learning through retelling, discussion and peer feedback.

Chapters 5 and 6 focus on two approaches to using network-based technologies to enhance learning both inside and outside of the classroom. The authors of Chapter 5, Victoria Hasko, Robert Moser, Fernanda Guida, Mary Elizabeth Hayes and Viviane Klen Alves, focus on a joint project in telecollaboration between the Portuguese Flagship at the University of Georgia and the State University of São Paulo, Brazil, in which students communicated via Skype during class, in both Portuguese and English, as part of a semester-long language course. The authors of the study examined the effects of this telecollaboration on the spoken abilities of Portuguese Flagship students, as shown through measurements of fluency, repair fluency and syntactic complexity in truncated, pre- and post-course institutional oral proficiency interviews (TIOPIs). The study also focused on varieties of collaborative assistance that was solicited, offered and appropriated during these sessions.

Chapter 6, co-authored by Sharon Bain, former co-director of the Russian Flagship at Bryn Mawr College, and Madeline K. Spring, director of the Chinese Flagship and co-director of the Language Flagship Technology Innovation Center at the University of Hawai'i at Mānoa, describes another technology-mediated instructional project: two online collaborative-learning communities, or 'language cafés', developed by instructors from Chinese and Russian Language Flagship programs in cooperation with the National Foreign Language Resource Center (NFLRC) at the University of Hawai'i at Mānoa. These online language cafés, inspired by the Massachusetts Institute of Technology's *Cultura* Project, brought together students from US Flagship programs and students from China and Russia, respectively, into asynchronous online written discussion forums alternating between English and the L2. Student responses to surveys about the cafés suggest significant cultural learning experiences.

Chapter 7, by Olga Kagan, director of the Russian Flagship and the National Heritage Language Resource Center (NHLRC) at the University of California, Los Angeles, and Cynthia Martin, University of Maryland, draws on the results of two surveys, one of Flagship directors and one of heritage speakers in Flagship programs, and on the results of a study on heritage speakers' language proficiency conducted by the NHLRC and ACTFL. Working with data from these sources, this chapter focuses on the inclusion of a group of students with great likelihood of high-level achievement: heritage language learners, students who 'speak a language other than English in the home, exclusively or in combination with English, while using English in most other interactions and in all educational settings' (Kagan & Dillon, 2004) and who are studying that language formally in an educational context. The authors point out that those very advantages which heritage students, in comparison with L2 learners, bring to the foreign language classroom – most notably, their greater fluency in the language, their deeper knowledge of the target culture and their greater sense of cultural difference in general – can become disadvantages when they study abroad. The authors make several recommendations for adapting Flagship programs to meet the needs of heritage learners, from individualized instruction to a shortened study abroad period. Most importantly, as Kagan has stressed in other publications as well (see, for example, Kagan & Dillon, 2004), the authors emphasize that instruction of heritage speakers should focus not on deficits to be repaired, but on strengths to be developed, as heritage speakers bring deeper cultural knowledge to their study and could, with further study and cultural immersion, serve as great resources in various workplace settings.

Along with language proficiency, one of the foremost goals of the Language Flagship is the development of intercultural competence. Chapter 8, by Dan Davidson, Nadra Garas and Maria Lekic, American Councils for International Education, examines the relationship between language proficiency as measured by the ACTFL Oral Proficiency Interview (OPI) and intercultural development as measured by the Intercultural Development Inventory (IDI), in a study abroad setting. The authors posit that language proficiency both influences and is influenced by intercultural development. Data from this important study indicate that overseas immersion, with or without language study but featuring a carefully structured curriculum, has a positive influence on students' intercultural development at all levels of language study, but most notably at early and middle stages, providing a rationale for overseas immersion at earlier stages.

Among the salient features of effective study abroad programs in promoting intercultural development noted in Davidson *et al.* are professional internships. Chapter 9, authored by Language Flagship director Samuel Eisen, describes the goals and structure of several Flagship overseas internship programs. Eisen discusses academic support systems to help students maximize language proficiency gains and cultural learning in their internships; he then turns to a discussion of student reflections on their overseas internship experiences. Students' observations on their experiences and insights gained from internships provide support for the conclusions in Davidson *et al.*: internships in an immersion setting promote the development of various intercultural competencies.

In Chapter 10, Mahmoud Al-Batal and Christian Glakas of the Arabic Flagship at the University of Texas at Austin present the results of their extensive survey of Language Flagship alumni in all languages with

Flagship programs, focusing on alumni perceptions of the program and its usefulness for the development of their intercultural awareness and global perspectives, intellectual development, career development or further academic study and development of communication skills necessary for success in graduate school and employment. The authors encourage discussion among alumni, educational institutions and employers to gain further information about the skills necessary for jobs requiring high-level foreign language proficiency and how educators can better prepare students for such positions.

The final chapter in this volume addresses one of the most important questions that readers are likely to ask with regard to the Language Flagship: how can Flagship-like principles and aspects of the program's design be applied when federal or other outside funding is not available? Thomas Garza, Director of the Texas Language Center and the Arabic Flagship at the University of Texas at Austin, shares the perspective of someone from outside the Flagship who oversaw the adoption of practices for intensive language learning that come as close as possible to those embedded in the Flagship. Garza describes the establishment of an intensive program of language study at the University of Texas at Austin in which students complete two years' worth of instruction in certain foreign languages within one year. While this model was borne of economic necessity and requires intensive instructor training, it produced extraordinarily positive results: high post-program language proficiency scores, robust participation in summer study abroad programs after the academic-year intensive course and unexpectedly higher retention rates in third-year language classes. Garza closes on an even more optimistic note: the founding in 2013 of Partners for Language in the United States (PLUS), a national non-profit organization of language programs dedicated to establishing and maintaining high standards for post-secondary L2 programs through a process of accreditation based on external peer review by fellow institutional members. Given ever-declining federal and state resources, accreditation requirements to establish and assess program learning outcomes and pressures to adapt to new teaching methods in order to accommodate the larger classes and lower contact hours likely to result from increasing economic pressures, this organization could provide a way to bring Flagship-like principles of intensive language instruction in and outside the classroom, proficiency-based assessment and accountability to a far greater number of language programs. Educational institutions, language teaching and our students will benefit.

The volume concludes with closing remarks by the co-editors that describe, from the perspective of program directors, some of the challenges in establishing and sustaining Language Flagship programs on US campuses. The challenges have been and remain formidable, but the goals articulated above are well worth the effort. We hope that readers of this volume will agree.

Notes

(1) In this volume, the 'Language Flagship' (also Flagship) is used to refer to the federal initiative and to the collective efforts of faculty, staff and students to meet the initiative's goals. Programs at individual universities are referred to as Language Flagship programs, or by title (e.g. the Arabic Flagship Program at the University of Maryland).
(2) The languages that are funded through the Language Flagship at the time of this writing are Arabic, Chinese, Hindi, Korean, Persian, Portuguese, Russian, Swahili, Turkish and Urdu. See Appendix B for a list of US and overseas universities in which these programs are housed.
(3) See Tschirner (2012) for a discussion of some of the issues involved in establishing correspondences between these frameworks and the Common European Framework of Reference.

References

Brown, T. and Bown, J. (eds) (2015) *To Advanced Proficiency and Beyond: Theory and Methods for Developing Superior Second Language Ability.* Washington, DC: Georgetown University Press.

Byrnes, H., Maxim, H. and Norris, J. (2010) Realizing advanced foreign language writing development in collegiate education: Curricular design, pedagogy, assessment. *Modern Language Journal* 94 (s1), 1–235.

Christensen, M. and Bourgerie, D. (2015) Chinese for special purposes: Individualized instruction as a bridge to overseas direct enrollment. In T. Brown and J. Bown (eds) *To Advanced Proficiency and Beyond: Theory and Methods for Developing Superior Second Language Ability* (pp. 87–103). Washington, DC: Georgetown University Press.

Davidson, D.E. (2010) Study abroad: When, how long, and with what results? *Foreign Language Annals* 43 (1), 6–26.

Davidson, D.E. (2015) The development of L2 proficiency and literacy within the context of the federally supported overseas language training programs for Americans. In T. Brown and J. Bown (eds) *To Advanced Proficiency and Beyond: Theory and Methods for Developing Superior Second Language Ability* (pp. 117–150). Washington, DC: Georgetown University Press.

Davidson, D.E. and Lekic, M. (2010) The overseas immersion setting as the contextual learning variable in adult SLA: Learning behaviors associated with language gain to level-3 proficiency in Russian. *Russian Language Journal* 60, 55–78.

Davidson, D.E. and Lekic, M. (2013) The heritage and non-heritage learner in the overseas immersion context: Comparing learning outcomes and target-language utilization in the Russian Flagship. *Heritage Language Journal* 10 (2), 88–114.

Eisen, S. (2014) The Flagship model and the humanities. *Russian Language Journal* 64, 5–23.

Falsgraf, C. and Spring, M.K. (2007) Innovations in language learning: The Oregon Chinese Flagship model. *Journal of the National Council of Less Commonly Taught Languages* 4, 1–16.

Falsgraf, C. and Bourgerie, D. (2008) The Language Flagship: Multiple approaches to creating global professionals. In S. Laughlin (ed.) *U.S.-China Educational Exchange* (pp. 83–97). New York: Institute of International Education.

Jiao, D. and Huang, Y. (eds) (2012) Special Issue for the Language Flagship. *The Journal of Chinese Teaching and Research in the U.S.* 4.

Kagan, O., and Dillon, K. (2004) Heritage speakers' potential for high-level language proficiency. In H. Byrnes and H. Maxim (eds) *Advanced Foreign Language Learning:*

A Challenge to College Programs. Issues in Language Program Direction (pp. 99–112). Boston, MA: Heinle.

Kagan, O. and Kudyma, A. (2012) Heritage language learners of Russian and L2 learners in the Flagship Program: A comparison. *Russian Language Journal* 62, 27–46.

Leaver, B.L. and Shekhtman, B. (eds) (2002) *Developing Professional Language Proficiency.* Cambridge: Cambridge University Press.

Lekic, M.D., Gorham, M. and Rivers, W.P. (eds) (2012) The Russian Language Flagship: Results 2012 [special issue]. *Russian Language Journal* 62.

Spring, M.K. (2012) Languages for specific purposes curriculum in the context of Chinese-Language Flagship Programs. *Modern Language Journal* 96 (s1), 140–157.

Spring, M.K. (2015) The monolingual international: Support of language learning through national initiatives. *ADFL Bulletin* 43 (2), 19–25.

Tschirner, E. (ed.) (2012) *Aligning Frameworks of Reference in Language Testing: The ACTFL Proficiency Guidelines and the Common European Framework of Reference for Languages.* Tubingen: Stauffenburg Verlag.

van Olphen, H. (2008) A new model for teaching South Asian languages: The University of Texas Hindi-Urdu Flagship. *South Asia Language Pedagogy and Technology* 1. See http://hindiurduflagship.org/assets/pdf/2008_01_01_SALPAT.pdf (accessed 17 September 2015).

1 The Language Flagship: Creating Expectations and Opportunities for Professional-Level Language Learning in Undergraduate Education

Michael Nugent and Robert Slater

Introduction

This chapter describes the first decade of the Language Flagship, beginning with a discussion of the national need for a systematic approach to creating opportunities for advanced- to superior-level language learning in US post-secondary education. It discusses how the Language Flagship was developed within the context of language education in US higher education and follows with an analysis of the initial implementation and subsequent evolution as the Flagship began involving increasing numbers of institutions of higher education, faculty and students. The chapter covers the programmatic decisions that established clear expectations necessary for professional-level language learning outcomes at universities while at the same time creating the realistic opportunities for undergraduate students to achieve proficiency. It discusses how the Language Flagship strived to maintain a balance between a process driven by federal needs and one that represented a strategic investment in the development of capacity and expertise to address a fundamental long-term shift in philosophy and approach.

The Flagship Concept

The Language Flagship is one of the more important national innovations to language learning within the US higher education system. Flagship established for the first time a responsible and accountable partnership between the federal government and higher education with a goal to produce high-level language proficiency skills, identified as a critical shortfall by the national security community throughout the 1980s and 90s (U.S. House of Representatives Committee on Armed Services, 2008). The events of 9/11 served to galvanize support for efforts to challenge higher education to enable students to graduate with certified foreign language proficiency. A 2002 review of the US Department of Defense language requirements identified the Interagency Language Roundtable (ILR) Level 3 (Appendix A), General Professional Proficiency, as the target proficiency level necessary for professionals to perform their duties adequately. College and university graduates with such language skills were seen as an important new resource for a civilian workforce (U.S. House of Representatives Committee on Armed Services, 2005). Increasingly, the need for such high-level language expertise was also felt in the private and non-profit sectors (National Security Education Program [NSEP], 2009).

Why was this expertise so difficult to find? Unlike most other countries, the US elementary and secondary school system has not historically recognized proficiency-based second language learning as a priority, particularly following an era of educational reform defined by efforts to test in other core areas (Rosenbusch, 2005). Fewer than 25% of colleges and universities require prior language study for entrance (Modern Language Association [MLA] Ad Hoc Committee on Foreign Languages, 2007); the US higher education system in general has not focused on language proficiency development as a skill set across the undergraduate curriculum. Instead, most language departments have defined their roles in terms of the foreign language major, emphasizing literature studies over more measureable language skills (MLA Ad Hoc Committee on Foreign Languages, 2007). In responding to this dilemma, the Language Flagship concept rests on a clearly defined purpose of challenging a limited set of universities to create a pool of educated university graduates with demonstrated professional-level language proficiency in speaking, listening, reading and writing (NSEP, 2004).

Creating the capability to reach these proficiency goals presented significant challenges to US higher education. The liberal arts tradition of the US higher education system has contributed to a form of undergraduate study in the United States that is unique in providing a wide array of course requirements and electives that, in some ways, resembles the broader curriculum and requirements in advanced secondary schools in other countries (Geiger, 1986, 2015). As Clark (1985) has pointed out, such a broad focus of requirements within the US undergraduate curriculum has in some ways relieved US high schools from providing a similar preparation for US students in high school, creating a situation where basic language acquisition is a part of the US higher education curriculum along with students' major concentrations and other elective courses. Unfortunately, despite the ubiquitous rhetoric about globalization by many university leaders over the last two decades, fewer universities require language study for graduation, and the overall enrollments in foreign language remain low relative to those in many other industrialized countries (Skorton & Altschuler, 2012).

Producing such capabilities in US college graduates in meaningful numbers and making language learning available to a broader cross section of students (i.e. to those whose area of specialization is not in language) meant that a critical mass of higher education institutions would have to agree to change the way that Americans learn languages within an already crowded post-secondary curriculum. Essentially, programs had to agree on setting new and much higher expectations for students who were selected into these special-focus language programs and then to create the opportunities to meet these expectations. The expectations were quite straightforward: to enable students to graduate with the same kinds of language capabilities that educated non-native English-speaking professionals from other industrialized countries use in their daily professional lives when using English or another language foreign to them. Given the historical lack of attention to articulated and sustained language learning at the K-12 (i.e. primary and secondary) level, higher education would have to take this challenge on from beginning to end.

Despite these academic challenges, the NSEP, established by the US Congress in 1991 (The David L. Boren National Security Education Act of 1991) created the Language Flagship, designed to address the long-standing national need for language skills as well as the long-standing frustration of federal agencies with the inability of US academic language programs to produce graduates with higher-level language proficiencies. When established, NSEP joined a set of existing federal programs whose goals focused on the need for area studies and language expertise. The rationale for the program, outlined in Section 801 of the Act, included an 'interest in taking actions to alleviate the problem of American undergraduate and graduate students being inadequately prepared to meet the challenges posed by increasing global interaction among nations' (The David L. Boren National Security Education Act of 1991: 1).

In fact, the documented US government need for language skills, along with strong Department of Defense support for their development, has been evident since the establishment of the National Defense Education Act of 1958, which underscored the need for Americans to have language skills as well as science and technical skills (Lambert, 2010). This landmark legislation resulted in US congressional support for international studies and language learning at US academic institutions through programs that later came to be called 'Title VI and Fulbright-Hays Programs' (Brecht & Rivers, 2000). Over the years, such support helped to create excellent regional area studies centers (Title VI National Resource Centers) at over 100 key academic institutions to support advanced research and study abroad programs. Collectively, these programs have served to create many international and area studies experts in the academic, non-profit and public sphere, and have supported the teaching of a large array of less commonly taught languages (Wiley & Glew, 2010).

Despite this federal support, certified language acquisition to the American Council on the Teaching of Foreign Languages (ACTFL) Advanced and Superior levels of proficiency has not been a priority of the Title VI National Resource Centers, especially at the undergraduate level (Lambert, 2010). The 2007 National Research Council's Report on Title VI and Fulbright-Hays programs underscored a lack of focus on the part of the US Department of Education on foreign language education, stating that, '[the Department of Education] has not made foreign language and culture a priority and its several programs appear to be fragmented. There is no apparent master plan or unifying strategic vision' (National Research Council, 2007: 4). Moreover, much of the support over the years for language learning through the Title VI and Fulbright-Hays programs had not supported proficiency-based language instruction, meaning that there was no tie between federal funding and any specific proficiency goals, outcomes or measurements (National Research Council, 2007).

The Title VI and Fulbright-Hays programs had the additional challenge of attempting to support language study within an existing two-tiered faculty structure in language departments, as characterized by the 2007 MLA Report. The report criticized US language departments for perpetuating a system where 'language instructors often work entirely outside departmental power structures and have little or no say in the educational mission of their department, even in areas where they have particular expertise' (MLA Ad Hoc Committee on Foreign Languages, 2007: 2). This division is even more pronounced, according to the MLA Report, at doctorate-granting institutions, which receive the bulk of the US Department of Education Title VI support. As a result of these structural factors, faculty members involved in language instruction have struggled for a voice in determining their role as academic professionals. As the MLA Report states,

> Such a configuration defines both the curriculum and the governance structure of language departments and creates a division between the language curriculum and the literature curriculum and between tenure-track literature professors and language instructors in non tenure-track positions. At doctorate-granting institutions, cooperation or even exchange between the two groups is usually minimal or nonexistent. (MLA Ad Hoc Committee on Foreign Languages, 2007: 2–3)

This observation from the MLA Report is critical in understanding the challenges over the years of establishing effective language programs in the US post-secondary education system. Ultimately, any program that sets high expectations for language proficiency must be able to create opportunities for students to meet those expectations. Departments must reward faculty for building and executing these programs, even if it takes them away from the demands of a tenure-driven system requiring research publications. Without professional autonomy and power, the majority of language faculty, tenured or not, have traditionally lacked the organizational power to change the system: the weight of power often rests with faculty who do not have language instruction as a primary area of focus or as their means of being rewarded at the institutional as well as the professional level. As discussed in the MLA Report: 'This two-track model endows one set of language professionals not only with autonomy in designing their curricula but also with the power to set the goals that the other set of professionals must pursue' (MLA Ad Hoc Committee on Foreign Languages, 2007: 4).

In addition to this challenge, it is important to point out that the bulk of Title VI-Fulbright Hays funding to Title VI National Resource Centers supported programming and research in area studies. Such support did little to challenge the two-tiered system criticized by the MLA Report and may have even created another level of unequal differentiation between those involved in area studies and those involved in language instruction at Title VI-supported institutions. As a result, little clear advocacy or consistent support for ACTFL Advanced- to Superior-level language learning (ILR 2-3) existed within the higher educational system before the creation of the Language Flagship. Some federal programs, such as the Title VI Undergraduate International Studies and Foreign Language program, the NSEP grants to institutions of higher education and the Fund for the Improvement of Postsecondary Education (FIPSE), attempted over the years to provide support to spur innovation in language teaching approaches and practice (Nugent, 2011). In addition, funding awarded through the Title VI Language Resource Centers and the International Research and Studies programs supported a range of efforts to sustain and improve language learning on US colleges and university campuses (National Research Council, 2007). Some programs, such as the Fulbright-Hays Group Projects Abroad program, did support more advanced language training overseas and, in the case of Russian, carefully measured language proficiency (Davidson, 2010), even though language proficiency was not a required goal of the federal program. The most rigorous efforts to produce language gains in languages such as Russian, which is classified by the federal government as being more difficult than many other languages for speakers of English (Jackson & Kaplan, 2001), were able to achieve the level of ILR 1+, with some of them reaching ILR Level 2 by the end of their study (Davidson, 2010; Watson et al., 2013). Lastly, the FIPSE International Cooperative programs were established in the mid-1990s to create opportunities for academic and professional programs to integrate language study with academic and professional disciplines in an overseas learning environment (Nugent, 2011). However, missing in many of these programs were specific standards to outline what the students should be able to achieve in their language skills upon completing their undergraduate study and strategies to enable them to attain these standards. One notable exception was the FIPSE-supported University of Rhode Island International Engineering program (IEP) that successfully integrated language learning and engineering studies as a general program practice, rather than as an exception for individual students (Grandin, 2011).

Flagship: Early Years

Within this national context and following extensive consultations with national security agencies within the federal government, NSEP announced in 2000 that it would transition and repurpose its Institutional Grants program toward a pilot National Flagship Language Initiative (NFLI) (NSEP, 2003). Based on its statutory mission and its experience working with colleges and universities, NSEP proposed to raise standards by creating a program that would advocate movement toward 'advanced language capacity in the U.S.' (NSEP, 2000). The goal was to refocus existing NSEP funding (only about $2 million per year) toward specific efforts to 'produce higher proficiency levels in critical languages in the United States' (NSEP, 2003). In September 2002, Congress officially authorized NSEP to implement the NFLI, and NSEP made its first awards for Arabic, Mandarin Chinese, Korean and Russian (NSEP, 2004).

The Language Flagship was conceived as an inventive and quasi-experimental approach to federal funding arrangements. Unlike many existing federal funding models, NSEP's goal, through Flagship, was to establish a more business-like partnership between the funder and the grantee. This partnership was based on the principle that universities were not simply entitled to long-term funding. Instead, a relationship that emphasized accountability required that universities receiving this funding would need to demonstrate that they were meeting performance-based expectations. Given the serious need for long-term investment in an enduring language-learning infrastructure, NSEP would commit to sharing the financial burden required to achieve the goals with its partners. Embedded in the Flagship funding model was a commitment to rewarding performance and a requirement that each funded partner would, over time, institutionalize the programs both through curricular modifications and by sharing an increasing percentage of the cost. For example, NSEP/Flagship would consider funding new tenure-track faculty lines, but only if the university offered a three-year plan to assume full responsibility for the cost. The overriding goal was to create a productive and accountable environment where both parties shared the burden of responsibility and cost, and to avoid a sense of entitlement to long-term support if the project continued to fail to meet its goals and expectations as outlined in the mutually agreed upon plan.

Because of the unprecedented challenge of getting students to the ILR 3 level in a second language, the original NFLI initially settled on a post-baccalaureate (post-BA) program design, drawing on the potential for a more immediate return on investment of NSEP's very limited funds by supporting qualified students who had already reached ILR 1-2 levels of language proficiency as undergraduates. This approach reflected US higher education's capacity, at that time, to respond to NFLI's goal and was based not only on a careful assessment of programs, but on intensive and lengthy on-campus meetings with language experts. In its early stages, the Flagship initiative was therefore conceived as a set of national post-BA programs supported by a number of regional undergraduate programs that would act as feeder programs. At the time, this approach seemed like the most expedient and cost-effective option for building a pipeline of students with the advanced language skills needed by employers.

The original post-BA program, which started with three domestic institutions in 2003, eventually expanded to 13 US-based centers by 2007, including a Russian Consortium and eight overseas centers (NSEP, 2004, 2008b). Each of the programs was charged with responsibility for graduating students at the ACTFL Superior level through a combination of domestic and overseas study. The post-BA approach relied on an effort to recruit college graduates nationwide to participate in two-year language-intensive programs consisting of carefully articulated domestic (US) and overseas study: one year at a designated domestic Flagship program on a university campus, and one year at an overseas program that included internships and direct enrollment in courses intended for matriculated students at the host institution. It was the goal of Flagship, in its early years as well as today, to foster the development of programs that would be both useful and attractive to students with a wide variety of specializations (majors). At a minimum, Flagship programs were required to establish clear proficiency goals; admitted Flagship students agreed to language proficiency assessment during and at the conclusion of the program.

Transition to the Undergraduate Flagship

In 2006, based on a review of the program, NSEP determined that it needed to redirect its focus to undergraduate education. In spite of the considerable success of the post-BA programs, they were not sustainable, given high per student costs, nor were they scalable for a national effort. Each program required funding to sustain both domestic and overseas infrastructure, with an average of $50,000 in student scholarship support over the course of the two-year effort. Additionally, it required a commitment on the part of students to two additional years of study without a degree that acknowledged their accomplishments.

Therefore, the Language Flagship shifted its focus toward undergraduate education. Most federal funding for language learning had targeted graduate students (e.g. Foreign Language and Area Studies [FLAS] fellowships); the transition to supporting undergraduate programs was intended to provide a far more cost-effective and sustainable way to meet the goal of enabling a large number of US students to gain professional language skills and international experience before continuation to graduate study. Instead of a single-focus, language-specific approach for the post-BA program students, the idea of the new Flagship undergraduate program was to allow students to integrate language study into their undergraduate major. Moving the program to the undergraduate level provided a clear opportunity not only to affect how students learned languages in the university, but also to enable these programs to have an impact on the K-12 community, with the goal of linking all levels of US language instruction more closely (NSEP, 2006). NSEP envisioned this as a major paradigm shift.

Flagship transitioned to the undergraduate level at a time when US federal agencies, Congress and the White House were fully embracing the idea that something had to be done to increase the number of students engaged in articulated language learning for federal service, especially for large agencies such as the Department of Defense. In a report published in 2008, the US House of Representatives Armed Services Committee (HASC) criticized the nation's lack of language proficiency, citing the lack of an 'educational infrastructure that can produce the dramatically increased numbers of highly-proficient individuals needed, not only to support national security, but also for economic competitiveness.' (U.S. House of Representatives Committee on Armed Services, Subcommittee on Oversight and Investigations, 2008: 55). The HASC specifically pointed out that the Department of Defense therefore found 'itself involved in programs aimed at increasing the availability of foreign language study opportunities for both its personnel and members of the U.S. public...starting in kindergarten and continuing through advanced graduate work' (U.S. House of Representatives Committee on Armed Services, Subcommittee on Oversight and Investigations, 2008: 55).

While the structural issues inherent in academic language learning posed significant challenges in establishing undergraduate Flagship programs at US universities, equally challenging were the widely held assumptions at the time about the role and limits of language learning in the United States. During the initial years of the undergraduate Flagship, beliefs at colleges and universities about what could and could not be achieved created challenges for the Language Flagship. Some university faculty and administrators voiced their concerns to NSEP that it would be very difficult, if not impossible, to expect undergraduate students to reach the goal of ILR Level 3 in any of the four modalities (speaking, listening, reading, writing) during the course of undergraduate study, and continued to push for an approach that supported the post-BA programs.

Another major challenge that the program faced in transition was that the general academic structure of undergraduate language programs was considerably different from the existing small, specialized and, in many cases, non-degree granting post-BA Flagship programs that had been created during the pilot phase of the Language Flagship. Many of the post-BA Flagship programs were created in parallel to existing MA language programs and, in many cases, were completely separate from those graduate programs, both structurally and organizationally. For this reason, creating new undergraduate Flagship language programs turned out to be a much more complex administrative endeavor than creating programs at the post-BA level. While the post-BA programs were designed primarily to serve students already possessing higher levels of proficiency to continue full-time study in specially focused language-intensive programs, undergraduate programs were designed to provide language instruction for students of all majors entering with lower or no proficiency and were integrated into the students' undergraduate program of study. In other words, unlike post-BA efforts, undergraduate programs had to work within the confines of the college curriculum and infrastructure, taking approaches that would effectively embed the Flagship program into the fabric of the undergraduate experience.

As a result, many of the participating institutions were put into the position of rethinking the structure, organization and support of language learning within the context of undergraduate education. Undergraduate Flagship students were encouraged to combine their language studies with a major in a field other than language. The undergraduate Flagship thus focused much more on language learning not only in formal language courses, but also in other courses and in extra-curricular experiences. New programs were provided with federal funding to integrate language study into content-based learning (e.g. courses in specific disciplines taught in the target language; see Freels et al., this volume) and opportunities for language use that matched students' areas of study, their majors and general university requirements. Programs were encouraged to create language houses that provided students with language-focused living environments, and to use extra-curricular cultural events, Flagship-specific student centers and trained tutors to provide Flagship undergraduates with as much exposure to the language as possible, in and outside the classroom. Undergraduate Flagship programs thus faced the challenge of re-engineering not only their language curriculum, but also the overall pathway through undergraduate study for their students.

Expansion and Change

The transition to the undergraduate Flagship occurred while the Language Flagship was undergoing a major national expansion (NSEP, 2008b). As mentioned above, additional support came to the program as a result of the National Security Language Initiative (NSLI) (U.S. Department of Education, Office of Postsecondary Education, 2008) and from Congress. Between 2007 and 2014, responding to strong congressional interest, the Language Flagship underwent a transition of its existing post-BA to undergraduate programs while at the same time undergoing a very ambitious institutional expansion of new undergraduate programs. By 2014, the Language Flagship consisted of 28 separate programs at 25 US institutions as well as an additional 10 overseas centers (Appendix B). During this time of rapid expansion, NSEP also decided to begin implementing an approach, planned earlier, that made institutional commitment and support a necessary criterion for funding. As a result, NSEP demonstrated a willingness to fund programs that had a somewhat weaker existing language infrastructure but a very strong commitment to build capacity. This approach responded to a need to invest in institutions that were committed to building vibrant new programs, rather than focusing only on transforming existing language departments that were sometimes less willing to engage in major change. All Flagship initiatives, new and old, were put into the position of rethinking the structure, organization and support of language learning within the context of the entire undergraduate program of study. None of the individual Flagship programs became successful without strong support from the faculty as well as from the institutional leadership. Those programs that did not have the combination of such support did not in the long run succeed as part of the Language Flagship.

At the same time that the Language Flagship program increased institutional participation, the primary measurable goal of expansion during this period was rising student enrollment in the Flagship languages. Starting with just 42 undergraduate students in 2007, enrollment of undergraduate Flagship students increased rapidly during the expansionary period as new undergraduate Flagship programs were established and new students recruited. Students who wished to receive support from the Language Flagship were required to register with Language Flagship in the Flagship Student Certification System (SCS), designed to ensure that Flagship student progress was recorded and documented so that students could receive certification of their participation and success at the end. By 2014, nearly 1000 students were registered as participants in the Language Flagship SCS (Figure 1.1). In registering for the program, students pledge to make all possible efforts both to enroll in the year-long Flagship capstone overseas program and to reach ILR Level 3.

Although students are required to register in SCS in order to be admitted to the capstone, and to receive Flagship scholarship funding for study abroad or domestic summer intensive study, the total number of students participating in Flagship programs at campuses across the country amounts to over twice the number recorded in the Flagship SCS, since many

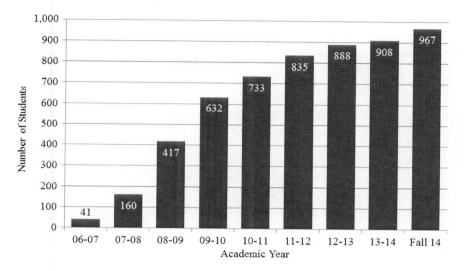

Figure 1.1 2006–2014 undergraduate Flagship enrollments

students participate in and benefit from Flagship in some way without being registered participants. They can often, for example, enroll in courses designed for Flagship students. In 2014, the total number of students involved in the Language Flagship amounted to just over 2500, including 967 registered and another 1591 either not yet registered or participating but unable to complete the entire domestic and overseas portions of the program due to other academic or extra-curricular commitments (NSEP, 2015). Some of these 1591 students will eventually register in the program; others will gain valuable language skills without completing the overseas components. Since the beginning of the Language Flagship, one overarching purpose of the program was to improve the overall language learning enterprise for as many students as possible (NSEP, 2007).

Articulation with Flagship Overseas Centers

Recognizing the importance of rigorous and intensive overseas study, the Language Flagship worked closely with its partners to ensure that an overseas academic year would be fully integrated with the curriculum. Compelling research on overseas language attainment coupled with the ongoing experience of Flagship supports the dramatically increased likelihood that students will reach the goal of ILR 3 if they (1) achieve ILR 2 before they begin the overseas study and (2) study for a full academic year in an intensive overseas program (Davidson & Lekic, 2010; NSEP, 2015). Additional experience with Flagship has also demonstrated that students at lower levels of proficiency can benefit from an intensive summer or semester-long program at the appropriate stages in their programs. The Language Flagship requires overseas study at programs specifically designed to include language instruction, direct enrollment in university classes at the host institution and internships to provide the student with well-rounded language and cultural experiences necessary to reach higher levels of language proficiency. The capstone requires a carefully planned and executed articulation between what the students have learned on campus and what they will study while overseas.

The Language Flagship partnered with universities to support and create specialized and articulated overseas programs at partner universities and colleges in countries including China, Egypt, India, Korea and Russia that would enroll future cadres of higher-level language learners. The development of overseas programs had an important synergistic effect on standards not only for the overseas but for the domestic programs as well. Flagship directors, recognizing the evidence of the potential for significant proficiency gains in overseas programs, coalesced around a requirement that students demonstrate proficiency at ILR 2 before admission to the capstone. The establishment of an objective proficiency-based requirement (along with other evidence of student preparation, including essays, grade point averages and faculty recommendations) created an opportunity for program directors to select only those students who would be likely to succeed in a difficult and intensive overseas environment. With admissions decisions to the overseas program made by language-specific national councils, the process provided an opportunity for peer review that enabled comparisons of assessment data across language modalities at the time of application to the capstone.

Building a Community of Innovators

An important innovation of the Language Flagship has been the strategic support and development of a Flagship community of innovators (NSEP, 2008a) around a goal of setting agreed upon expectations and creating opportunities for American students to reach professional-level proficiency in languages (Nugent, 2010). As the former NSEP director and Flagship founder, and co-author of this chapter, Robert Slater (2010: 1), wrote, 'we designed the Language Flagship to be a collaborative, evidence-based enterprise that builds on best practices and research. The program's collective success is based on a willingness to collaborate within as well as across languages'.

In order to promote a collaborative approach to achieving the goals of the program and to support faculty ownership of each program's future, the Language Flagship formed a number of academic councils to discuss goals, standards, pedagogical approaches, language curricula, testing and assessment, funding and support and recruitment (NSEP, 2010). In

2007, the Flagship Directors' Council, comprised of the directors of all Flagship programs, was established to provide a forum for the discussion and establishment of standards and protocols across languages, and to share information about program changes made to improve student learning at partner campuses. The following year, the Language Flagship supported the development of individual language-specific councils for those languages such as Arabic, Chinese and Russian that had more than one institutional program. In order to ensure that Flagship pedagogy and standards were developed in a collaborative manner, NSEP also supported the establishment of an Assessment Council to ensure that test development, delivery and standards were approached collectively across Flagship programs.

To further support collaboration, the Language Flagship provided supplemental funding to programs in the form of collaborative innovation grants, which provided support for programs to work together on the development of new approaches to teaching languages at high levels. Such support included, as outlined by Freels *et al.* (this volume), the support of content-based or interdisciplinary language learning and the innovative use of technology for language learning, also discussed by Bain and Spring (this volume). In 2015, NSEP funded faculty training and development workshops as well as a new Flagship Technology Innovation Center at the University of Hawaii, the purpose of which is to 'develop a resource center that coordinates and collaborates with NSEP-funded Language Flagship Programs in one or more of the Flagship-supported languages' (NSEP, 2015: 2).

All of these efforts served to create a community of innovators and leaders in the field for advanced language learning. In keeping with the recommendations of the MLA Report, the Language Flagship worked closely with the administrative and academic leadership at all partner institutions to ensure that each of the programs had support from senior faculty whose primary academic interest was in the improvement of language learning. Since 2010, NSEP supported the Deans' Roundtable each year at the Flagship annual meeting to ensure input and support from key decision-makers. As the program evolved, Flagship worked closely with institutions to ensure that they had the resources to hire tenure-track faculty who would be fully engaged in the design, delivery and mentorship of students in the target language. This collaborative approach served two purposes. First, it bolstered the effectiveness of individual Flagship programs by ensuring that the key participants were not only nationally recognized experts in their respective language fields, but also had decision-making power on their home campuses. Second, it served the long-term goal of institutionalization and sustainment, assuring that newly developed programs under Flagship were not built on grant-funded, part-time, adjunct positions, but rather on positions funded by the institutions for the long term.

Building a collaborative community helped program directors, faculty and staff address significant innovations and challenges, many of which are described in greater detail in this volume. Long-standing academic and pedagogical discussions specific to certain languages, such as the approach in Arabic instruction to teaching Modern Standard Arabic versus spoken Arabic dialects, were discussed and resolved as participating faculty set common standards and goals for language proficiency. The Flagship Council of Directors helped coordinate institutions across the nation in developing new educational standards and common practices that promote high-level language learning through common experiences including internships, enrollment in advanced language instruction and capstone experiences. Through established peer review processes supported by NSEP, individual Flagship programs began sharing best practices, helping them meet new standards.

Creating Success through Measured Standards, Practices and Outcomes

One of the most important areas of Flagship innovation was the development of rigorous approaches to the testing and assessment of language proficiency. In many ways, this effort proved as challenging as the development of the programs themselves. For more than half a century, proficiency-based language learning and assessment, especially at higher levels, had primarily been the domain of government language training centers such as the Defense Language Institute Foreign Language Center in Monterey, California and the US Department of State's Foreign Service Institute in Washington, DC (Wing & Mayewski, 1984). Based on the recommendations of US President Jimmy Carter's Commission on Foreign Language and International Studies, the Educational Testing Service (ETS) and ACTFL received funding from the US Department of Education in the 1980s to establish a new language proficiency framework based on the government ILR numeric scale, to which they tied the Oral Proficiency Interview, or OPI (Wing & Mayewski, 1984). Though the OPI has been used extensively by government training facilities alongside the Defense Language Proficiency Tests in reading and listening created by the Defense Department, the actual use of proficiency testing at universities and colleges was very limited and not, until the establishment of the Language Flagship, systematically employed across a number of academic institutions.

The goal of the Language Flagship, however, was to test not only speaking, but also reading, listening and writing. This was no easy task. Whereas the ACTFL OPI provided an established means to test oral proficiency, few established tests existed in the Flagship target languages that were adequate for assessing reading, listening and writing in the academic environment. In addition to the lack of adequate tests, the lack of tradition, experience and logistics in language testing in the academic setting across institutions and time zones meant that the implementation of testing and assessment on a large scale had never been done before. For this reason, starting in 2008, the Language Flagship began the development of new academic language tests based on the ILR language proficiency framework for Flagship languages. By 2014, the Language Flagship had created a Flagship Assessment Battery that included web-delivered tests in reading and listening in Arabic, Chinese, Hindi, Korean, Persian, Portuguese, Russian, Swahili, Turkish, Urdu and Yoruba that were designed to cover both the lower and upper ranges of proficiency in the ILR framework, from 0+ to 2, as well from ILR 2 to 3+. In the case of Arabic, a writing test was also developed (NSEP, 2013).

The challenge was not only to test students but also to demonstrate accurately the impact of the Language Flagship through the verification of student and program success. It is important to note that success for Flagship came through a combination of testing procedures, peer program review, faculty-based reviews of candidates for overseas study and faculty review of candidates for final Flagship Certification. In order for students to be certified, they not only need to reach a score of ILR 3 in speaking; they must also complete the capstone and all programmatic requirements of the undergraduate Flagship program at their institution. In 2015, the Flagship Council of Directors agreed at its annual meeting to expand the certification requirement for future Flagship students to require that students reach ILR 2+ in reading and listening along with an ILR 3 in speaking.

Flagship Results

The National Security Education Act directs NSEP to create initiatives under the Language Flagship to enable students to acquire 'advanced' language skills (The David L. Boren National Security Education Act of 1991). Yet since the beginning, NSEP established an aggressive goal for the Language Flagship at ILR Level 3. By 2014, over 76% of the 101 Flagship students who completed the program that year had reached the goal of ILR 3, with over 95% of students across Flagship programs and languages reaching Level 2+ and above (Figure 1.2; NSEP, 2015).

Flagship students are assessed at key junctures in their programs, such as when they enter the program, before they embark on summer intensive overseas or domestic programs and after their completion. The two most important points of assessment are when students apply to participate in the capstone (pre-capstone) and when they return from the capstone (post-capstone). Figure 1.3 shows the speaking proficiency levels on the ACTFL scale of 290 students across the Flagship languages, tested over three years from 2012 to 2014, with the light gray demonstrating the pre-capstone scores and the black depicting the post-capstone OPI test scores.

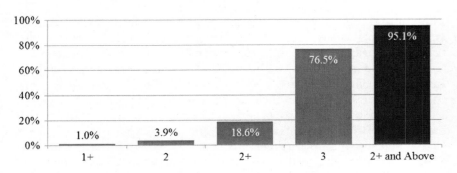

Figure 1.2 2014 Post-overseas capstone ILR speaking proficiency outcomes (*n*=101)

Based on a review of student results, the Language Flagship made a key decision that beginning in 2013, all students applying to participate in the capstone were required to have achieved proficiency at least at ILR Level 2 in speaking as well as in one other modality, with the third modality at least at ILR 1+. The goal was to ensure that a higher number of students could reach the ILR Level 3 program goal. In some cases, strong students who came close to reaching the required levels by the time of application were given additional time and support to meet this challenge and were tested again for review and admission by the Flagship Council to the capstone.

In addition to these changes, the Language Flagship began to test students with the ACTFL OPI using the ILR scale rather than the ACTFL scale, in order to ensure that student results from the program would better match workplace expectations for jobs which require professional-level language proficiency. In addition to oral skills, Flagship began testing all students in reading and listening skills. Whereas all students must submit

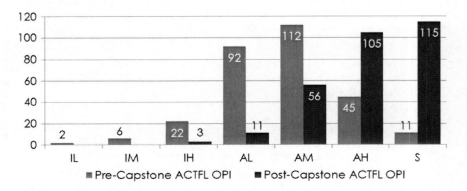

Figure 1.3 2012–2014 Flagship pre- and post-overseas capstone ACTFL speaking proficiency (*n*=290)

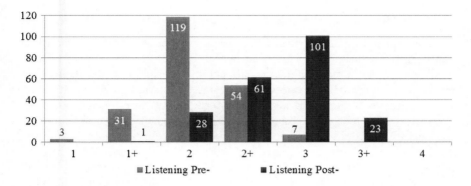

Figure 1.4 2012–2014 Flagship pre- and post-capstone ILR listening proficiency (214 tested)

writing samples for review, only Arabic students were formally tested in writing skills, using the ILR scale, at the time this chapter was written. It is the plan that eventually all four skills will be formally tested before departure for the capstone. Figures 1.4 and 1.5 show listening and reading pre- and post-capstone outcomes over a period of three years using the ILR scale. In 2014, a smaller group of 20 Flagship students were also formally tested using two government tests, the Foreign Service Institute test of Reading and Speaking and the Defense Language Proficiency Test for Reading and Listening. Of that group, 85% of the students tested reached ILR 3 or above in at least one modality on both tests, and 100% of the students tested reached at least ILR 2+ in one modality on either of the government tests (NSEP, 2015: 36). As the program matures, Flagship intends to continue to explore the use of various tests to better understand the outcomes of its programs.

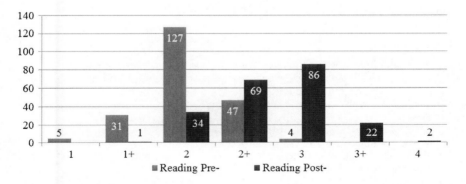

Figure 1.5 2012–2014 Flagship pre- and post-capstone ILR reading proficiency (214 tested)

Transforming Undergraduate Education

One of the most important national impacts of the Language Flagship has been not just language learning per se, but the overall impact on the quality of undergraduate education at each of the partner institutions. For years, researchers in effective undergraduate education have investigated and documented the impacts of the undergraduate experience by delving not only into effective means of learning but also into improvements to the entire undergraduate experience (Kuh, 2008; Pascarella & Terenzini, 2005). Successful Flagship programs have become important centers of innovation for the undergraduate experience, creating meaningful liberal arts experiences. Most importantly, students in a wide range of disciplines study not only languages, but also the history and the culture of the region.

From the very beginning, the Language Flagship represented an experiment in funding collaboration and innovation. After more than a decade of planning, investing, expansion and readjustment, the key to success remains in the ability to produce concrete results, while at the same time institutionalizing programs so that they become an integral part of the fabric of undergraduate education. NSEP has worked closely with its partner institutions to help support new tenure-track faculty lines, new curricula, overseas language learning centers, testing and assessment practices and new proficiency-based standards for language. Continued success requires an innovative and resilient community supported by its own and partner institutions, as well as the larger language-learning community. In the end, the goal of the Language Flagship is to make high-quality language learning the norm throughout the US educational system, rather than the exception, creating a critical mass of college graduates who carry with them into their personal and professional world advanced skills in language and culture.

Disclaimer: The contents of this chapter are the opinions of the authors and not of the US Department of Defense.

References

Brecht, R. and Rivers, W. (2000) *Language and National Security in the 21st Century: The Role of Title VI/Fulbright-Hays in Supporting National Language Capacity.* Washington, DC: U.S. Department of Education.

Clark, B.R. (ed.) (1985) *The School and the University.* Berkeley, CA: University of California Press.

The David L Boren National Security Education Act of 1991, as amended, 50 U.S.C. § 1902 – Scholarship, fellowship, and grant program (2006).

Davidson, D.E. (2010) Study abroad: When, how long, and with what results? *Foreign Language Annals* 43 (1), 6–26.

Davidson, D.E. and Lekic, M. (2010) The overseas immersion setting as the contextual learning variable in adult SLA: Learning behaviors associated with language gain to level-3 proficiency in Russian. *Russian Language Journal* 60, 55–78.

The Language Flagship 27

Geiger, R.L. (1986) *To Advance Knowledge. The Growth of the American Research Universities, 1900-1940.* Oxford: Oxford University Press.

Geiger, R.L. (2015) *The History of American Higher Education: Learning and Culture from the Founding to World War II.* Princeton, NJ: Princeton University Press.

Grandin, J.M. (2011) Bridging two worlds. In G.L. Downey and K. Beddoes (eds) *What is Global Engineering Education For? The Making of International Educators* (pp. 321–342). San Rafeal, CA: Morgan & Claypool.

Jackson, F.H. and Kaplan, M.A. (2001) Lessons learned from fifty years of theory and practice in government language teaching. In J.E. Alatis and Ai-Hui Tan (eds) *Georgetown University Round Table on Languages and Linguistics 1999: Language in Our Time* (pp. 71–87). Washington, DC: Georgetown University Press.

Kuh, G.D. (2008) *High-Impact Educational Practices: What They Are, Who Has Access to Them, and Why They Matter.* Washington, DC: Association of American Colleges and Universities.

Lambert, R.D. (2010) The changing form and function of Title VI since its beginnings in the 1960s. In D.S. Wiley and R.S. Glew (eds) *International and Language Education for a Global Future* (pp. 155–164). Lansing, MI: Michigan State University Press.

MLA Ad Hoc Committee on Foreign Languages (2007) Foreign languages and higher education: New structures for a changed world. See https://www.mla.org/flreport (accessed 28 May 2015).

National Research Council, Center for Education, Division of Behavioral and Social Sciences and Education, Committee to Review the Title VI and Fulbright-Hays International Programs. (2007) *International Education and Foreign Languages: Keys to Securing America's Future.* Washington, DC: National Academies Press.

National Defense University (2000) National Security Education Program 2000 Annual Report. See https://nsep.gov/docs/2000-NSEP-Annual-Report-Scanned-1.pdf.

National Security Education Program (2000) National security education program 2000 annual report.

National Security Education Program (2003) Report to the United States Congress. See http://www.nsep.gov/docs/2003%20NSEP%20Report%20to%20Congress.pdf (accessed 23 July 2015).

National Security Education Program (2004) *Combined Annual Report for Years 2003 and 2004.* See http://www.nsep.gov/docs/NSEP%202003%20and%202004%20Report.pdf (accessed 23 July 2015).

National Security Education Program (2006) 2005–2006 combined annual report. See http://www.nsep.gov/docs/NSEP%202005-2006%20Combined%20Annual%20Report.pdf (accessed 23 July 2015).

National Security Education Program (2007) Changing the way Americans learn languages. *Discourse: Newsletter of the Language Flagship* (1) 1–2.

National Security Education Program (2008a) Building a community of innovators. *Discourse: Newsletter of the Language Flagship* 2, 3.

National Security Education Program (2008b) Flagship expands in 2008. *Discourse: Newsletter of the Language Flagship* 4, 1–2.

National Security Education Program (2009) What business wants: Language needs in the 21st century. See http://www.thelanguageflagship.org/media/docs/reports/what_business_wants_report_final_7_09.pdf (accessed 23 July 2015).

National Security Education Program (2010) 2010 annual report. See http://www.nsep.gov/docs/2010%20NSEP%20Annual%20Report.pdf (accessed 23 July 2015).

National Security Education Program (2013) 2013 annual report. See http://www.nsep.gov/docs/2013-NSEP-Annual-Report.pdf (accessed 23 July 2015).

National Security Education Program (2015) 2015 annual report. See https://nsep.gov/sites/default/files/NSEP%202015%20Annual%20Report.pdf (accessed 23 July 2015).

Nugent, M. (2010) Word from Flagship. *Discourse: Newsletter of the Language Flagship* 8, 2.

Nugent, M. (2011) Linking language proficiency and the professions. In G.L. Downey and K. Beddoes (eds) *What is Global Engineering Education For? The Making of International Educators* (pp. 269–294). San Rafeal, CA: Morgan & Claypool.

Pascarella, E.T. and Terenzini, P.T. (2005) *How College Affects Students: A Third Decade of Research*. San Francisco, CA: Jossey-Bass.

Rosenbusch, M.H. (2005) No Child Left Behind Act and teaching and learning in U.S. schools. *Modern Language Journal* 89, 250–261.

Skorton, D. and Altschuler, G. (2012) America's foreign language deficit. *Forbes Online Magazine.* See http://www.forbes.com/sites/collegeprose/2012/08/27/americas-foreign-language-deficit/ (accessed October 1 2014).

Slater, R. (2010) Flagship founder reflects on the program, with an eye to the future. *Discourse: Newsletter of the Language Flagship* 8, 1–2.

U.S. Department of Education, Office of Postsecondary Education (2008) Enhancing foreign language proficiency in the United States, preliminary results of the national security language initiative. See https://www.lep.gov/resources/nsli-preliminary-results.pdf (accessed 23 July 2015).

U.S. House of Representatives Committee on Armed Services, Subcommittee on Oversight and Investigations (2008) Building language skills and cultural competencies in the military: DoD's challenge in today's educational environment. *See* http://prhome.defense.gov/Portals/52/Documents/RFM/Readiness/DLNSEO/files/LanguageCultureReportNov08_HASC.pdf (accessed 23 July 2015).

Watson, J., Siska, P. and Wolfel, R.L. (2013) Assessing gains in language proficiency, cross-cultural competence, and regional awareness during study abroad. *Foreign Language Annals* 46 (1), 62–79.

Wiley, D.S. and Glew, R.S. (eds) (2010) *International and Language Education for a Global Future*. Lansing, MI: Michigan State University Press.

Wing, B.H. and Mayewski, S.F. (1984) *Oral Proficiency Testing in College-Level Foreign Language Programs. A Handbook for Foreign Language Departments*. Hastings-on-Hudson, NY: American Council on the Teaching of Foreign Languages.

2 Laying the Groundwork: Programmatic Models in US Language Flagship Programs

Dianna Murphy, Karen Evans-Romaine, Valerie Anishchenkova and Zhuo Jing-Schmidt

Introduction

Nugent and Slater (this volume) describe the US Language Flagship program from the perspective of individuals involved in spearheading and administering the federally funded initiative to address national needs in both the public and private sectors for US citizens with advanced abilities in certain languages (National Security Education Program [NSEP], 2003). This chapter, authored by directors of Language Flagship programs at three different US universities, provides a description of how the goals of the national program have been realized in practice by educators at the local level, on their home campuses. The chapter shows how different Language Flagship programs have built on existing strengths at their universities to develop ways for undergraduate students of any major – many of whom have had no formal instruction or exposure to the foreign language (second language [L2]) prior to matriculation – to combine the study of an L2 with other academic interests or specializations to achieve a high level of proficiency in the L2 and an in-depth understanding of the cultures and societies in which the L2 is spoken.

The chapter is descriptive, focused primarily on the design of domestic (US) Language Flagship programs that aim to enable undergraduate students to reach Interagency Language Roundtable (ILR) 2 (American Council on the Teaching of Foreign Languages [ACTFL] Advanced; Appendix A) in the L2, in preparation for a year-long Language Flagship capstone overseas program for students at ILR 2 to reach ILR 3 (ACTFL Superior) by graduation. The chapter begins with a broad overview of foreign language education at the post-secondary level in the United States, including a brief description of current enrollment trends in languages other than English

(LOEs) and a discussion of the typical design of L2 undergraduate majors. This overview is followed by a discussion of the shared goals of all Language Flagship programs to provide opportunities for US undergraduate students of all majors, both within and outside of the humanities (Eisen, 2014), to reach a high level of proficiency in a LOE by graduation. The main body of the chapter is a description of six different program characteristics shared by US undergraduate Language Flagship programs, with examples from the three Flagship programs with which the authors are affiliated: the Arabic Flagship at the University of Maryland (UMD), the Chinese Flagship at the University of Oregon (UO) and the Russian Flagship at the University of Wisconsin-Madison (UW).

US Foreign Language Education at the Post-Secondary Level

Despite repeated calls to address the national need for speakers of LOEs (Brecht *et al.*, 2015; Jackson & Malone, 2009; cf. Kramsch, 2005; Robinson *et al.*, 2006), passionate rhetoric about the critical importance of educating students who are 'equipped linguistically and culturally to communicate successfully in a pluralistic American society and abroad' (National Standards in Foreign Language Education Project, 2015: 7), unflagging advocacy by professional organizations such as the ACTFL and the Joint National Committee for Languages, as well as by individuals such as Brecht *et al.* (2015) and various forms of federal investment in language education, the national capacity of speakers of LOEs has remained 'stubbornly stable' (Rivers & Robinson, 2012: 369). In 2008, approximately one quarter of the US population reported being able to speak an LOE, roughly the same proportion of the population as in 1980 (Rivers & Robinson, 2012). Only 10% of those speakers of LOEs who reported being able to speak the language very well, however, learned the language in school (Rivers & Robinson, 2012).

Certainly, national educational policies that have neglected LOEs (Abbot *et al.*, 2014) are part of this problem. Levine (2014), in an analysis of public discourses on LOE learning in the United States, argues that long-held beliefs about LOEs must also be taken into account and that

> the marginalization of foreign language education in the U.S. ... originates in a long and entrenched history of language learning as a luxury, peripheral to the life of a U.S. citizen and consequently not deemed a critical component of education for all but a select number of exceptionally well-educated individuals. (Levine, 2014: 57)

Blake and Kramsch (2007: 248), in a discussion of national education policies, suggest that speaking LOEs in the United States may even be viewed as a somewhat suspect activity, reflecting 'a national ideology that considers speaking and using other languages [other than English] as a slightly un-American activity'. Levine (2014) does describe alternate public discourses that emphasize the various personal benefits of L2 learning to individuals, as well as the political, economic and other benefits to society, that L2 education advocates commonly invoke. The effect of these alternate discourses does not yet seem to be making an impact on decisions by post-secondary students to study LOEs, however, as the next section will discuss.

Post-secondary enrollments in LOEs

The most recent national survey of post-secondary enrollments in courses in LOEs conducted by the Modern Language Association (MLA) showed that for the first time in recent years, the number of students who enrolled in courses in LOEs has decreased by 6.7% from 2009 to 2013 (Goldberg *et al.*, 2015). The proportion of enrollments in LOEs relative to enrollments in other academic subject areas has been decreasing for quite some time. In 1960, enrollments in modern LOE courses accounted for 16.2 for every 100 overall enrollments; in 2013, the most recent year for which there are published national data, the ratio was 8.1 for every 100 (Goldberg *et al.*, 2015). Perhaps even more discouraging, given the strong interest among many US students enrolled in beginning-level L2 courses in 'achieving fluency' (Magnan *et al.*, 2014: 204), the MLA data show that the overwhelming majority of US students who enroll in a course in an LOE do not continue to study the language beyond the second year of instruction, typically the maximum required at US universities that have a foreign language requirement (Lusin, 2012). In 2013, for example, advanced courses (defined by the MLA as third- and fourth-year language courses) accounted for just 17.2% of all undergraduate LOE course enrollments (Goldberg *et al.*, 2015).

Degrees conferred in LOEs

Given the relatively small number of US undergraduate students who continue to study the language beyond the second year of instruction, it is perhaps not surprising that the number of students who graduate with an undergraduate major in a LOE is also very small. In 2011–2012, the most recent year for which national statistics are available, only 1.26% of all bachelor's degrees conferred by US post-secondary institutions were in foreign languages, literatures and linguistics (FLLs) (Snyder & Dillow, 2015).[1] These 2011–2012 data are not atypical: the percentage of majors in FLLs of all US bachelor's degrees awarded has remained fairly stagnant since at least 1980, following a precipitous drop in the 1970s. Moreover, the range of languages represented by this small proportion of US undergraduates who major in a LOE is quite limited, largely representing those languages, Spanish, French and German, most widely taught at the primary and secondary levels (Pufahl & Rhodes, 2011): of those students who earned a bachelor's degree in 2010–2011 in an LOE, the largest numbers of students were in Spanish (8918), French (2492) and German (1019) (Snyder & Dillow, 2015). Far fewer students in 2010–2011 earned a bachelor's degree in the languages taught by the authors of this chapter: Arabic (141), Chinese (449) and Russian (340).

The structure of the LOE majors

The much discussed report on LOE post-secondary education in the United States by the MLA (MLA Ad Hoc Committee on Foreign Languages, 2007: 2) describes the typical US undergraduate LOE program as representing a 'narrow model' comprised of a 'a two- or three-year language sequence [that] feeds into a set of core courses primarily focused on canonical literature'. To determine the extent to which current undergraduate programs seem to follow the model described in the MLA report,[2] Rifkin (2012) reviewed the coursework requirements for 213 language programs in 19 languages at 35 US colleges and universities. He concluded that in fact 'a preponderance' of majors (Rifkin, 2012: 69) do reflect this structure, adding that 'very few of the programs require students to take courses in which they use the target language in nonliterary contexts' (Rifkin, 2012: 69).

This strong emphasis on literary studies in upper-level LOE courses may not reflect the goals and interests of all students who choose to study the language. Unfortunately, the authors of the MLA report did not seem to take into account student perspectives in drafting their recommendations, a point not lost on Berman (2012), who noted the report's exclusive focus on faculty stakeholders. Indeed, the student perspective is sorely lacking in much of the scholarly literature about L2 program design; it has also been conspicuously absent in the development of national frameworks for L2 education such as the *World-Readiness Standards for Language Learning* (National Standards in Foreign Language Education Project, 2015) that set forth goals for students' learning. Magnan *et al.* (2014), who surveyed over 16,000 students enrolled in introductory LOE courses at 11 US universities to look at the fit of students' goals for their language learning with the goals of the Standards, found that students' main goals for language learning were related to using the language to interact and to develop relationships with others. For that same study, Magnan *et al.* conducted structured interviews with 200 students at two universities to ask about students' goals and expectations related to their L2 learning. The analysis of responses to an open-ended interview question about students' goals revealed 22 themes, not one of which had to do with the study of literature.

The authors of the present chapter firmly believe in the intrinsic value and the educational imperative for including literary studies in the design of the LOE major, in line with the recommendations of the MLA Ad Hoc Committee on Foreign Languages (2007: 4) report to 'situate language study in cultural, historical, geographic, and cross-cultural frames within the context of humanistic learning', and of the MLA Teagle Foundation

Working Group (2009: 292–293), which urged departments to 'resist the impulse to increase coverage [in other areas] at the expense of intensive engagement with great and complex works of literature'. At the same time, however, our experience in designing, overseeing and teaching in Language Flagship programs has shown us the value of finding ways to attempt to meet the varied interests and goals of students which may include, but are not limited to, the study of canonical works of literature.

Proficiency attainments of graduates in LOEs

The level of proficiency in the L2 attained by US undergraduate students has been the subject of much concern for almost 50 years, beginning with Carroll's (1967: 1) study of the 'foreign language competence'[3] of over 2700 US graduating seniors majoring in five languages (French, German, Italian, Russian and Spanish) at 203 US colleges and universities. Carroll (1967: 205) concluded, 'the foreign language proficiency of the typical graduating senior majoring in a foreign language was considerably poorer, especially in listening and speaking skills, than what might be desired or expected'. Leaver and Shekhtman (2002) argue that US educators seem to assume that ACTFL Advanced High is the maximum that students can achieve. The scholarship to date on the proficiency attainment of US undergraduate students of LOEs suggests that Advanced High is far above the proficiency level than most students reach by graduation. (See Malone & Montee, 2010 for a review.) Levine (2014) grimly states:

> second-language researchers as a whole seem to agree that language education in the U.S. has failed to bring the majority of the students in classroom settings either to a significant level of communicative competence (Hymes 1992), or, more recently, what the MLA (2007) has called translingual/transcultural competence — the ability of the bi- or multilingual person to use all the languages at any learning level to acquire knowledge and negotiate communicative exchanges (Canale and Swain 1980; Swain 1985). (Levine, 2014: 60)

Along similar lines, Falsgraf and Spring (2007: 1) describe a 'culture of low expectations' for language learning in the United States; Reagan and Osborne (2002, cited by Levine, 2014: 59) decry a 'social expectation of failure' for learning LOEs.

The Language Flagship: Shared Goals and Program Characteristics

Language Flagship programs aim to foster a culture of high expectations intended to help undergraduate students see themselves as capable language learners who can reach 'professional-level language proficiency'

(The Language Flagship, 2015): ACTFL Superior (ILR 3) in the L2 by graduation. This goal, shared by all Flagship programs, is also shared early and often with students, who formally commit to working to reach ACTFL Superior when they are admitted to the program or accept federal Language Flagship scholarship funding. All Language Flagship programs also share the goal of offering the opportunity of developing advanced L2 abilities to a broad range of students – not only to those students who choose to major in the language and focus primarily on language, literary and cultural studies, but also to students with majors in the natural and physical sciences, social sciences, business, the arts, education, etc. A third shared goal, one that has profound implications for the curriculum, offers an alternative to the 'narrow model' (MLA, 2007: 1) of current US LOE majors: all Flagship programs aim to provide ways for students to link their language study to their other academic interests or to professional goals.

Responding to the goals of the national initiative and the requirements of the federal funding,[4] all Flagship programs are designed to provide opportunities for participating undergraduate students with very different profiles, including L2 and heritage learners with varied backgrounds and abilities (Kagan & Martin, this volume), to reach ACTFL Advanced (ILR 2) on their home campus, then to participate in a 9- to 12-month overseas Flagship program designed for students to reach ACTFL Superior (ILR 3). Described by Brecht et al. (2015: 180) as 'the most visible embodiment of sustained and intensive language programming' in the United States today, Language Flagship programs, while varied in their specific curricula and pedagogical approaches, share certain characteristics and program practices (Falsgraf & Bourgerie, 2008; Jackson, 2015; Spring, 2012) that support students in reaching these goals.[5] Taken individually, these shared program characteristics and practices are not necessarily unique. As Spring (2012: 141) argues, what is 'somewhat unusual [is] for all components to be linked together as part of the fundamental curricular design'.

The remainder of this chapter will discuss six program components shared by Language Flagship programs, with examples from the UMD Arabic Flagship, the UO Chinese Flagship and the UW Russian Flagship programs:

(1) A persistent focus on language development and proficiency-based assessments throughout the student's course of study.
(2) Options for intensive and accelerated programs of study, as well as advanced coursework on the student's home campus that prepares them for advanced overseas study.
(3) Opportunities for disciplinary learning in the L2, connecting the students' L2 development with learning in other subject areas.
(4) Focused attention and support for individual learners, including individual or small-group tutoring in the L2.

(5) Extensive co- and extra-curricular programming that provides opportunities for language use outside of traditional classroom environments.

(6) Articulated domestic and overseas programs of study, with direct enrollment and professional internships during advanced overseas study on a capstone program that targets ILR 3 proficiency in the L2.

Persistent focus on language development and proficiency-based assessments

All Language Flagship programs are characterized by a consistent and persistent focus on the students' developing language proficiency throughout their course of study. In the UW Russian Flagship, satisfactory progress in the program is based in part on students' meeting proficiency-based goals tied to the Russian language curriculum, as shown in Table 2.1. (Table 2.1 also provides information about weekly and yearly instructional contact hours. Information about weekly contact hours for non-credit small-group and individual tutoring is not included in the table.)

These proficiency-based goals are discussed with students at program recruitment and orientation meetings, in advising and tutoring sessions and in workshops for students on strategies for meeting proficiency goals. The goals also inform the types of professional development activities provided to program faculty and instructional staff, including graduate student teaching assistants and tutors.

To assess the students' developing language proficiency, the UW Russian Flagship follows an assessment protocol that makes use of both local and national resources. To assess speaking, instructors who are certified (or in the process of becoming certified) ACTFL Oral Proficiency Interview (OPI) Testers conduct unofficial OPIs. To assess listening and reading, the program uses a series of proctored and timed online proficiency-oriented assessment instruments developed at UW. Finally, the program administers a grammar test which, while not proficiency based, has proven to be useful in helping to identify areas related to accuracy in which individual students might need attention. This battery of assessments is administered to incoming students to determine their baseline level of proficiency, and then to all students annually. Students also participate in annual Flagship tests, assessments of reading and listening proficiency developed and administered annually by American Councils for International Education to all students enrolled in US Russian Flagship programs (Appendix B).

The purpose of both the UW assessments and the Flagship tests is to document gains in proficiency in different skill areas for the purpose of providing students with information about their developing language abilities. This information is also provided to program faculty, tutors and staff who use the assessment data to inform plans for tutoring, in advising

Table 2.1 UW Russian Flagship program curricular sequence, instructional contact hours and proficiency goals

Level in Russian	Instructional contact hours (academic year OR summer for each level)[6]		Proficiency goal (ACTFL scale)
	Academic year (AY)	8-week summer session	
Prerequisite courses: can be completed in two calendar years, through coursework during the academic year and in intensive summer programs at UW and overseas	First-year Russian (8 credits) Optional Honors Tutorial (2 credits)	5–6 hours/week=150–180 hours/year[7] at UW	20 hours/week=160 hours/ summer at UW	Intermediate Low
	Second-year Russian (8 credits)	5 hours/week=150 hours/year at UW	20 hours/week=160 hours/ summer at UW	Intermediate Mid
	Third-year Russian (8 credits) Russian Language and Culture (4 credits)	5 hours/week=150 hours/year at UW	20 hours/week=160 hours/ summer at UW or intensive Russian overseas[8]	Intermediate High in reading/ listening; Intermediate Mid in speaking/writing
	Fourth-year Russian (8 credits)	3 hours/week=90 hours/year at UW	Not offered at UW; option of intensive Russian overseas[8]	Advanced Low in reading/listening; Intermediate High in speaking/ writing
Advanced Flagship coursework completed at UW (10 credits): • History of Russian Culture (3 credits) • Contemporary Russian Culture (3 credits)	Average 5 hours/week = 150 hours/year at UW	n/a	Advanced Mid in reading/listening; Advanced Low in speaking/writing

- Advanced Elective: Capstone Seminar in Russian Literature and Culture *or* Special Topics in Russian (3 credits)
- Russian Across the Curriculum Tutorial (1 credit; taken fall or spring semester)

Subtotal of instructional hours in curricular plan at UW to support students reaching ACTFL Advanced in all modalities: 690–720 hours/year[9]

Russian Overseas Flagship Capstone program, administered by American Councils for International Education	21 hours/week (fall); 30 hours/week (spring)*	n/a	Superior

* See Davidson and Lekic (2013) for the breakdown of instructional contact hours on the Russian Overseas Flagship (ROF) program and for more information about the curriculum for that program at St. Petersburg State University and at Al-Farabi Kazakh National University in Almaty, Kazakhstan. Davidson (2010) reports that students on the ROF average 65 hours per week in the language, including both instructional contact hours and self-reported language use outside of class.

students about study plans and to monitor students' proficiency-based progress over time. In addition to these relatively low-stakes assessments, American Councils also administers higher-stakes assessments to those students applying to participate in the Russian Overseas Flagship (ROF) capstone program.

To be eligible for admission to the ROF capstone program, students must demonstrate proficiency at ILR 2 in speaking and in either listening or reading (and at ILR 1+ or higher in the other modality). The pre-capstone assessments consist of an official OPI administered by Language Testing International (LTI) and the Flagship tests in reading and listening, all rated according to the ILR scale. Assessment continues on the ROF in three waves over the course of the academic year. Assessments include the OPI, Flagship tests in reading and listening described above and the *Test of Russian as a Foreign Language*, developed in Russia and based on the Common European Framework of Reference. To successfully complete the full program, and to be eligible for Flagship certification by NSEP, students must receive a minimum OPI rating of ILR 3 and, as of the 2016–2017 academic year, ratings of at least ILR 2+ in reading and listening at the end of their capstone year.

Accelerated programs of study and advanced coursework options to prepare students for advanced overseas study

To enable students to reach Flagship proficiency goals, Flagship programs have expanded curricular options beyond those available in the traditional foreign language major. At UW, for example, the typical coursework sequence for a student with no prior exposure to Russian begins with four years of Russian language instruction, taken either during the academic year or, in the case of first- through third-year Russian, possibly as a summer intensive course equivalent to a full year of instruction in the academic year. Students can complete the equivalent of third- or fourth-year Russian in an intensive overseas summer program. These intensive summer options enable students to progress through the four-year sequence in two calendar years of study: two academic years and two summers. Students then take three advanced content courses, including a two-semester sequence in the history of Russian culture and options from courses in Russian literature, culture and media (Table 2.1). Basic shared principles across levels include an emphasis on the development of both functional language abilities and on intercultural competency, a recognition of the importance of both interaction and textual analysis in language study and a focus on personalizing and contextualizing language learning for all students.

These principles apply to advanced-level courses as well. The goal of the year-long cultural history sequence is to provide students with an understanding of aspects of Russian cultural history most relevant to contemporary political, scholarly, journalistic and everyday discourse in Russia and the Russian-speaking world. Students in this course sequence read texts that represent varied discourses and viewpoints to gain a nuanced understanding of overarching themes in Russian cultural history. The emphasis in another advanced course, focused on listening and both presentational and interpersonal communication, is on discussion of current issues in Russia and the Russian-speaking world as represented through online Russian-language media from Russia, the United States and elsewhere, again representing a variety of viewpoints and discourses. Topics in the capstone seminar vary by instructor but generally focus on cultural discourses as expressed through literature, from a major novel to political satire. Although approaches and topics vary at the advanced level, all advanced courses share the goals of enabling students to develop functional language abilities in a variety of settings and modalities; a nuanced understanding of culturally complex topics; analytical and critical thinking skills gained through both individual research and group interaction; and awareness of individual personal, academic and professional language and cultural learning goals and a variety of ways to pursue them.

In the UMD Arabic Flagship, the curricular sequence begins with intensive language instruction, with three years of intensive core Arabic language courses designed to build communicative abilities across a variety of functions (Glanville, this volume), followed by classes in Egyptian dialect and culture offered during the third year of study, content courses taught in Arabic and offered during third and fourth years of study and courses in English that students can take at any time during their college study. The conceptual model behind the UMD Arabic language curriculum is the 'integrated approach' (Younes, 1990), which implies simultaneous learning of the formal register of Arabic (*fusHa*) and Arabic dialects. Using the third edition of *Al-Kitab fi Ta'allum al-Arabiyyah* as the core language textbook (Brustad *et al.*, 2011), students learn both registers and develop strategies for code-switching from the very first semester. The two primary dialects are Egyptian and Levantine; each of the first-, second- and third-year courses focuses on one of these dialects, depending on the dialect spoken by the teaching faculty. Students, however, are not required to follow with the same dialect from one semester to the next. In fact, they are encouraged to try at least a second dialect in different years of their study, with the goal of developing a level of comfort with both dialects, then gradually prioritizing one of them, depending on their personal preference and future career goals. This aspect of the program's design allows students to meet the desired learning outcome of developing ACTFL Superior in one dialect and at least ACTFL Advanced in one more dialect by the end of their study.

In addition to the integration of dialect into all core language classes, the UMD Arabic Flagship offers a specialized two-semester sequence in Egyptian dialect and culture for students who have completed two years of core language coursework. These two courses expand and refine students' knowledge of Egyptian cultural discourses and promote deeper and more nuanced ability in the Egyptian dialect: students learn to produce complex discourses in Egyptian colloquial, including diverse idiomatic language, and develop knowledge of different social and generational vernaculars and regional subdialects. Additional dialects are integrated into curricular and co-curricular programs in various ways. First, the program offers dialect workshops, run by either faculty or Language Partners. Currently these workshops, which focus on Moroccan and Levantine dialects, are usually offered for a semester, during which small groups of five to seven students meet for one hour per week. In addition, several lower-level content courses are organized around a particular sociocultural area of the Arab world, offering students region-specific knowledge in both linguistic and cultural terms. Currently, two such courses are offered: *The Arabian Gulf: Dialect and Culture* and *Practicum in Arabic Language and Culture: Lebanon*. Typically, students take these courses simultaneously with the last sequence of core language courses (during their third year of Arabic). Finally, the program employs a team of Language Partners, recruited from the UMD community, including our Flagship alumni, as well as Arabic-speaking communities in the Washington, DC area, for one-on-one weekly meetings with students with the objective of advancing their communicative abilities in Arabic. The UMD Arabic Flagship purposefully recruits as Language Partners speakers of various dialects – Palestinian, Syrian, Iraqi, Moroccan, Egyptian and so forth, which further diversifies the students' experience with multiple dialects.

Disciplinary learning in the L2

Spring (2012: 141) claims that 'in addition to linguistic proficiency, students who strive to reach Superior Levels must be able to link content knowledge, such as an in-depth understanding of the target culture's history, literature, and contemporary social issues, with their work in language acquisition'. The acquisition and application of the L2 beyond the traditional language classroom is a hallmark of the Language Flagship: all Flagship programs offer some form of content-oriented instruction. Generally, three models of content-based instruction are used (Freels *et al.*, this volume): (1) theme-based, content-infused language instruction by a language instructor, (2) sheltered content instruction by a content expert who is a native speaker of the target language and (3) content-oriented one-on-one tutorials led by native or Superior-level speakers of the L2 who are trained in the content area. Theme-based language instruction 'is structured around topics or themes, with the topics forming the backbone of the course curriculum' (Brinton *et al.*, 2003: 14). Sheltered content instruction is defined as 'content courses taught in the second language to a segregated group of learners by a content area expert, such as a university professor who is a native speaker of the target language' (Brinton *et al.*, 2003: 15). The tutorial model caters to individual students' disciplinary needs and interests; it focuses on providing help with materials related to that discipline, rather than providing full-fledged instruction. In a study comparing the two content-based instruction models in terms of linguistic proficiency gains, Jing-Schmidt (2012) showed that learners under the theme-based condition achieved gains in accuracy, and learners under the content condition achieved significant gains in lexical and syntactic complexity. Furthermore, gains in complexity came at the expense of fluency under both conditions. The study suggests the complexity and non-linearity of proficiency development, and the need to balance between content and language instruction.

The UO Chinese Flagship program offers both theme-based language courses and sheltered content courses. The theme-based language courses are designed for students at the ACTFL Novice High to the ACTFL Advanced Low levels; they cover diverse topics from the humanities, social sciences and natural sciences. For students at the Advanced level, the UO Chinese Flagship offers sheltered content courses in various academic disciplines such as journalism, folklore, cinema studies, public policy and planning, geography, linguistics and Chinese literature. These courses are taught in Chinese by UO faculty members who are content area experts and native speakers of Chinese. The reading materials for these courses are from Chinese undergraduate textbooks or academic journal articles, providing students with the opportunity to gain experience in reading academic works in Chinese before embarking on the capstone program in China.

The UO Chinese Flagship currently offers two sheltered content courses per academic year. Most content courses are offered on a three-year rotation, with the exception of two online Chinese Academic Language Learning Modules (CALLM) courses that have been offered every other year. The sheltered content courses enroll both advanced UO Chinese Flagship students and UO native Chinese students, enhancing the immersion experience by increasing UO Chinese Flagship students' linguistic exposure through interaction and collaboration with Chinese peers. The courses also replicate, to a certain extent, the learning environment typical of direct-enrollment courses in the overseas capstone, further preparing Flagship students for their overseas capstone experience.

Content courses in the UMD Arabic Flagship likewise aim to prepare Flagship students for overseas study. The Arabic content courses are taught in a two-tiered model. First, in the students' third year of Arabic, UMD Arabic Flagship students enroll in lower-level content courses taught in Arabic – 'bridge' courses that aim to link language-focused and content-focused courses. Bridge courses provide intensive linguistic training, while increasing and diversifying cultural content. These are usually thematic, focusing on a particular cultural area. In their fourth year of Arabic, UMD Arabic Flagship students register for upper-level content courses taught in Arabic with more advanced and sophisticated content and tasks. These classes provide students with a full year of learning in the language before their overseas capstone year, and allow them to build domain-specific vocabulary and to expand and refine their cultural knowledge. With the growth of the UMD Arabic Summer Institute (offering three levels of Arabic, each covering a full academic year in accordance with the UMD Arabic curriculum), a population of students has emerged who, having completed one language level over the summer, take two full years of upper-level Arabic content courses. The program also offers various content courses taught in English, focusing on analytical perspectives toward Arab societal, cultural and ideological discourses, and development of critical thinking skills. Typically, the UMD Arabic Flagship offers 1 or 2 bridge content courses and 8 to 10 upper-level content courses per academic year, such as *Culture Wars: Controversial Issues in Arabic Literature, Film and Cyberspace, Arabic Linguistics: Roots and Patterns, Arabic Media* and *Contemporary Arab Political Thought.*

In the UMD Arabic Flagship, content courses taught in Arabic focus on training in linguistic proficiency and on cultural discourses in the target language. Content courses taught in English, on the other hand, provide students with analytical tools to approach Arab societies and cultures with a global perspective. Courses taught in English include *Contemporary Egyptian Pop Culture, Filming War Zones: Cinematic Representations of Wars in Iraq and Chechnya* and *Fascinating Monsters: Middle Eastern and American Stereotypes in Popular Film and Television.* Some of these courses are cross-listed and team-taught. One such course is *The Arab-Israeli Conflict Through Film*, team-taught by faculty from the Arabic program, Hebrew program and Film Studies, and offering students the opportunity to participate in a unique intercultural dialogue.

Finally, the newest course model within the UMD Arabic Flagship's content curriculum is an English–Arabic fusion course that combines a three-hour upper-level content course taught in English with an additional hour taught in Arabic. This type of course is typically taught by one of the Arabic faculty under the supervision of the Flagship director. The main goal of this twofold structure is to help students to advance their language skills and to expand specialized vocabulary in Arabic, while simultaneously developing their critical thinking, analytical skills and cultural awareness.

Focused attention and support for individual learners

Disciplinary learning in Language Flagship programs may be supported by individualized instruction or tutorials. In the UW Russian Flagship, theme-based content courses are supplemented by *Russian Across the*

Curriculum (RAC) tutorials, one of several forms of tutoring offered by the program to provide focused attention and support for individual learners that meets their developing language needs as well as their disciplinary interests and professional goals. UW Russian Flagship students participate in three different types of weekly tutorials: (1) weekly pair or small-group tutoring for students at all levels of Russian; (2) additional weekly individualized tutoring beginning in the third- or fourth-year level of Russian study; and (3) a one-credit, semester-long RAC tutorial linked to a credit-bearing course in the student's major or area of special interest, or to a general area of study (e.g. microbiology, physics, macroeconomics).

Tutors for the first two types of tutorials are generally UW graduate students in Slavic Languages and Literature or in another program (such as another foreign language or Second Language Acquisition [SLA]). In the case of RAC tutorials, tutors are graduate students from a department in the area of the tutorial or, if a graduate student with appropriate expertise cannot be found, a specialist from the university or community. UW Russian Flagship tutors are native or ACTFL Superior-level speakers of Russian, except for those leading first- and second-year small-group tutorials, who must have Advanced-Mid or higher levels of proficiency. Most tutors are also experienced instructors of Russian or another language and have taken a graduate course in foreign language teaching methods. All tutors participate in professional development opportunities such as pedagogy-focused workshops on campus and national workshops sponsored by ACTFL. Formative program evaluation consistently shows that students find the tutorial program to be, by far, the most important aspect of the program in enabling them to make progress in Russian (Murphy *et al.*, 2012).

Topics of the UW RAC tutorials have varied widely, including history, political science, economics, physics, environmental studies and literature. At the end of the semester-long RAC tutorial, students submit a paper in Russian on a related topic. If the RAC tutorial is linked to a course in which the faculty member teaching the course is a speaker of Russian (as has been the case for courses in political science, history and literature), students may also incorporate Russian-language primary or secondary sources into papers for that course, and meet with the faculty member for discussions about the course material in Russian.

The UO Chinese Flagship offers peer tutoring as well as language clinics designed to provide individualized student support. Facilitated by Chinese language instructors, the language clinics focus on one modality (i.e. reading, listening, speaking or writing) at a time, providing a forum for students with needs in a specific skill area to receive focused support. These language clinics have proven to be especially helpful in meeting the needs of Chinese Flagship students who come from increasingly diverse language-learning backgrounds and enter the program with very diverse language abilities.

Co- and extra-curricular programming to support language and culture learning

These tutoring programs and language clinics are one way that language and culture learning is supported in Flagship programs outside of formal course environments. Language Flagship programs also provide many other kinds of opportunities for language use and culture learning in extra-curricular contexts. In the UMD Arabic Flagship, for example, students participate in language workshops, cultural clubs, internships, communicative practice with Language Partners and regular lectures delivered by native speakers of Arabic. In the UW Russian Flagship, students can live in *Russkii dom* (Russian House), a Russian language floor in the International Learning Community dormitory staffed by a residential Russian language coordinator, and participate in weekly structured Flagship social hours, Russian tea and conversation hours, film screenings, lectures in Russian and community events.

Alongside similar types of co- and extra-curricular programming, the UO Chinese Flagship offers a unique technology-enabled and tutor-facilitated program, the Mobile Attrition Prevention Program (MAPP), that helps students to remain active in their language use when they are not enrolled in a course (e.g. over the summer, if they are not able to participate in a language program or internship), thus reducing their L2 attrition during that period. The UO MAPP is a learning program designed for advanced students to engage online in independent habitual language practices in reading, listening, speaking and writing. Students read at least two news reports and view at least two news videos in Mandarin daily. At the end of the week, students write a news review including a list of 20 new expressions learned, a 300-character summary of three news reports using new vocabulary and a 200-character commentary on those news reports. A MAPP tutor who reviews the students' work provides weekly feedback on recurrent errors in grammar, vocabulary and discourse structures. Students also participate in a 15-minute weekly Skype session with the MAPP tutor, during which the tutor elicits narration of and commentary on the news reports and then provides feedback on aspects of the student's language use.

Articulated domestic and overseas study

The capstone experience[10] for students in all Language Flagship programs is the capstone overseas program, designed for students who have reached ILR 2 with the goal of helping them attain ILR 3 (Davidson *et al.* and Eisen, this volume). As described by Davidson (2015):

the overseas capstones emphasize small-group language training and individual tutorials but place increased stress on direct enrollment in courses at the overseas university as well as professional-level internships. The overseas capstone places a special emphasis on in-class and public presentational or project work. (Davidson, 2015: 135)

In the UMD Arabic Flagship, students complete their capstone year in a Flagship-designated overseas program to which they apply during their last year of domestic coursework. Students typically complete all of their university breadth and major requirements prior to their capstone year abroad and apply for graduation while abroad. Many UMD Arabic Flagship students also choose to participate in an intensive summer program abroad, either in the Flagship overseas center in Meknes, Morocco, or through programs in other Arab countries. (Due to the continuing political instability in the Middle East, the only currently operating overseas site for the Arabic Flagship is the Arabic American Language Institute located in Meknes.) The program, administered by American Councils in collaboration with the five domestic Arabic Flagship programs, employs a team of Moroccan and Egyptian faculty, trained to deliver instruction that meets the Language Flagship's objectives. The makeup of the faculty allows students to be trained simultaneously in Moroccan colloquial (Darijah), Egyptian colloquial and formal *fusHa*.

In order to prepare students for study abroad, the UMD Arabic Flagship offers two mandatory one-credit intensive workshops during the pre-capstone year: *Moroccan Darijah and Culture Workshop* and *Egyptian Language and Culture Workshop*. The Egyptian workshop is typically taught by visiting faculty from the University of Alexandria; the Moroccan workshop is taught by a Moroccan Language Partner. Additionally, students preparing for overseas study participate in mandatory weekly individual meetings and tutoring sessions run by Arabic faculty (see Christensen & Bourgerie, 2015). In these sessions, students work on both continuing to develop their language abilities and conducting targeted research in Arabic in their particular areas of interest. These pre-study abroad sessions are typically taught by either a visiting faculty member from overseas or by one of the UMD Arabic Flagship's regular faculty members.

In the UW Russian Flagship, as in all other Russian Flagship programs, students study overseas at least twice: for at least six weeks in a secondary or post-secondary academic setting before application to the academic year capstone, then on the ROF itself. Students commonly complete the prior study abroad requirement by participating in a Flagship-designated program administered by American Councils or the State Department-funded Critical Language Scholarship program. Increasingly, students are coming to the UW Russian Flagship after a summer or academic year in Russia at the high school level through the National Security Language Initiative for Youth (NSLI-Y).

During the academic year, ROF students live with host families and report and reflect on their language learning and use as related to a variety of activities in their academic and daily lives through biweekly language use reports (LURs). They enroll in 20 hours per week of formal coursework on Russian language and culture, complete independent research projects, engage in daily one-on-one tutoring, take one direct-enrolled course with native Russian-speaking students in the fall semester and take part in a weekly professional internship during the spring semester (Davidson & Lekic, 2013; Eisen, this volume).

Conclusion

Language Flagship programs offer an alternative to the traditional LOE major in the United States. This chapter described, from the perspective of educators of three different languages at three US universities, a number of shared goals and different aspects of the program design found in Language Flagship programs today. These programs have enabled undergraduate students of any major, even those with no prior experience in the language, to achieve a high level of proficiency in a targeted L2 (Nugent & Slater, this volume) and an in-depth understanding of the cultures and societies in which the L2 is spoken (Davidson et al., this volume) by graduation. The program components described here are not, however, based on a fixed model: the design of Flagship programs continues to evolve as a result of accumulated experience in working with students at higher levels of proficiency, growing research on L2 learning in Flagship and other programs and pedagogical and technological innovations that provide opportunities for further improvement. The Flagship, established in 2002, is a relatively new program in US colleges and universities. As the Flagship initiative expands and more Flagship alumni report on their post-graduation experiences (Al-Batal & Glakas, this volume), the design of our programs will continue to develop.

Notes

(1)   The data on degrees conferred in FLLs include majors in languages other than English as well as majors in fields such as linguistics and comparative literature.

(2)   The authors of the MLA report themselves bemoaned 'a chronic lack of reliable, systematically compiled data on the actual practices of language departments in post-secondary institutions' (Pratt et al., 2008: 287).

(3)   Carroll's 1967 study was based primarily on the (no longer used) MLA Foreign Language Proficiency Tests for Teachers and Advanced Students. The tests included skill-based assessments in speaking, listening, reading and writing as well as assessments in applied linguistics, civilization and culture and professional preparation.

(4)   See, for example, the 2014 Request for Proposals for a new Arabic Flagship program, which states that successful proposals will show how the university will 'transform the beginning and intermediate curriculum to include, for example, more contact hours, proficiency driven learning, integration of culture throughout and tutoring' (The Language Flagship, 2014: 4), provide 'customized and individualized language learning, ... content-based or domain-based language learning, ... integrated assessment planning, ... and articulation with the existing Overseas Flagship Program' (The Language Flagship, 2014: 5).

(5)   Faculty and instructional staff in the many US Language Flagship programs do not necessarily share assumptions, beliefs or theoretical frameworks for understanding the nature of language or the nature of L2 learning or acquisition in instructional contexts. Likewise, all Language Flagship programs do not necessarily share a set of specific student learning outcomes, beyond those associated with the shared goal of the achievement of a professional level of competence in the L2, currently assessed using proficiency-based measures. This chapter thus does not attempt to describe a particular theory of instructed SLA or a set of specific learning outcomes. As Spring (2012: 143) has argued, however, citing work by Krashen (1981, 1985) on comprehensible input, Swain (1995) on pushed output and contextualized language instruction, Oxford (1996) and Scarcella and Oxford (1992) on learning styles and strategies and Doughty and others (Doughty, 2001; Doughty & Williams, 1998; Ellis, 2003; Robinson, 2001) on task-based instruction, programmatic practices found in Language Flagship programs are 'firmly grounded in best pedagogical practices drawn from research in SLA'.

(6)   The number of instructional contact hours is based on two 15-week semesters in the academic year and on one 8-week summer session.

(7)   Students enrolled in first-year Russian courses at UW may enroll for an additional one-credit Honors Tutorial. The tutorial meets for one hour per week during the academic year; it is not offered in the intensive summer session. The Honors Tutorial is open to all students, not only students in the university's Honors program.

(8)   Students may complete the equivalent of third- or fourth-year Russian by participating in the overseas Russian Language and Area Studies program (RLASP), administered by American Councils in Russia and Kazakhstan. Intensive fourth-year Russian is not offered in the summer at UW.

(9)   Rifkin (2005: 12) suggested that students of Russian may need at least 600 contact hours to reach ACTFL Advanced proficiency in one or more modalities. As shown in Table 2.1, the UW Russian Flagship program provides up to 720 credit-bearing contact hours in Russian to enable students to reach ACTFL Advanced, the level required for admission to the Russian Overseas Flagship capstone program.

(10) Language Flagship students participating in the overseas capstone, as well as in intensive domestic or overseas summer study, are eligible for significant merit-based federal scholarships. Without this scholarship support, many of our students would not be able to participate in, much less successfully complete, a Language Flagship program.

References

Abbot, M., Brecht, R., Davidson, D., Fenstermacher, H., Fischer, D., Rivers, W., Slater, R., Weinberg, A. and Wiley, T. (2014) The language enterprise: Languages for all? Final report. See http://www.americancouncils.org/sites/default/files/LFA2013_FinalReport.pdf (accessed 22 June 2015).

Berman, R. (2012) Foreign languages and student learning in the age of accountability. *ADFL Bulletin* 42 (1), 23–30.

Blake, R. and Kramsch, C. (2007) The issue: National language educational policy. *Modern Language Journal* 91 (2), 247–249.

Brecht, R., Rivers, W., Robinson, J. and Davidson, D. (2015) Professional language skills: Unprecedented demand and supply. In T. Brown and J. Bown (eds) *To Advanced Proficiency and Beyond: Theory and Methods for Developing Superior Second Language Ability* (pp. 171–184). Washington, DC: Georgetown University Press.

Brinton, D.M., Snow, M.A. and Wesche, M. (2003) *Content-Based Second Language Instruction*. Ann Arbor, MI: The University of Michigan Press.

Brustad, K., Al-Batal, M. and Tunisi, A. (2011) *Al-Kitaab fii ta'allum al-'Arabiyya =: A Textbook for Beginning Arabic*. Washington, DC: Georgetown University Press.

Carroll, J.B. (1967) *The Foreign Language Attainments of Language Majors in the Senior Year: A Survey Conducted in U.S. Colleges and Universities*. Cambridge, MA: Laboratory for Research in Instruction, Graduate School of Education, Harvard University.

Christensen, M. and Bourgerie, D. (2015) Chinese for special purposes: Individualized instruction as a bridge to overseas direct enrollment. In T. Brown and J. Bown (eds) *To Advanced Proficiency and Beyond: Theory and Methods for Developing Superior Second Language Ability* (pp. 87–103). Washington, DC: Georgetown University Press.

Davidson, D.E. (2010) Study abroad: When, how long, and with what results? *Foreign Language Annals* 43 (1), 6–26.

Davidson, D.E. (2015) The development of L2 proficiency and literacy within the context of the federally supported overseas language training programs for Americans. In T. Brown and J. Bown (eds) *To Advanced Proficiency and Beyond: Theory and Methods for Developing Superior Second Language Ability* (pp. 117–150). Washington, DC: Georgetown University Press.

Davidson, D.E. and Lekic, M.D. (2013) The heritage and non-heritage learner in the overseas immersion context: Comparing learning outcomes and target-language utilization in the Russian Flagship. *Heritage Language Journal* 10 (2), 88–114.

Doughty, C. and Williams, J. (eds) (1998) *Focus on Form in Classroom Second Language Acquisition*. Cambridge: Cambridge University Press.

Eisen, S. (2014) The Flagship model and the humanities. *Russian Language Journal* 64, 5–23.

Ellis, N. (2003) Constructions, chunking and connectionism: The emergence of second language structure. In C. J. Doughty and M.H. Long (eds) *The Handbook of Second Language Acquisition* (pp. 63–103). Malden, MA: Blackwell.

Falsgraf, C. and Spring, M.K. (2007) Innovations in language learning: The Oregon Chinese flagship model. *Journal of the National Council of Less Commonly Taught Languages* 4, 1–16.

Falsgraf, C. and Bourgerie, D.S. (2008) The language flagship: Multiple approaches to creating global professionals. In S. Laughlin (ed.) *U.S.-China Educational Exchange* (pp. 83–97). New York: Institute of International Education.

Goldberg, D., Looney, D. and Lusin, N. (2015) Enrollments in languages other than English in United States institutions of higher education, Fall 2013. See http://www.mla.org/pdf/2013_enrollment_survey.pdf (accessed 2 July 2015).

Jackson, F. (2015) Expanded understandings and programmatic approaches for achieving advanced language ability. In T. Brown and J. Bown (eds) *To Advanced Proficiency and Beyond: Theory and Methods for Developing Superior Second Language Ability* (pp. 185–204). Washington, DC: Georgetown University Press.

Jackson, R. and Malone, M. (2009) Building the foreign language capacity we need: Toward a comprehensive strategy for a national language framework. Center for Applied Linguistics. See http://www.cal.org/resource-center/publications/building-foreign-language-capacity (accessed 2 July 2015).

Jing-Schmidt, Z. (2012) Differential effects of content-based instruction models on advanced Chinese language acquisition. *Journal of Chinese Teaching and Research in the U.S.* 4, 16–26.

Kramsch, C. (2005) Post 9/11: Foreign languages between knowledge and power. *Applied Linguistics* 26 (4), 545–567.

Krashen, S. (1981) *Second Language Acquisition and Second Language Learning*. Oxford: Pergamon.

The Language Flagship (U.S.) (2014) *Request for proposal: Undergraduate Arabic Flagship Program.* Arlington, VA: National Security Education Program, Institute of International Education, The Language Flagship.

The Language Flagship (2015) The next generation of global professionals. See www.thelanguageflagship.org (accessed 25 September 2015).

Leaver, B.L. and Shekhtman, B. (2002) *Developing Professional-Level Language Proficiency.* Cambridge, MA: Cambridge University Press.

Levine, G.S. (2014) The discourse of foreignness in U.S. language education. In J. Swaffar and P. Urlaub (eds) *Transforming Postsecondary Foreign Language Teaching in the United States* (pp. 55–76). Dordrecht: Springer.

Lusin, N. (2012) The MLA survey of postsecondary entrance and degree requirements for languages Other Than English, 2009–10. See http://www.mla.org/pdf/requirements_survey_200910.pdf (accessed July 2, 2015).

Magnan, S., Murphy, D. and Sahakyan, N. (2014) Goals of collegiate learners and the standards for foreign language learning. *The Modern Language Journal* 98 (s1), 1–293.

Modern Language Association (MLA) Ad Hoc Committee on Foreign Languages (2007) Foreign languages and higher education: New structures for a changed world. See http://www.mla.org/pdf/forlang_news_pdf.pdf (accessed 2 July 2015).

Modern Language Association (MLA) Teagle Foundation Working Group (2009) Report to the Teagle Foundation on the undergraduate major in language and literature. *Profession* 1, 285–312.

Malone, M. and Montee, M. (2010) Oral proficiency assessment: Current approaches and applications for post-secondary foreign language programs. *Language and Linguistics Compass* 4 (10), 972–986.

Murphy, D., Evans-Romaine, K. and Zheltoukhova, S. (2012) Student and tutor perspectives of tutoring in a Russian flagship program. *Russian Language Journal* 62, 107–127.

National Security Education Program. (2003) *Report to the United States Congress.* See http://www.nsep.gov/docs/2003%20NSEP%20Report%20to%20Congress.pdf (accessed 23 July 2015).

National Standards in Foreign Language Education Project (2015) *World-Readiness Standards for Learning Languages.* Alexandria, VA: American Council on the Teaching of Foreign Languages.

Oxford, R. (1996) *Language Learning Strategies Around the World: Cross-cultural Perspectives.* Mānoa: University of Hawaii Press.

Pufahl, I. and Rhodes, N. (2011) Foreign language instruction in U.S. schools: Results of a national survey of elementary and secondary schools. *Foreign Language Annals* 44 (2), 258–288.

Pratt, M.L., Geisler, M., Kramsch, C., McGinnis, S., Patrikis, P., Ryding, K. and Saussy, H. (2008) Transforming college and university foreign language departments. *Modern Language Journal* 92 (2), 287–292.

Reagan, T. and Osborn, T.A. (2002) *The Foreign Language Educator in Society: Toward a Critical Pedagogy.* Mahwah: Lawrence Erlbaum Associates.

Rifkin, B. (2005) A ceiling effect in traditional classroom foreign language instruction. Data from Russian. *Modern Language Journal* 89 (1), 3–18.

Rifkin, B. (2012) Learners' goals and curricular designs: The field's response to the 2007 MLA Report on Foreign Language Education. *ADFL Bulletin* 42 (1), 68–75.

Rivers, W. and Robinson, J. (2012) The unchanging American capacity in languages other than English: Speaking and learning languages other than English, 2000–2008. *Modern Language Journal* 96 (3), 369–379.

Robinson, P. (2001) Task complexity, cognitive resources, and syllabus design: A triadic framework for examining task influences on SLA. In P. Robinson (ed.) *Cognition and Second Language Instruction* (pp. 287–318). Cambridge: Cambridge University Press.

Robinson, J., Rivers, W. and Brecht, R. (2006) Speaking foreign languages in the United States: Correlates, trends, and possible consequences. *Modern Language Journal* 90 (4), 457–472.

Scarcella, R., and Oxford, R. (1992) *The Tapestry of Language Learning: The Individual in the Communicative Classroom*. Boston: Heinle & Heinle.

Snyder, T. and Dillow, S. (2015) *Digest of Education Statistics 2013* (NCES 2015-011). National Center for Education Statistics, Institute of Education Sciences. Washington, DC: U.S. Department of Education.

Spring, M. (2012) Languages for specific purposes curriculum in the context of Chinese-language flagship programs. *Modern Language Journal* 96 (s1), 140–157.

Swain, M. (1995) Three functions of output in second language learning. In G. Cook and B. Seidlhofer (eds) *Principles and Practice in the Study of Language* (pp. 125–144). Oxford: Oxford University Press.

Younes, M. (1990) An integrated approach to teaching Arabic as a foreign language. *al-Arabiyya* 23 (1–2), 105–122.

3 Adding Breadth to the Undergraduate Curriculum: Flagship Approaches to Interdisciplinary Language Learning

Sandra Freels, Olesya Kisselev and Anna Alsufieva

Introduction

One of the distinctive features of Language Flagship programs is an overt strategy for developing language skills across a wide range of subject matter. The effect is an expansion of the traditional undergraduate foreign language curriculum to include general education topics, area studies and work in the students' respective major disciplines. Individual Flagship programs, while sharing this common goal, have tailored their pedagogical approaches to interdisciplinary language learning to meet the needs of local students and conditions. Some programs provide individualized tutorials; some offer content classes taught in the target language by an expert in the field and some favor a language across the curriculum approach that permits language specialists to teach subject matter not normally associated with foreign language study. The strategies that programs have adopted to foster interdisciplinary language learning, and the pedagogical approaches that accompany them, are the focus of this chapter.

Traditionally, foreign language programs in the United States have concentrated somewhat narrowly on the language and literature of the target culture, often with the intent of preparing students for graduate work in the same discipline. The Language Flagship program, on the contrary, aspires to create global professionals, that is, individuals with a strong disciplinary background in their diverse areas of expertise combined with Interagency Language Roundtable (ILR) 3 (Appendix A) proficiency in at least one language in addition to English. ILR 3, General

Professional Proficiency, requires an ability 'to speak the language with sufficient accuracy and vocabulary to participate effectively in most formal and informal conversations on practical, social and professional topics' (Interagency Language Roundtable [ILR], 2015). The challenge for domestic Flagship programs, in order to realize this goal, has been to expand traditional language and literature curricula to include the practical and social topics that characterize global professionals and, because Flagship students major in so many different disciplines, the professional topics that students will need in their future careers. Meeting this challenge has necessitated the development of new instructional materials and the adoption of non-traditional pedagogical approaches as well as a willingness and ability to cross disciplinary boundaries in the search for solutions.

In this chapter, the authors review the practices of 26 domestic Flagship programs to ascertain how they have addressed the challenge of expanding the traditional foreign language curriculum and whether there are discernible trends and tendencies in interdisciplinary language learning now in use that have proven particularly effective for work with students at higher levels of proficiency. Data for the chapter come from a self-study of Flagship programs conducted in 2011, a survey of Flagship directors administered in January 2014 (Appendix 3.1), websites of the 26 programs and personal communication with program directors.

The Case for Interdisciplinary Language Learning

The term *interdisciplinary language learning* implies a departure from narrowly focused language and literature curricula and a widening of the contexts in which language learning occurs with concomitant changes in pedagogy. Research on pedagogical practices associated with interdisciplinary language learning often focuses either on the use of authentic materials, that is, unedited materials that might be used by a native speaker (content-based instruction, Content and Language Integrated Learning [CLIL]) or on authentic tasks requiring the use of the target language in a practical, often work-related context (Experiential Language Learning [EX-LL]).

Second language acquisition (SLA) theory and research has been largely supportive of content-based approaches to foreign language instruction, since these pedagogical practices meet the conditions that numerous SLA experts consider crucial for successful language learning. These conditions can be briefly summarized as: (1) having a clear purpose for using the language; (2) focusing on meaning and communication of ideas rather than form; (3) increasing students' exposure to the language; (4) engaging students in meaningful use of language with appropriate amounts of support, which creates a relatively anxiety-free environment; and (5) exposing students to naturalistic language through the use of authentic materials, discourses and tasks (Lightbown & Spada, 2013; Nunan, 2004; Swain, 2000).

The use of authentic texts, although potentially limiting for the purposes of language instruction, provides contextualized, meaningful and repeated exposure to particular vocabulary items and grammatical and discourse patterns. Such 'contextualized redundancy' can result in deeper knowledge and greater automaticity in the use of target structures; moreover, the more complex cognitive processes that are required of learners when dealing with subject matter and tasks that require real-life cognitive skills such as problem solving can also lead to better retention of new linguistic information (Brinton *et al.*, 2003).

Schema theory provides additional support for interdisciplinary language learning on the basis that familiarity with the subject matter, no matter how slight, decreases the learners' cognitive burden and allows them to compensate for missing language knowledge by predicting and/or inferring meanings based on their existing knowledge of the world (Brinton *et al.*, 2003). Research on working memory has also convincingly shown that new knowledge is better retained when incorporated into existing knowledge (frames or schemas). In interdisciplinary classrooms, new knowledge (language) can be built into the frame of the existing knowledge (content) and vice versa. To summarize the above in the words of Jim Cummins (1984, cited by Navés, 2009: 26), 'successful learning takes place when the task is cognitively demanding yet heavily contextualized. The integration of language and subject matter content offers the possibility of meeting the two conditions'.

Theoretical arguments for interdisciplinary language learning are supported by research on the effectiveness of integrating content and language learning. On the surface, one notices greater exposure to the target language in integrated classrooms, as well as more speaking of the target language by students. Higher levels of motivation and cognitive stimulation are also observed (Brinton *et al.*, 2003; Dalton-Puffer, 2011; Marsh, 2009). Additionally, students dealing with meaningful tasks in a content-based setting, when compared with students in a traditional foreign language class, demonstrate higher levels of comprehension, increased ability to deal with more complex information in the target language and better developed *strategic* ways of dealing with new information, unlike traditional learners who tend to employ word-by-word comprehension strategies (Wiesemes, 2009). These skills may, arguably, result in higher gains in proficiency. Leaver (1997), for example, reports that the introduction of content-based methodology at the beginning of a 10-month intensive program resulted in the percentage of students graduating at ILR 3 rising from 52% to 83%.

At the level of discrete linguistic features, content-based approaches to instruction have been shown to be advantageous on such different levels of language command as phonology, various aspects of vocabulary acquisition, morphosyntax and academic discourse patterns (Ruiz de Zarobe & Jiménez Catalán, 2009). Even in content-based courses that emphasize one skill (such as listening or reading), students may improve their speaking skills compared with students attending traditional foreign language classes (Burger & Chrétien, 2001; Gallardo del Puerto et al., 2009). Wiesemes (2009) further asserts that content-based methodologies contribute to higher learner motivation and raise standards in the study of foreign languages while having no negative impact on the levels of subject matter learning.

Recent studies of task-based learning in foreign language instruction have also shown that experiential learning has the potential to influence an array of learning outcomes, including increased interpersonal and intercultural communication skills, heightened sensitivity to class distinctions in the target culture and improved foreign language skills. Askildson et al. (2013), for example, noted a dramatic increase in the language command of students of English (more than three times the expected outcome) in a service learning program that included targeted language instruction, guided reflection and corrective feedback in an immersion environment. Lafford (2013) notes that domestic service learning programs may provide the one thing that most reliably and consistently correlates with success in study abroad programs: the integration of learners into communities of native speakers. She also notes, however, that foreign language studies to date have tended to focus on gains in cultural awareness rather than on actual language acquisition.

Research on the efficacy of content-based language learning, although generally positive, nonetheless remains equivocal (Dalton-Puffer, 2011). First of all, what different researchers mean by traditional foreign language classes varies from study to study, as do researchers' understanding of practices that may be regarded as content based; teasing apart different methodological and contextual issues can be difficult if not impossible. Possibly due to the lack of clarity in the definitions, some comparative studies show no clear benefits of content-based approaches to language learning over traditional approaches. More importantly, as Dalton-Puffer (2011) points out, some studies disregard important issues like the fact that students often take content-based courses in addition to, rather than instead of, traditional courses.

Language as a medium of instruction enthusiasts have also been criticized for overselling the benefits of 'naturalistic environment' and 'painless language acquisition' (Dalton-Puffer, 2011). Such claims sit well with the public (parents, students and administrators) but are unsustainable in reality, as any language practitioner or language learner will attest. Evaluation of incidental or contextual learning outcomes, unsurprisingly, shows that although effective for promoting receptive and some productive fluency, language immersion without overt focus on forms fails to promote accurate usage. Errors and native language-influenced patterns persist especially in those instances where meaning is not dramatically affected by the misuse of forms or errors (Brinton et al., 2003).

Clearly, interdisciplinary language learning paradigms, whether content based or task based, must include language learning per se, either in the form of corrective negative feedback, overt language analysis or the implementation of language-sensitive content-based tasks (Brinton *et al.*, 2003; Dalton-Puffer, 2011). To focus on content or context to the exclusion of linguistic forms is to miss the point of any study, be that of language or other subject matter. As Thorne (2013: 1) reminds us, 'relevant to all academic and professional pursuits is the fact that human knowledge is fundamentally mediated by specialized and technical language, often in tandem with other semiotic systems'. Mastery of discipline-specific language (which includes non-specialized and specialized vocabulary and patterns of use, as well as genre- and text-specific grammatical and discourse patterns) is positively correlated with learning outcomes in science, technology, engineering and mathematics and leads to fuller participation in academic and professional communities (Halliday, 2007).

The design of Flagship programs takes into account that full membership in professional communities requires knowledge of subject matter and professional skills, as well as well-developed facility with the discourse particular to the community. Interdisciplinary language learning, with a strong focus on language, within the domestic Flagship programs is key to the acquisition of that facility.

Approaches to Interdisciplinary Language Learning

Much of the terminology associated with interdisciplinary language learning derives from practices in primary and secondary bilingual education and from the teaching of English to speakers of other languages (Dalton-Puffer, 2011; Navés, 2009). The Language Flagship program works almost exclusively with undergraduate college students, the majority of whom enter their studies with no prior experience in the target language. In selecting terminology for this chapter, therefore, the authors have limited themselves to terms that are most often applied to foreign language teaching at the post-secondary level. (For a discussion of heritage language teaching see Kagan & Martin, this volume.)

In the United States, *content-based instruction* is the term that is most often associated with interdisciplinary language learning (Brinton *et al.*, 2003; Stryker & Leaver, 1997). Content-based instruction is often understood to refer either to theme-based courses taught in the target language by a foreign language teacher within the context of a foreign language program, e.g. 'Hindi Drama and Film', or to courses taught in the target language by an expert in another discipline, e.g. 'Economics and Politics of the Arab World'. In Europe, the term *content and language integrated learning* is equally well established (Dalton-Puffer, 2011; Smit & Dafouz, 2012). Smit and Dafouz (2012) in their introduction to *Integrating Content and Language in*

Higher Education, after reviewing some of the prevailing terminology and noting that some terms seem to be used interchangeably, ultimately opt to distinguish between 'integrating content and language' as a distinct pedagogical practice and 'English-Medium Instruction'. Following their lead, we will use 'integrated content and foreign language' (ICFL) and 'foreign language medium instruction' (FLMI) to distinguish classes with explicit language-learning objectives from those classes taught in the target language in which mastery of subject matter is paramount.

Among the pedagogies associated with interdisciplinary language learning there are a number of other well-established, widely recognized approaches including 'Culture and Language across the Curriculum'. These initiatives may focus either on efforts to infuse international perspectives into non-language courses or on broadening the cultural component of lower-level foreign language classes. For the purposes of this chapter, we will use the more restrictive term *foreign language across the curriculum* (FLAC) to refer to small discussion sections in the target language provided in conjunction with regular course offerings taught in English in a variety of disciplines.

Classes of the kinds described above are often referred to collectively as *content classes*, that is, classes where students acquire language skills within the context of studying something other than language. Language for Specific Purposes (LSP) is yet another approach to language instruction with interdisciplinary implications (Grosse & Voght, 2012; Lafford, 2012; Spring, 2012). LSP is quite well developed within the teaching of English to speakers of other languages where one finds courses such as 'English for Hotel Management' that purport to teach the students only the vocabulary and grammar that they will need for one specific vocational purpose without addressing broader applications. Foreign language classes with a narrow vocational purpose are relatively rare in US institutions of higher education, but interest in foreign language for professional purposes ('Business Arabic', for example), which does have implications for Flagship programs, is on the rise (Lafford, 2012). Of particular relevance to Flagship programs are the practices associated with English for academic purposes, which trains speakers of languages other than English in the conventions of academic discourse that they will need to succeed when attending university in English-speaking countries. Since all domestic Flagship programs are, by definition, preparing their students to take part in university classes in other countries, all of them necessarily provide substantial training in the academic discourse of the target culture. Indeed, Spring (2012: 141) asserts that 'LSP instruction plays an integral part in all Flagship programs'.

Content classes provide broader exposure to a wide range of subject matter, but Flagship programs are still faced with the challenge of providing language expertise in the many different majors of Flagship students. Some Flagship programs meet the challenge by providing LSP courses devoted to the students' majors, while others opt for some sort of individualized instruction or practical experience. Individualized language instruction (ILI) focusing on a specific academic discipline may often be provided by graduate-level tutors or other content experts (native informants) in the student's field of study. EX-LL, sometimes known as community-based learning, community-based service learning or service learning (Lafford, 2013), offers yet another well-developed and widely recognized approach to integrating language learning with an individualized professional experience. The Language Flagship program has built EX-LL into its overall program design by requiring all students to complete a substantial professional internship during their capstone overseas program, but domestic Flagship programs also encourage their students to use their language skills in a wide variety of applied settings ranging from volunteer work (after-school tutoring, for example) to professional internships either in the public or in the private sectors preceding the capstone. Domestic EX-LL courses provide students with authentic tasks in meaningful contexts supported by the home institution with language instruction and opportunities for reflection, integration and personal growth.

All Flagship programs integrate high levels of interdisciplinary language learning into their curricular design. They combine elements of the approaches described above in configurations that are most effective and practical given the needs of their student population and the affordances and constraints of their academic settings. In the section that follows, the authors will explore how each of the approaches described above, including ICFL, FLMI, FLAC, LSP, ILI and EX-LL, are utilized by Flagship programs in their ongoing efforts to add breadth to the undergraduate language curriculum.

Interdisciplinary Language Learning in the Language Flagship

The Language Flagship program prioritizes interdisciplinary language learning, making special reference to content classes, ILI and EX-LL both on its website (http://www.thelanguageflagship.org/) and in all of its promotional materials. The emphasis on interdisciplinary language learning is reflected, in turn, in the curricular design of each of the domestic Flagship programs. In response to the survey question, 'Why is interdisciplinary language learning important to your program?', program directors named goals to be attained through interdisciplinary language learning, such as: (a) a general ability for speakers at ILR 3 to converse about the 'literature, culture, geography, politics, economics and history' of the target culture; (b) a command of academic discourse across a broad range of subject matter; and (c) knowledge of the terminology specific to the speaker's discipline. Directors also focused on the benefit of interdisciplinary studies to students' analytical abilities. One of them responded:

Interdisciplinarity enriches language learning through exposing students to complexities and multiple perspectives that they inevitably face in the complex professional and academic world. Developing critical thinking skills, making connections between different views and fields, and being better prepared for future careers are the added values of interdisciplinary language learning.

Integrated content and foreign language

All of the 26 Flagship programs reviewed use the term *content class* in their program descriptions. For the most part, they distinguish between lower-division language classes (first and second year), where information about the target culture is integrated into classes whose purpose is primarily language acquisition, and upper division (third year and higher), where students hone their language skills while studying something other than language. The majority of Flagship programs require that students complete a certain number of content courses taught in the target language, often during or after the third year of study, when the students have reached ILR 1+/2 proficiency. Typically, ICFL courses are taught by faculty within language programs who have disciplinary expertise in fields such as literature, cinema or cultural studies while at the same time being experienced in and thoroughly conversant with foreign language pedagogy.

Since literature and culture courses have traditionally held a privileged place in foreign language curricula, they rarely register as interdisciplinary or content based in the discussion of ICFL practices. However, teaching literature, culture and similar text-based courses with a regional focus may well satisfy the best conditions for language learning discussed above. These courses employ authentic materials with highly contextualized subject matter (plots, characters, settings) and allow for repeated exposure to and practice with vocabulary and grammatical patterns. Discussion of literary texts requires a focus on linguistic structure as well as an ability to analyze events and motives in relevant cultural and historical contexts.

'Russian Socio-Political Satire', a semester-long (15-week) course at the University of Wisconsin-Madison, provides an example of a theme-based ICFL class. Intended for students who have attained an ILR 1+/2 level of proficiency, the course has explicit content goals (studying the 'literary, cultural and historical context' of works of Russian satirical literature) combined with overt language goals (learning to 'read between the lines' while simultaneously developing a 'stronger understanding of the norms of Russian academic writing') (Tumarkin, 2014). The course is intended to approximate a course on the same subject taught at a university in Russia to prepare students for, among other things, eventual study overseas.

ICFL courses are relatively common in the United States, but within the context of Flagship programs they are pervasive. The combination of informational content with the focus on academic discourse in preparation for university study abroad is certainly one of the distinguishing (and beneficial) features of these courses. Additionally, an important advantage of theme-based ICFL courses is that they take advantage of the particular expertise of the faculty in the programs and are relatively easy to implement from an administrative point of view.

Foreign language medium instruction

Although developing an ICFL course for ILR 1+/2 students is pedagogically challenging, there are no structural barriers in US institutions of higher education that prevent teachers in foreign language programs from teaching courses in their own areas of expertise and tailoring the linguistic level of difficulty of those courses to meet the needs of their students. Programs that provide FLMI courses taught by faculty from other academic units cite very different structural and pedagogical obstacles, however. Structural problems most often involve either the difficulty of finding qualified faculty who are willing to teach FLMI courses or issues of faculty and departmental compensation. Programs that successfully incorporate FLMI courses often provide the qualified faculty member's home department with funding to hire a substitute. Pedagogical concerns include the willingness and ability of the faculty member to work with students with limited proficiency (Airey, 2012) along with the difficulty of obtaining level-appropriate instructional materials in the target language that meet the academic requirements of the home instructional unit.

The Chinese Flagship Program at the University of Oregon has successfully integrated FLMI components into its undergraduate language program. The Oregon program is distinctive in that it can expect that each of its entering classes will include students who have completed Portland Public Schools' Chinese Immersion Program at ILR 2 or higher and are thus fully capable of taking prerequisite LSP classes and transitioning to FLMI classes conducted in Chinese. In addition, the Oregon program is able to work with a fairly large number of Chinese-speaking faculty from numerous disciplines (business, chemistry, East Asian literature, English, human physiology, journalism and communications, planning and public policy). This combination of qualified students and faculty permits the program to offer a series of quarter-long (10-week) FLMI classes on a three-year rotation. The courses are open to any qualified student, including native speakers, which provide a rich learning environment for the less proficient Flagship students, but also potentially puts them at a considerable disadvantage. The Oregon program prepares and supports these students by requiring them to take a prerequisite three-quarter LSP sequence (topics in natural sciences, social sciences and humanities) and later a concurrent advanced topics language strategies sequence designed to support students taking FLMI content classes not necessarily tailored to their existing levels of proficiency. Co-Director Zhuo Jing-Schmidt (personal communication) reports that the most frequently taught subjects in this program include 'sustainable urban planning' (public policy and planning), 'sociolinguistics' (linguistics), 'journalism and media' (journalism) and 'green energy' (physics). (For further discussion of the Oregon model see Murphy *et al.*, this volume.)

Foreign language across the curriculum

The FLMI model used by the University of Oregon and a number of other Flagship programs requires that ILR 1+/2 students take courses taught in the target language but then provides additional language support to ensure student success. Programs that cannot mount a sizable number of courses taught in the target language sometimes do the opposite: that is, they require the students to take parent classes taught in English but then provide parallel language courses (sometimes known as *adjunct* or *trailer* sections) that teach the students how to talk about the material covered in the parent class. Programs that take this approach do not cite difficulties identifying suitable parent classes, and instructors of the parent classes, who do not necessarily speak the target language, are generally happy to recommend either original or translated works for students in the parallel sections. When teachers of the parent classes cannot recommend level-appropriate works, however, teachers of the target language sections may find it difficult to find instructional materials, particularly for those courses whose subject matter changes from year to year. Proponents of FLAC models find that the students' increased control of the subject matter leads to increases in their language gains, while the faculty who teach the parent classes cite the ability to bring international perspectives into their teaching as a positive advantage. Davidova (2011), for instance, reports on the highly positive experience of integrating the goals and objectives of a parallel Flagship course into her university-wide English-language course at Portland State University. Among the improved learning outcomes, Davidova lists heightened cultural awareness, greater tolerance of multiple and differing perspectives and increased motivation to study foreign languages and cultures for all students enrolled in the course.

Most commonly, FLAC models require that students take area courses taught in English that are related to the culture and history of the countries that they study. The Swahili Flagship Program at Indiana University calls on the expertise of faculty in such disparate fields as business, political science, history and religious studies to create 'clusters of content and language courses emphasizing interpretation, analysis and presentation of Swahili cultural concepts and events from a global perspective' (Swahili

Flagship Center, 2015). FLAC courses taught in the past have included 'Politics in International Development', 'International NGO Management in Comparative Perspectives', 'Kenya Today', 'Culture and Health', 'Africa since 1800' and 'Dress Cultural Analysis', with new classes being added every year ('Field Methods in Linguistics', 'Language in Africa', 'Race, Gender and the Media' and 'Children's Health' in 2013–2014). Flagship students enrolled in these classes also take a concurrent FLAC course on the same subject supervised by the program director and, working with tutors, prepare a research paper in Swahili for public presentation (program director Alwiya Omar, personal communication).

The Russian Flagship Program at Portland State University has taken the FLAC model a step further by aligning its advanced content classes not with Russian area studies but with the university's general education program. According to this model, students who enter university at ILR 1+/2 will simultaneously take a required year-long first-year seminar taught in English on 'Globalization' along with a parallel course on the same topic taught in Russian. At the sophomore level, students repeat the process, taking three quarter-long (10-week) classes taught in English on 'American Culture', 'European History' and 'Environmental Sustainability' along with parallel classes taught in Russian. An obvious challenge in all FLAC models is the lack of content expertise of language instructors in such a variety of topics. At Portland State University, this difficulty was overcome by soliciting assistance from the content experts to help with curriculum design for the parallel courses. Working closely with the teachers of the parent courses, obtaining their advice and help on the selection of topics and discussing readings and assignments in both parent and parallel sections ensured the quality and appropriateness of content in the parallel language courses. Upon completion of an initial pilot period, instructors in this program took the unusual step of freezing the content of the parallel sections to ensure that the linguistic needs of the students would be consistently met despite changing materials and assignments in the parent classes. The result is something like the LSP model at the University of Oregon: a series of classes that introduce students to the language of the humanities, the social sciences and the natural sciences in preparation for discipline-specific work the following year.

Language for specific purposes

Spring's (2012) assertion that LSP is integral to all Flagship programs is well taken. In a sense, all of the approaches to interdisciplinary language learning described above have the purpose of increasing the students' command of academic language, particularly in the traditional areas of social sciences, natural sciences and humanities. A number of programs either instead of or in addition to interdisciplinary content classes also offer

LSP classes, either under the title of 'Advanced Language' or, less often, under 'Language for Academic Purposes' or 'Language for Professional Purposes'. In addition, nearly all domestic Flagship programs offer some training, either embedded in advanced language classes or as a stand-alone class, in language of the media. Finally, those Flagship programs that have a sizable number of students with similar professional interests are able to offer courses tailored to students' future professional needs ('Advanced Business Arabic', for example).

The Chinese Language Flagship Program at the University of Rhode Island offers an excellent example of an LSP approach to foreign language instruction. Rhode Island's International Engineering Program offers undergraduate students the option of majoring in engineering along with a number of foreign languages, including Chinese. The large number of engineering majors in the Chinese Flagship Program makes it possible, in turn, for the program to offer 'Advanced Technical Chinese' to all students of science, technology, engineering and mathematics. In the future, the program plans to expand its LSP offerings downward by developing 'Chinese for Science' courses for students in their second and third year of Chinese language instruction (program director Wayne He, personal communication).

At Portland State University, where students come to the Russian Flagship Program from a number of different majors, disciplinary language expertise is provided in an LSP course called 'Russian in the Major'. In this course, students whose academic interests range from fine and performing arts to mechanical and electrical engineering meet as a group and learn to speak of their academic programs in terms that the other students in the group, non-specialists in each other's respective disciplines, can understand. The students begin by exploring how their particular major is taught in Russia; they then develop a personalized glossary of professional vocabulary and prepare a research paper in Russian, which they deliver at a public symposium at the end of the academic year. This approach has the advantage of not requiring the instructor to be a specialist in each of the disciplines. The students are the specialists, while the instructor answers for the quality and clarity of the language and the conventions of academic discourse.

Individualized language instruction

LSP classes, whether focusing on a single area of specialization, like technology, or integrating work in multiple disciplinary areas, serve a number of purposes, the most notable being training in the general conventions of academic discourse and in those of the students' professional disciplines. Other programs address the same goals by providing ILI for students in the program either instead of or in addition to LSP classes.

ILI sometimes implies self-paced instruction, often computer assisted, with periodic interaction with native informants. Within Flagship practice, ILI generally takes the form of regularly scheduled individual or small-group meetings with educated native speakers (tutors, peer mentors, coaches) either for the purpose of language training (tutoring) or for training either in general academic or discipline-specific discourse (tutorials). All Flagship programs provide some form of ILI.

The benefits of ILI, which can be tailored to meet individual students' needs, are great (Christensen & Bourgerie, 2015), but the concomitant difficulties can also be considerable. Flagship directors cite problems of expense and of recruiting, training and supervising tutors. Flagship programs housed in departments with graduate programs in the target language often recruit their own native or highly proficient graduate students. Programs with large numbers of international students recruit advanced undergraduate or graduate students from other departments. Programs with access to large immigrant populations take advantage of local community resources. In some programs, foreign language instructors themselves serve as language coaches for advanced students.

ILI tutorials run the gamut from conversation practice to fully articulated coursework. The Russian Flagship Program at the University of Wisconsin-Madison, in addition to language tutoring for beginner language learners and language for academic purposes tutorials for intermediate-level students, offers a one-credit language across the curriculum tutorial that requires each advanced student to select a course, generally either in Russian area studies or in the student's major, and then to work with a native or near-native graduate student or, less frequently, with a community or faculty member on a program of individual study based on the content of the parent class. This FLAC-ILI approach culminates with a research paper written in Russian and based on original Russian resources that is then submitted to and evaluated by the supervising faculty member.

ILI is the hallmark of the Chinese Flagship Program at Brigham Young University (Christensen & Bourgerie, 2015). The Brigham Young program provides a regularly scheduled ILI course for upper-level students with proficiency at ILR 2. The course requires students to select and read appropriate materials in their respective disciplines and to meet twice a week with two separate instructors: first with a graduate student to work on the language of the material that they have chosen, and then with a faculty member to discuss the content. In addition to individualized tutorials, students in this class meet weekly with their classmates and, as in 'Russian in the Major' described above, prepare a personalized lexicon and develop a research paper in Chinese for public presentation. Brigham Young has addressed the considerable difficulty of locating appropriate instructional materials by creating an online repository of materials selected by students over the years and vetted by their language instructors.

Experiential language learning

EX-LL, which provides students opportunities to apply their language skills in non-instructional settings, can facilitate considerable gains in intercultural awareness and language acquisition (especially language pragmatics); however, unless they are appropriately supported both by the host organization and the students' academic institutions, they can run the risk of reinforcing inaccurate language production (fossilized patterns of errors) as well as misapprehensions about the target culture (Askildson *et al.*, 2013). All Flagship programs value EX-LL, as evidenced by the numerous references to volunteer opportunities in settings such as after-school programs, refugee resettlement and health care, as well as professional internships in the public or private sectors; however, because of the expectation that all Flagship students complete an internship during their capstone overseas program, few domestic Flagship programs have integrated a formal EX-LL requirement into their curricular design. Hunter College, located in New York City, is a notable exception.

The Chinese Flagship Program at Hunter College requires all Flagship students to perform 20 hours of community service during their first year in the program. The program has numerous partners within the large Chinese-speaking community of New York, which ensures that students will be appropriately supervised and supported at their host sites. Because students during their first year of study may be true beginners (ILR 0+), one of the primary goals of the requirement, according to program director Der-Lin Chao (personal communication), is community engagement, and one of the benefits to students, in addition to intercultural awareness and linguistic gains, is increased motivation: 'We want to give the students the opportunity to go into the community and see how useful Chinese is'. Following best practices as described by Askildson *et al.* (2013), the Hunter program director meets weekly with all Flagship students, providing students in their first year of study with opportunities to reflect on their community experiences and to integrate their observations and insights into their growing linguistic and cultural knowledge.

Due to geographic location, not all Flagship programs are able to provide access to the host sites the way the Hunter College Chinese Flagship Program can. Nonetheless, the majority of the programs work on providing their students with opportunities to apply their skills beyond the classroom. Students from the Arabic and Persian Flagship Programs at the University of Maryland, for example, have opportunities for internships in Washington, DC, working at local businesses, print and broadcast media outlets and research institutes and think tanks whose work focuses on the Middle East. The Arabic Flagship Program at the University of Texas at Austin partners with several non-profit agencies where students work with Arabic-speaking refugees. A number of other programs are directly engaged in K-12 immersion and/or summer language camps for schoolchildren, where Flagship students assist in the classroom or work as counselors. Others partner with a variety of local organizations, from police bureaus to health services to local businesses, to broaden the learners' experiences with the language and culture of the workplace.

Conclusion

All Flagship programs prioritize interdisciplinary language learning, that is, a significant broadening of the undergraduate language curriculum, delivered in non-traditional ways. All Flagship programs at US universities include content-based instruction and ILI, and all of them anticipate EX-LL in an immersion environment during the students' capstone overseas program. All Flagship programs incorporate pedagogical strategies that facilitate interdisciplinary language learning, especially at higher levels of instruction. It is interesting to note that no single program employs any one approach exclusively, but rather, as one director put it, all favor a holistic approach combining the approaches described above (ICFL, FLMI, FLAC, LSP, ILI and EX-LL) in different configurations depending on the resources available to the program (international students, graduate students, immigrant community, interdepartmental partnerships and so forth), the interests and abilities of individual faculty members and the needs of the students. It is also worth noting how often the various pedagogies seem to intersect while leading toward similar learning outcomes. The FLMI classes at the University of Oregon are supported by LSP classes that are similar to the FLAC classes at Portland State University. The Indiana University FLAC class is similar to the University of Wisconsin FLAC-ILI, which in turn resembles Brigham Young University's LSP-ILI training in the major discipline. In each case, the outcomes are comparable: the development of a personalized professional lexicon leading to an original research project and the eventual authentic task of a public presentation or final report (paper) in the target language.

No matter what particular configuration of interdisciplinary language teaching approaches a Flagship program takes, all programs are distinguished by their focus on academic discourse in general, as well as on the discourse of the students' many and varied areas of academic and professional specialization. This focus on the discourse practices essential to particular subject matter or a particular discourse community allows Flagship students to achieve the high levels of language proficiency required of global professionals.

A review of the websites of the 26 Flagship programs under consideration reveals more than 40 original content classes on a wide variety of topics including media studies and cinema, issues in contemporary society, economics, political issues and the history of the regions where the target languages are used. All Flagship programs require that students take such content classes, usually at the ILR 1+/2 level of proficiency. The most common model is the theme-based ICFL class, generally taught by faculty in the language program, but FLMI and FLAC models are also fairly widespread. Typically, students are required to take one or more content classes during the third year of study in preparation for study at a foreign university in the coming year.

All of the 26 Flagship programs reviewed in this chapter employ varying amounts of ILI, ranging from individualized language tutoring for true beginners to conversation practice for intermediate students to intensive disciplinary training for advanced students. In addition, a number of programs augment their formal ILI offerings by recruiting international undergraduate students or advanced Flagship students from their own programs to serve as informal peer mentors for other students in the program. Anecdotal evidence, including internal program evaluations, suggests that Flagship students find ILI to be one of the most valuable aspects of the program.

All Flagship programs provide a considerable amount of LSP training as they prepare students for study at foreign universities. In addition to being one of the primary goals of ILI and content classes, LSP may also be embedded in advanced language classes. Less commonly, one also encounters stand-alone classes on 'Language for Business' or, when student interests warrant, on 'Language for Technology'.

Given the documented benefits of EX-LL (Askildson *et al.*, 2013), it is somewhat surprising that relatively few of the domestic Flagship programs, which clearly place a high value on all forms of experiential learning, systematically incorporate EX-LL into their program design. The *ad hoc* nature of experiential learning in domestic Flagship programs may in part be a result of the inherent difficulties in organizing and monitoring meaningful EX-LL experiences, but it may also simply reflect the reality of already heavy student workloads. It is also possible that domestic programs do not formally integrate experiential learning because of the certainty that students will complete a substantial professional internship during their year abroad, when they are more proficient and can benefit most from working in an immersion environment.

Implementing interdisciplinary practices into language instruction is not always easy. 'Integration often means challenging the status quo. It means breaking former boundaries, inviting controversy and especially in the case of CLIL, re-examining discipline-specific territories in education' (Marsh, 2009: vii). However, the mounting evidence from interdisciplinary classrooms from all over the globe, including the Flagship programs reviewed here, points to the obvious advantages of expanding the traditional undergraduate language curriculum and adjusting pedagogical approaches appropriately. Interdisciplinary approaches provide better opportunities for meaningful and engaged language learning, enrich learning of discipline-specific discourse in English and the target language and improve academic, interpersonal and professional skills. When asked to provide examples of student success, most survey respondents referred either to gains in proficiency (ILR 2 within 3 years; ILR 3 upon completion of the overseas program) or to the kinds of employment their students have found upon graduation (Al-Batal & Glakas, this volume). All Flagship directors agree that interdisciplinary language study is essential for the attainment of the ILR 3 proficiency required of global professionals.

References

Airey, J. (2012) 'I don't teach English'. The linguistic attitudes of physics lecturers in Sweden. In U. Smit and E. Dafouz (eds) *Integrating Content and Language in Higher Education: Gaining Insights into English-Medium Instruction at European Universities (AILA 25)* (pp. 64–79). Philadelphia, PA: John Benjamins.

Askildson, L., Kelly, A. and Mick, C. (2013) Developing multiple literacies in academic English through service-learning and community engagement. *TESOL Journal* 4 (3), 402–438.

Brinton, D., Snow, M. and Wesche, M. (2003) *Content-Based Second Language Instruction* (Michigan Classics edn.). Ann Arbor, MI: University of Michigan Press.

Burger, S. and Chrétien, M. (2001) The development of oral production in content-based second language courses at the University of Ottawa. *Canadian Modern Language Review* 58 (1), 84–102.

Christensen, M. and Bourgerie, D. (2015) Chinese for special purposes: Individualized instruction as a bridge to overseas direct enrollment. In N.A. Brown and J. Bown (eds) *To Advanced Proficiency and Beyond: Theory and Method for Developing Second Language Ability* (pp. 87–103). Washington, DC: Georgetown University Press.

Cummins, J. (1984) *Bilingualism and Special Education: Issues in Assessment and Pedagogy.* Clevedon: Multilingual Matters.

Dalton-Puffer, C. (2011) Content and language integrated learning: from practice to principles? *Annual Review of Applied Linguistics* 31, 182–204.

Davidova, E. (2011) Internationalizing general education from within: Raising the visibility of heritage language students in the classroom. *InSight: A Journal of Scholarly Teaching* 6, 52–59.

Gallardo del Puerto, F., Gomez Lacxbex, E. and Garcia Lucumberri, M.L. (2009) Testing the effectiveness of content and language integrated learning in foreign language contexts: The assessment of English pronunciation. In Y. Ruiz de Zarobe and R.M. Jiménez Catalán (eds) *Content and Language Integrated Learning: Evidence from Research in Europe* (pp. 63–80). Bristol: Multilingual Matters.

Grosse, C.U. and Voght, G.M. (2012) The continuing evolution of languages for specific purposes in the United States. *Modern Language Journal* 96, 190–202.

Halliday, M.A.K. (2007) Language and education. In J.J. Webster (ed.) *The Collected Works of M.A.K. Halliday* (Vol. 9). London: Continuum. See http://www.bloomsbury.com/us/languageand-education-9781847065766/.

Interagency Language Roundtable (ILR) (2015) 'Interagency Language Roundtable Skill Level Descriptors – Speaking'. See http://govtilr.org/Skills/ILRscale2.htm (accessed 4 June 2015).

Lafford, B.A. (2012) Languages for specific purposes in the United States in a global context: Commentary on Grosse and Voght (1991) Revisited. *Modern Language Journal* 96, 1–27.

Lafford, B.A. (2013) The next frontier: A research agenda for exploring experiential language learning in international and domestic contexts. In J. Cabrelli Amaro, G. Lord, A. de Prada Pérez and J.E. Aaron (eds) *Selected Proceedings of the 16th Hispanic Linguistics Symposium* (pp. 80–102). Somerville, MA: Cascadilla Proceedings Project.

Leaver, B.L. (1997) Content-based instruction in a basic Russian program. In S. Stryker and B.L. Leaver (eds) *Content-Based Instruction in Foreign Language Education: Models and Methods* (pp. 30–55). Washington, DC: Georgetown University Press.

Lightbown, P. and Spada, N. (2013) *How Languages are Learned* (4th edn). Oxford: Oxford University Press.

Marsh, D. (2009) Foreword. In Y. Ruiz de Zarobe and R.M. Jiménez Catalán (eds) *Content and Language Integrated Learning: Evidence from Research in Europe* (pp. vii–viii). Bristol: Multilingual Matters.

Navés, T. (2009) Effective content and language integrated learning (CLIL) programmes. In Y. Ruiz de Zarobe and R.M. Jiménez Catalán (eds) *Content and Language Integrated Learning: Evidence from Research in Europe* (pp. 22–40). Bristol: Multilingual Matters.

Nunan, D. (2004) *Task-based Language Teaching*. Cambridge: Cambridge University Press.

Ruiz de Zarobe, Y. and Jiménez Catalán R.M. (eds) (2009) *Content and Language Integrated Learning: Evidence from Research in Europe*. Bristol: Multilingual Matters.

Smit, U. and Dafouz, E. (2012) Integrating content and language in higher education: An introduction to English-medium policies, conceptual issues and research practices across Europe. In U. Smit and E. Dafouz (eds) *Integrating Content and Language in Higher Education: Gaining Insights into English-Medium Instruction at European Universities* (*AILA 25*) (pp. 1–12). Philadelphia, PA: John Benjamins.

Spring, M.K. (2012) Languages for specific purposes curriculum in the context of Chinese-language flagship programs. *Modern Language Journal* 96, 140–157.

Stryker, S. and Leaver, B. (1997) *Content-Based Instruction in Foreign Language Education: Models and Methods*. Washington, DC: Georgetown University Press.

Swahili Flagship Center (2015) 'Key Components'.

Swain, M. (2000) French immersion research in Canada: Recent contributions to SLA and applied linguistics. *Annual Review of Applied Linguistics* 20, 199–212.

Thorne, S. (2013) Language learning, ecological validity, and innovation under conditions of superdiversity. *Bellaterra Journal of Teaching & Learning Language and Literature* 6 (2), 1–27.

Tumarkin, A. (2014) Content course development. See http://www.thelanguageflagship.org/content/presentations (accessed 3 June 2014).

Wiesemes, R. (2009) Developing theories of practices in CLIL: CLIL as post-method pedagogies? In Y. Ruiz de Zarobe and R.M. Jiménez Catalán (eds) *Content and Language Integrated Learning: Evidence from Research in Europe* (pp. 41–62). Bristol: Multilingual Matters.

Appendix 3.1 Survey of language flagship directors

Questions 3–9 included space for narrative explanations of affirmative answers.

(1) Which Flagship program do you represent?

(2) Why is interdisciplinary language learning important to your program?

(3) Do you employ tutorials in your Flagship program? (Tutorials are generally individual or small-group training sessions provided by individuals, often native speakers, with expertise in a non-language discipline. Typically, tutorials are linked to a content course or to the student's major discipline.)

(4) Do you employ content courses taught by experts in a non-language discipline in your Flagship program? (Content courses are generally independent courses in an academic discipline taught in a language other than English. Typically, content courses taught by experts in a non-language discipline are structured around content objectives rather than language learning objectives. Although there are variations, credit for such courses is typically awarded in the discipline, for example, biology, rather than in the language, for example, Chinese.)

(5) Do you employ content courses taught by language professionals in your Flagship program? (Content courses are generally independent courses in an academic discipline taught in a language other than English. Typically, content courses taught by language professionals are based on the disciplinary expertise of the faculty, for example, literature, linguistics, cinema, cultural history and so forth. Courses in this category are usually structured around both content objectives and language objectives.)

(6) Do you employ language across the curriculum courses in your Flagship program? (Language across the curriculum courses typically are either formally attached to or predicated upon courses in non-language disciplines. Typically, these courses are structured around language objectives rather than content objectives. Courses of this type typically award credit in the language, for example, Chinese, rather than in the discipline, for example, biology.)

(7) Do you employ service learning (practicum, internship) in your Flagship program?

(8) Do you employ extra-curricular activities as a form of interdisciplinary language learning in your Flagship program?

(9) Do you employ any other types of interdisciplinary language learning in your Flagship program?

(10) What evidence do you have that your approach to interdisciplinary language learning is successful?

(11) Please share one or two examples of student successes.

4 The Road Through Superior: Building Learner Independence

Peter John Glanville

Introduction

Increased interest in the United States in promoting the study of languages considered critical to US national security requires language programs to address two important goals. The first is to increase the number of learners who achieve high levels of language proficiency (Interagency Language Roundtable [ILR] 3; Appendix A). While every language program has one or two stars who seem to instinctively know how to learn a language, other students seem to require explicit strategy training to achieve similar results (cf. Rubin, 1975). At the same time, bringing learners to a certain level of proficiency does not, on its own, ensure that they can or will continue learning once the course ends, though many of them will pursue careers where language maintenance and/or improvement will be necessary. A second goal, therefore, is to produce learners who can achieve superior proficiency (ILR 3) in a formal educational setting and be capable of continuing independently to distinguished proficiency (ILR 4) and beyond.

In this chapter, I present a model for building learner independence used in the Arabic program at the University of Maryland to achieve these two goals. The model is a course component that can be added to any existing language course. It consists of independent listening, reading, speaking and writing assignments designed to train learners to exploit linguistic resources and keep progressing in their acquisition of the language by processing a text, noticing and documenting new language and activating this new language in their linguistic production. The assignments combine to function as a learner record that is used as a teaching tool and as a method of assessment that provides an alternative to standard examinations (cf. Syverson, 2014).

I begin the chapter by defining learner independence and situating it within the larger concept of learner autonomy. I then outline the model I have developed for building independence in the specific context of the University of Maryland Arabic Flagship Program, providing assignment details for each linguistic skill, examples of student work to illustrate key points and follow-up class activities. The chapter finishes with a summary and suggestions on how the model can be modified for other teaching situations.

Learner Independence

For career professionals who have achieved ILR 3-level proficiency, the ability to continue their linguistic development as autonomous learners is a valuable skill. The concept of learner autonomy has been expanded since first defined by Holec (1981) as the learner taking charge of his or her own learning. Benson and Voller (1997) identify several different uses of the term, which simultaneously describes agency in self-study, the possession of an innate capacity to direct one's learning and the right to exercise this capacity. Benson (1997) also distinguishes among three spheres of learner autonomy: technical, involving the skills necessary to take charge of the learning process; psychological, where a learner accepts that he or she is responsible for his or her own learning; and political, referring to control over both the content of learning and the process (how content is learned). An autonomous learner is therefore technically able, psychologically motivated and politically free to select content and decide how best to use it. Autonomy in this sense occurs when the learner is reliant solely on himself or herself, with no teacher or textbook directing learning. In the context of second language (L2) education, this type of learner autonomy is a long-term goal. It does not necessarily come about on its own, but language programs can prepare learners for the day when the teacher and textbook are no longer around (cf. Nunan, 1997).

Learner independence as I define it here is a precursor to full learner autonomy. It refers to the ability and willingness of a learner to operate within a formal educational setting as an active partner in the learning process, rather than as a passive consumer. An independent learner is perhaps best defined through contrast with a dependent learner. The latter relies on the textbook to provide vocabulary (which is often pre-taught before a reading or listening skills activity); reads or listens in order to answer comprehension questions posed by the book or teacher; may study a linguistic structure (determined by the book) and rely on the teacher to provide contextualized practice; and primarily aims in class activities and homework to complete the task.

An independent learner is focused on the learning process itself and has developed what Sheerin (1997) terms an educational philosophy that informs personal learning practices. When engaging with texts, an independent learner identifies and solves comprehension problems; notices and documents new instances of language use; creates contexts to use this new language in spoken and written production; monitors and evaluates personal language use; sets goals for improvement and evaluates progress in achieving these goals and responds to feedback and error correction by actively using the feedback in new contexts.

There is no suggestion here that dependent learners are less motivated or exert less effort than independent learners. The difference is one of learning strategy, or how they go about learning the language. In a study of A-level (pre-university qualification) language learners in the United Kingdom, Graham (1997) found that most learners had developed strategies, but they were not always effective. She concludes that teachers need to address *how* students are learning, not just the language content of a given course. The importance of learner training in strategies for effective language learning is well established (see, for example, Cohen, 2007, 2009, 2012; Dickinson, 1992; Ellis & Sinclair, 1989; Esch, 1997; Griffiths, 2008; O'Malley & Chamot, 1990; Oxford, 1990, 2011; Wenden, 1991; Willing, 1989), but the final goal of autonomy depends on more than strategy training. As Littlewood (1997) notes, ability is of little use if it is not accompanied by a willingness to act, which, he states, depends on motivation and confidence. Building learner independence by training learners *how* to be partners in the learning process cannot be separated from ensuring their confidence and motivation to participate.

An early attempt to characterize motivational factors in second language acquisition comes from Gardner and Lambert (1959, 1972), and later Gardner (2010), who distinguish between the motivational goal of integration into an L2 community and more instrumental goals like employment or future study. In addition to this, Oxford and Shearin (1994) point out that a simple interest in the human faculty of language can be a motivational factor, and Noels (2001: 54) adds several intrinsic orientations, noting that 'individuals are motivated to develop their competencies by seeking out and overcoming challenges, in part because being competent can strengthen their control over their own behavior'. Work by Norton (1995, 1997) links motivation to a learner's identity, and this is developed further by Dörnyei (2001, 2005), building on Markus and Nurius (1986). In Dörnyei's (2005) L2 self model, learners envisage possible selves (positive and negative aspects of their future identities), and the desire to make certain selves a reality, while ensuring that other possible selves do not materialize, drives learners to act.

Encouraging a drive to action through building confidence and an ongoing sense of achievement is an integral part of building learner independence, and learners need motivations other than task completion if they are to persevere with language study up to ILR 3 and beyond.

To summarize, dependence, independence and autonomy represent points on a continuum. At the dependence end, learner behavior centers on efforts at memorization, comprehension and producing a correct answer. The continuum ends with full autonomy where the learning process continues without guidance or oversight from any other source but the learner. In the middle of this continuum is a set of behaviors which characterize the independent learner. While still in a formal educational setting, such a learner accepts responsibility for learning by engaging with texts in a way that ensures growth, not just comprehension; noticing language and creating contexts to use it and monitoring his or her production for errors and gaps in knowledge. Learner independence may happen to be part of the learning style of some students, but if the number of effective learners in a university language program is to be increased, skills for learner independence should be built into syllabi and developed consistently as students move from course to course. In the next section, I illustrate one way that learner independence can be developed within the context of any existing language program.

Building the skills

The independent learning skills component used at the University of Maryland is integrated into Arabic language classes from the third semester onward once students have learned the alphabet, know how to use an Arabic dictionary, are acquainted with Arabic morphology and have a solid foundation in terms of vocabulary and grammatical knowledge that they can begin to build upon independently. Most students finish this semester at the ILR 1 to ILR 1+ level. Typically students completing the third year of the program reach ILR 2, and some reach ILR 2+ after content courses in their fourth year of Arabic study. In line with Cohen's (1998) observation that learners need explicit instruction in the development and application of language learning strategies (see also Oxford & Leaver, 1996), students in our program receive explicit strategy instruction that raises their awareness of what they are doing and why, as it relates to their language learning and language use. At the beginning of each course, the instructor discusses key independent learning skills with students, who are given a set of instructions to follow when completing independent listening and reading tasks, audio assignments (spoken recordings in response to a prompt) and writing tasks. The totality of assignments constitutes a learner record of improvement over time, and individual assignments are graded according to how well they illustrate skill development. The course progresses, based largely around the textbook, and independent skills are developed in tandem, using the model presented below.

Independent listening and reading

Texts for listening and reading assignments cover a variety of genres and levels of difficulty. Examples from fourth-semester Arabic include news stories, summaries of medical studies (for non-specialists), investigative reports, biographies and interviews. In later semesters, texts may be editorials and opinion pieces, political commentary, discussions (either in the form of talk shows or interviews) and excerpts from literary works or television dramas. All texts are authentic, having been produced for a native-speaker audience. The incorporation of these authentic texts places learners in contact with real-life language use at an early stage in their linguistic development (in line with Little, 1997). The instructions supplied at the beginning of the semester provide students with a framework for dealing with each text, which they work with outside of class.

Listening

The instructions for listening assignments explain the goal of the task, the specific steps to be followed and provide information on grading. The steps are as shown below:

Independent listening instructions

In listening, we aim to train you to identify the main idea of a text, and any details that you can get; and then to identify a part of the text that you do not immediately understand and to attempt to figure out what it means. Once you have gone as far as you can go with comprehension, you can exploit the text for language, by taking away some useful vocabulary and expressions, or maybe a new way of saying something that you never heard before. You will note down this new language and then use it in your writing and audio assignments. With each independent listening, follow this procedure:

- Listen once, then make a few notes (in English is fine) about the general meaning of the text. What is the main point? A short sentence is good.

- Listen again, and note any further details. (Don't spend long on this – short notes leave you more time for listening.)

- Now identify one part of the text that you didn't quite get (write the time in your notes, e.g. 00:25–00:40). Write down what you think is being said.

- Listen three more times to that one bit, using the pause button as necessary. Write down any new thoughts. If possible, identify certain words that are giving you trouble. Write down a guess as to what they may mean, and then check them in the dictionary.

- Now choose a bit for detailed listening. Write the time in your notes, and write the Arabic that you hear word for word. (Start short – 20 seconds? And get longer as the course progresses.) Leave gaps where you get stuck.

- Check what you have written. Does it look correct to you? Are there any bits that just can't be right, based on your grammatical knowledge, etc.? Can you fix them? Can you fill any gaps? Can you get the root of a problem word?

- Note down any new vocabulary, expressions or any language that you like the sound of, so that you can use it in your writing and speaking later.

These steps train learners both to interact with the text as a whole unit, building global comprehension, and to analyze discrete elements within it to arrive at a more finely grained understanding. Establishing the general meaning and then going back to pick up further details requires learners to formulate and test hypotheses about what they hear as they try to relate chunks of input (N. Ellis, 2003) to each other and to background knowledge that they bring with them to the task. R. Ellis (2003) makes a distinction between listening to comprehend, which involves a process of prediction, hypothesis testing and inference, and listening to learn, where the listener creates meaning using bottom-up strategies focused on putting linguistic constituents together (see also Lynch, 2009). In a similar vein, Brown (2007), building on Richards (1983), lists a set of macro-skills and micro-skills for listening. Broadly speaking, macro-skills may be defined as skills necessary for understanding the overall meaning of a spoken message, such as the ability to link cause and effect, to determine the communicative function of a text and to identify the main idea and supporting details. Micro-skills may be defined as those that enable the learner to process the linguistic elements that are brought together to convey this meaning: to focus at the sentence level, including the ability to discriminate sounds, to recognize the grammatical class of a given word and to identify the constituents of a sentence.

Part of the appeal of the approach used here is that individual learners are free to focus on aspects of a text (and of language) that are salient to them, rather than relying on a textbook or teacher to select excerpts for them to focus on. Learners are asked to identify a problem area in the text, guess the meaning and then check this guess; different learners will select different areas of a text. The point is to train students not to hypothesize randomly, but to build and refine an interpretation based on evidence, and ideally to get better at making initial hypotheses as a result. An example of this process at work is given below (from a fourth-semester student). Italicized words are written in Arabic in the student's original assignment.

Solving a problem in a listening text
  Main idea: Plastic surgery in Saudi Arabia
  Details:
  - The number of young people getting surgery is growing. (*to grow*)
  - In the US, China, Mexico and India plastic surgery is spreading.
  - Saudi became the first Arab country in terms of the number of surgeries performed.

- Total number of surgeries: Saudi Arabia 141,000; world 18.5 million.
Difficult bit: 0:56 – 1:01
Guess: Men are getting plastic surgery as well.
After completion of the assignment: Men keep quiet about getting plastic surgery.
New vocabulary: *plastic surgery; surgeon; line up; keep quiet; to include.*

The first guess made here is plausible, but the student has refined it by identifying which piece of vocabulary is standing in the way of a more certain interpretation, checking that word (meaning 'keep quiet') and then reformulating the guess based on this new evidence. Graham (1997) found that effective A-level language learners (studying for this pre-university qualification in the United Kingdom) monitor their comprehension, double-checking their interpretations and taking remedial action when necessary, while less successful learners did not check their initial interpretations. Training learners to interpret and then check not only provides them with a strategy for improving comprehension, but also contributes to motivation, since there is always a problem that is both identified and then solved by the learner, providing a sense of achievement.

The word-for-word listening approach focuses learners on recognizing individual sounds, segmenting a streaming text into words and then piecing these together to create meaning. It is important that learners do not simply write what they think they hear, as this does not involve relating words to each other to see if the larger text makes sense. An example, again from a fourth-semester student, is given below. The entire sentence is in Arabic in the original, and the italicized words are new to the student, who has used a dictionary to check them.

Word-for-word listening
It is strange that in _____ of the most _____ wars in history, there was *enthusiasm* among a number of the *participants*.

The gaps here represent words that the learner was unable to identify. An instructor giving feedback will typically write some clue in these gaps. For example, most Arabic words contain a three-consonant root arranged in a certain pattern consisting of vowels and perhaps other non-root consonants. An instructor might provide the root and leave the student to guess the word. In fact, students often submit work with gaps where they have written one or two of these root letters but have been unable to get the third. This approach is highly encouraged, as distinguishing individual sounds is a necessary step in word recognition.

The new vocabulary items from a listening activity are noted at the end of the assignment. I refer to this final stage as 'harvesting' language for future use. Schumann (2001) uses the term 'foraging' and suggests that learning involves a form of foraging behavior that is motivated by an incentive or goal. New language chosen by the learner is then logged in a personal vocabulary book and then activated in speaking and writing assignments. The idea of extracting language from a text is also advocated by Lynch (2009), who cites Samuda (2001) and Sherman (1998). Initially, the language chosen from a text is primarily in the form of vocabulary, but the important point is that the skill of harvesting language is developed, and this can easily be expanded to other areas as the learner becomes more autonomous. For example, Hughes (2002) considers the extent to which the grammar of speech differs from written grammar and comments that the structure of a conversation may differ from culture to culture. Learners who are trained to notice language use should be able to notice and then reproduce grammatical patterns that are unique to the spoken language (a point of particular importance to Arabic, with its multiple dialects).

This approach to listening is complemented by more traditional communicative listening activities in class time, where comprehension questions may be set, and lead-in activities are used to activate schemata, or background knowledge structures with reference to which the reader processes the information in the text (Anderson & Pearson, 1984; Carrell, 1983; Grabe, 2009). The independent listening assignments offer several benefits, complementing the in-class activities. First, the independent assignments always result in a gain for each individual student. When a textbook or a teacher sets a comprehension question, a student who is able to answer that question after listening may have practiced a variety of skills, but he or she has not necessarily had to work to solve a problem. Because independent listening is individualized, it is the learner who decides where in the text things start to get difficult, and who then works to deal with the problem area. Each learner decides what he or she will focus on. As Ellis and Sinclair (1989: 1) state, 'learning is more effective when learners are in control because they learn what they are ready to learn'. Second, this approach allows the use of texts that are far above the student's level and that may lead to frustration if used in a traditional listening activity. Because students are able to choose just one or two areas of a text to work on, they are able to set the difficulty level themselves. Student A may select a relatively simple part of a text, while student B may choose something that is a bit more of a challenge. Third, dealing with difficult texts and achieving so much develops confidence. Students are often initially intimidated by the speed of speech but are then surprised at how much of it they understand once they have completed the assignment. Finally, the independent listening assignments simply allow for increased exposure to authentic texts produced by and for native speakers, and because learners have a framework to help them to approach these texts, they are able to cope with them without feeling overwhelmed.

Reading

Reading assignments have goals similar to those of the listening tasks. The steps provided at the beginning of the semester are as shown here:

Independent reading assignment instructions
- Without using a dictionary, produce a general outline of what the text is about. (English is fine, and perhaps better.) Think of this as a map of the text, which shows where different points are raised or discussed. A short bulleted list works well.
- Now identify a paragraph of the text that you didn't quite get. (Write the paragraph number in your notes.) Write down (in one sentence) what you think is being said.
- Now read that paragraph sentence by sentence. Think about the relationships between the words in each sentence. What is the subject of the verb (if there is one)? What do pronouns refer to? Identify certain words that are giving you trouble. Write down a guess as to what they may mean, and then check them in the dictionary. Write an explanation to show the extent to which you have understood the paragraph, and indicate any bits that are still not clear. Give these your best guess.
- Now choose a part of the text to translate into English. (Keep it short, but increase the difficulty of this part as the course progresses.)
- Note new vocabulary, expressions or any language you like, in order to use later.

The reading assignments train learners in what Grabe (2009) refers to as higher-level processes used to determine what the text is about and how to interpret it, connecting it with existing knowledge and lower-level processes like word recognition and syntactic parsing (see also Eskey, 1988). In producing the initial outline of the text, learners read for general comprehension without getting distracted by potential pitfalls. They identify problem areas during this process, but do not attempt to analyze them. The student then returns to work on a problem area, piecing together a possible meaning and judging whether or not this makes sense in the context. An example of this problem-solving process is given below.

Solving a problem in a reading text
Paragraph 2 (guess):
The police recalled that the airplane was flying above the buildings in Melbourne city last Saturday.
After completing the assignment:
The statement issued by police mentioned that the airplane was circling above the prison yard in Melbourne last Saturday.

In the first guess here, the student has selected an inappropriate meaning for the verb ðakara ('to recall; to mention'). (Both meanings should be familiar to the student, as this happens to be a verb that has already been introduced in the textbook.) In the second attempt, the student has clearly identified some problem words and checked their meaning, which led him or her to select the 'mention' meaning of the verb, as it fits better in the context. This type of flexibility in generating meaning is a valuable skill that enables learners to reformulate an interpretation, rather than becoming hung up on an initial one. Such flexibility is also developed in the translation section of the assignment, in which learners focus on linguistic details to produce an accurate translation of a passage they select.

The entire assignment provides much more freedom for students to focus on what is salient to them than standard reading comprehension activities consisting of questions whose relevance has been determined by the instructor or textbook author. Sheerin (1997) observes that some supposedly independent study materials in self-access centers are basically tests in which there is a set of correct answers, with the traditional authority of the teacher residing in the answer key. Specifying how a learner should engage with a text, rather than what specific semantic or linguistic details he or she should focus on, transfers considerably more control to the learner.

In sum, both the independent listening and the independent reading assignments combine a focus on meaning with a focus on linguistic form (Long, 1991; Long & Robinson, 1998), training students to deal with a text for comprehension using different strategies and then to exploit the text for language development. The assignments are motivational, because there is always a problem that is solved and a corresponding linguistic gain; since students are given a degree of control over the outcome of the assignment, they are free to focus on what they can get from it rather than what they cannot. Speaking and writing are used to activate the language that has been harvested from these assignments. This is the topic of the next section.

Speaking and writing

Speaking and writing assignments in this model require learners to use new language while encouraging individual creativity. Such an approach pairs well with training good listeners and readers to focus on both meaning and form; it rests on the distinction between receptive knowledge, where a linguistic item is recognized and comprehended, and productive knowledge, where an item can be recalled and activated when needed (see Elgort & Nation [2010] for receptive versus productive knowledge of L2 vocabulary). Kumaravadivelu (1994) suggests that rather than comprehension, it may be production that really forces learners to pay attention to form. Asking learners to integrate some newly discovered element of the language (whether that be a word, an expression, a structure, a discourse pattern and so on) into their production requires them to move from being aware that the element exists to fully owning it as part of their own linguistic repertoire (cf. Swain, 1985).

Speaking

In first-year Arabic in our program, speaking is developed through a series of skits that require students to activate language learned from the textbook in a context of their choice. The skits are recorded. From the third semester onward the format changes: students receive a prompt and are asked to record an audio response using Audacity (free recording software available online). They create a sound file and submit it to their instructor via the course website. The aim of these assignments is to build fluency, complexity and accuracy (Skehan, 1996). The instructions for audio assignments are given below.

Audio assignment instructions
    For each audio assignment, follow these steps:
    - Read the assignment prompt.
    - Type a **very brief and simple** outline **in English** of what you want to say. This should be in simple list form, and is just to jog your memory when you start speaking.
    - Identify the new language that you want to activate (some of the **new** vocabulary, expressions and grammatical structures that you have studied since you submitted your previous recording).
    - Decide where you will use this new language, and add it to the relevant place in your outline. Do not write full sentences. This is just to jog your memory. You will lose points for reading rather than talking.
    - Record in Audacity, and Export (**not save**) as a WAV file.
    - You are now going to record yourself correcting your original file. Your teacher should be able to hear the original error, and then your correction.
    - Open the original WAV file in Windows Media Player (or some other program).
    - Start recording a new file in Audacity.
    - As you notice errors in your original, pause the original and say the correction out loud. Audacity will record the original that is playing in the background, and it will record the corrections you make, so the second sound file will be a corrected original.
    - Your completed assignment should consist of your preparatory notes and this second sound file.

Assignment prompts are posted every week on the course website. They are linked to course content, and they get more challenging as students advance. The first example below is from the fourth semester; the second is from the sixth semester.

Sample prompts for audio assignment

Why are some people more successful in life than others? What is success, anyway?

In your opinion, what social factors lead to a cohesive society, and what factors can be dangerous for its continuation as a coherent social group?

Audio assignments represent a type of planned discourse (Ochs, 1979) where learners are able to organize their thoughts prior to speaking, freeing them up to focus on how to express what they want to say when they record and enabling them to speak with greater fluency. R. Ellis (2003) observes that giving learners time to plan before they speak results in fewer production problems. In addition, because the planning stage also involves a focus on language, learners build complexity by planning to use more sophisticated linguistic features. For example, in spontaneous speech a student may avoid the passive voice or use of a relative clause (Schachter, 1974) simply to avoid linguistic breakdown. Likewise, familiar L2 vocabulary (e.g. *talk about the problem of* for a learner of English) is more likely to be used even when a less high-frequency expression (such as *address* or *delve into*) is known. Planning allows students to select linguistic items for activation before they need them and to place them into the point in the outline where they plan to use them. An example of the preparatory notes that accompany an audio assignment is given below. The original is planned in English (so that the learner does not read it aloud when recording in Arabic). The words in brackets are Arabic in the original, but I have italicized the English words that correspond with the Arabic to show what the student is targeting.

Sample preparatory notes

- some people are successful because of their personalities
- *smart* people (أذكياء)
- people who *discuss* (يناقشون) *important* things (مهم) with important people
- good studying and *morals* (أخلاق)
- *polite* (مؤدب) people
- people with many *friendships* (صداقات)
- success is not the *most important* thing (أهم)
- *confidence/trust* (ثقة) is important
- there people aren't *scared* (خائف) for the future or relationships
- some successful people are *kind* (قلبه أبيض)
- some *have no feelings* (البلادم) or are *obnoxious* (ثقيل دم)

These notes are submitted with the assignment so that the teacher is able to see evidence of planning and an effort to use new language. The assignment targets accuracy by requiring the learner to correct the original recording before submission. The aim is to train learners to monitor their linguistic production themselves without relying on correction from the teacher. Teacher feedback typically consists of drawing the learner's attention to errors that seem inappropriate for the student's level (and which should have been picked up during correction) and suggesting one or two useful linguistic items. Future recordings should illustrate an effort to act on this feedback by using any corrections and suggested language in addition to whatever new linguistic items the student has chosen to target.

A valid criticism of this type of assignment is that speaking is used primarily for language development rather than as a skill in its own right. Hughes (2002) points to a difference between teaching a language through speaking (where some language point is introduced and then used in a speaking activity) and genuinely teaching the spoken form of a language. In the case of English, she notes that teaching the spoken language involves deciding whether to teach common spoken expressions like *ain't*; *good thing you told me*; *the man I told you about, his brother's wife's bought my car* and so on, as well as decisions regarding dialect, correctness and discourse practices. Citing Scollon and Wong-Scollon (1991), Hughes points out that patterns of topic introduction differ in Asian culture (where a topic is rarely introduced immediately), and that true expertise in speaking any language requires a speaker to learn the cultural, social and perhaps even political factors that condition language use. Developing language through speaking need not miss these important elements, however, if language is defined broadly as encompassing not only linguistic items, but also conditions of use. These speaking assignments train students to notice and then use, and noticing is not limited to discrete vocabulary items but can incorporate differences in register, dialect and discourse patterns as exposure to the language increases. The point is that students get used to intentionally using new language, and the contexts in which certain language is used, setting their own goals for what they want to incorporate into their own linguistic production and creating contexts (in their assignments and in regular interaction) to do so. The habit of creating contexts to use new language is vital, whether this be in an assignment or in spontaneous conversation. Rowsell and Libben (1994) found that a learner's approach to use of the target language is an important factor that distinguishes high achievers from low, with high achievers actively creating contexts for language use and taking advantage of these opportunities to use what they have learned. The speaking assignments discussed here aim to train all learners to do this rather than leaving it to chance. The writing assignments are based on the same philosophy.

Writing

For writing, students receive prompts that at lower levels of instruction are accompanied by language-based requirements regarding how much new vocabulary should be used, how many examples of new linguistic structures must be included and so on. Students are encouraged to select these examples of new language before they start writing and then to construct their writing around them, creating contexts in which they make sense. Students submit a draft, get feedback and submit a second draft approximately two weeks later. The second draft has a higher word count, is expanded with new language learned in the intervening two-week period and incorporates the feedback on the original draft. In a study of good L2 writers, Gordon (2008) discusses a particular successful writer who makes notes of new vocabulary when reading, notes how it is used and then uses it in her own writing. Likewise Graham (1997) points to a link between a focus on form (Long, 1991; Long & Robinson, 1998) and accuracy in production. She found that good writers judged whether language used was accurate based on specific examples of how they had seen it used previously, while weaker writers referred to things 'just looking right' based on a hunch.

With their focus on language use, these writing assignments may be viewed as taking a focus on the written product to extremes: learners are encouraged to write with the aim of activating language rather than thinking about what they want to say and then finding suitable language to express that. Hyland (2003) remarks that an exclusive concern with language (form and function) divorces writing from the purpose and personal experience of the writer, and that writing tasks should therefore provide meaningful contexts for authentic expression. The provision of a prompt in our model aims to strike a middle ground. If assignments asking learners to use new language (with no prompt) focus too much on language, there is a risk in the opposite approach: giving students total freedom to choose a topic can lead to the problem that they are so keen to convey a given message that they spend considerable time and effort looking up new language which they then forget once the assignment is submitted. Nation (2001, 2007) emphasizes the importance of having students use L2 vocabulary that they already know in their linguistic output, and these assignments accomplish this while providing an opportunity for the learner to be creative as well. The writing assignment prompts typically ask a student for an opinion or stance. The example below is used in sixth-semester Arabic.

Sample writing prompt

Do you think that poverty is inevitable in a capitalist society? Do you think that the rich should help the poor, or is this the responsibility of the government?

Prompts are usually connected to the theme being studied in the textbook. Some activities that focus on the writing process, such as brainstorming ideas or forming connections between different areas of the topic, take place in class discussions before students write at home. By including a prompt, the assignments provide learners with a chance to express an opinion, and to be creative in doing so, while at the same time requiring them to use recently studied forms and vocabulary. This not only helps to cement what students have noticed, but as Williams (2005) asserts, it can help them to notice what they cannot yet do and may prime them to notice the language they are missing when they encounter it in future input.

In sum, the independent skills component described here trains learners to focus on form, to document and then use new language, with the consequence that they keep moving forward in their language acquisition. While this independent component can stand alone as part of a course and need not intrude into class time, it provides a valuable source of material for teachers to exploit in follow-up activities. The next section describes some ways that this may be done, together with information on using the component as a method of alternative assessment.

In-class work and assessment

The independent assignments that learners complete outside of class provide an excellent source of material for expansion in in-class communicative activities. Having students work in pairs or groups to discuss their interpretations of a text, exchange new language and to then give a personal response to the content of the text is a natural extension of the reading and listening assignments. This not only bolsters comprehension but also provides an opportunity to consolidate new language through use. Lynch (2009) advocates class activities that focus on how individual learners have interpreted a listening text; likewise, Grabe (2009) points out that comprehension of a reading text is supported and expanded by interaction in group work. These activities need not take a long time. Typically, the first 10 minutes of class following an independent reading or listening assignment are set aside for group work in which students exchange what they thought the text meant, what they learned and their opinions on the issues raised. They complete this activity in Arabic, using new language to summarize and discuss, followed by whole-class discussion that then highlights shared understandings of the text as well as variations in interpretations.

Following an audio assignment where students have planned and recorded a monologue in response to a prompt at home, class time is devoted to discussing the same topic in pairs. Students engage in conversation here, exchanging their opinions and asking questions to clarify or expand on what the other is saying. This activity is repeated three or four times with different partners in a kind of supported spontaneous speech. It is supported because the learner has thought through his or her position beforehand, and has rehearsed a response (planned speech). It is spontaneous because this planned speech is interrupted, deviated, clarified and so on because there is now an interlocutor who does not just passively listen but interacts with what is being said. Students have pre-prepared chunks of language to fall back on, but they have to think on their feet as well. Learners rarely appear bored by the repetition, but rather confident (since they have practiced at home); the more fluent speech that results motivates and encourages them. Larsen-Freeman (2010) suggests that much L2 use is iterative, and that repeated activity in different interactions is therefore a useful device for acquisition. R. Ellis (2003) also observes that rehearsal and repetition strengthen task performance. The content of writing assignments is exchanged orally in class in a similar way, with students questioning each other, clarifying and exchanging useful expressions included in their drafts.

Assessment of the independent skills work complements traditional assessment through tests and exams. The assignments function as a learner record that demonstrates the development of key skills over time. This model has its roots in Syverson's (2014) learning record, a method of documenting skill development and achievement in a variety of learning settings based on observation and samples of work (among several other methods). At the beginning of each Arabic course, the teacher discusses the learner record with the class, highlighting the key skill areas in which they will be assessed (as detailed in the independent assignment instructions). Learners are made aware that they need to demonstrate the development of these skills over time in order to maintain a high grade. For example, if a student produces a translation that makes little sense in an early reading assignment but gets consistently better as time goes on, no problem arises. If no improvement is made in response to feedback, the grade in consecutive assignments is decreased. This is not due to an incorrect translation in and of itself, but rather to the fact that the student is not developing the targeted skill of checking the plausibility of the translation (an independent learner skill).

In sum, the independent component aims to train language learners to work with but not depend on a teacher. It engages students with real language and can be motivational. It pairs well with in-class communicative activities and can be used as a method of alternative assessment based on skill development rather than an isolated instance of performance in the language.

Conclusion

The model for building learner independence presented in this chapter aims to increase the number of effective learners in a class, in turn increasing the likelihood that they will continue with the language and remain motivated to continue developing their proficiency. It also seeks to equip learners with the necessary skills to transition to full learner autonomy once they leave the classroom setting. The assignments outlined in this chapter train students to work on comprehension problems, harvest language from input and use that harvested language in their own linguistic production. It also trains them to monitor their production, notice areas for improvement and set goals to rectify gaps in their knowledge.

A student can continue to use this model in a variety of contexts. Upon transitioning to content classes taught in the language, he or she can continue to deal with texts in the same way and to use new language in class discussions and written work. The same is true for overseas study and in the workplace. Language teachers may also adapt the model. In a media class, for example, where students deal with real-time texts that have no accompanying materials, the model provides an ideal framework for student assignments and assessment. It is available as a course framework for teachers who accept advanced students for independent study and for graduate students who engage in research and work with a mentor to maintain their language skills. Because it is not linked to any specific material, the learner record model is extremely versatile. What remains constant is that skill development is structured, and eventually the autonomous learner is free to adapt the model as he or she sees fit.

References

Anderson, R. and Pearson, P. (1984) A schema-theoretic view of basic processes in reading comprehension. In P. Pearson (ed.) *Handbook of Reading Research*. New York: Longman.

Benson, P. (1997) The philosophy and politics of learner autonomy. In P. Benson and P. Voller (eds) *Autonomy and Independence in Language Learning* (pp. 18–34). London/New York: Longman.

Benson, P. and Voller, P. (1997) *Autonomy and Independence in Language Learning*. London/New York: Longman.

Brown, H.D. (2007) *Teaching by Principles: An Interactive Approach to Language Pedagogy* (3rd edn). White Plains, NY: Pearson.

Carrell, P. (1983) Some issues in studying the role of schemata, or background knowledge, in second language comprehension. *Reading in a Foreign Language* 1, 81–92.

Cohen, A. (1998) *Strategies in Learning and Using a Second Language*. London/New York: Longman.

Cohen, A. (2007) Coming to terms with language learner strategies: Surveying the experts. In A. Cohen and E. Macaro (eds) *Language Learner Strategies* (pp. 29–46). Oxford: Oxford University Press.

Cohen, A. (2009) Focus on the language learner: Styles, strategies and motivation. In R. Schmidt (ed.) *An Introduction to Applied Linguistics* (pp. 161–178). London: Hodder Education.

Cohen, A. (2012) Strategies: The interface of styles, strategies and motivation on tasks. In S. Mercer, S. Ryan and M. Williams (eds) *Language Learning Psychology: Research, Theory and Pedagogy* (pp. 136–150). Basingstoke: Palgrave.

Dickinson, L. (1992) *Learning Autonomy 2: Learner Training for Language Learning*. Dublin: Authentik.

Dörnyei, Z. (2001) *Motivational Strategies in the Language Classroom*. Cambridge: Cambridge University Press.

Dörnyei, Z. (2005) *The Psychology of the Language Learner: Individual Differences in Second Language Acquisition*. Mahwah, NJ: Lawrence Erlbaum.

Elgort, I. and Nation, I.S.P. (2010) Vocabulary learning in a second language: Familiar answers to new questions. In P. Seedhouse, S. Walsh and C. Jenks (eds) *Conceptualising 'Learning' in Applied Linguistics* (pp. 89–104). London: Palgrave Macmillan.

Ellis, N. (2003) Constructions, chunking and connectionism: The emergence of second language structure. In C. Doughty and M. Long (eds) *The Handbook of Second Language Acquisition* (pp. 63–103). Oxford: Blackwell.

Ellis, R. (2003) *Task-based Language Learning and Teaching*. Oxford: Oxford University Press.

Ellis, R. and Sinclair, B. (1989) *Learning to Learn English*. Cambridge: Cambridge University Press.

Esch, E. (1997) Learner training for autonomous language learning. In P. Benson and P. Voller (eds) *Autonomy and Independence in Language Learning* (pp. 164–175). London/New York: Longman.

Eskey, D.E. (1988) Holding in the bottom: An interactive approach to the language problems of second language readers. In P. Carrell, J. Devine and D. Eskey (eds) *Interactive Approaches to Second Language Reading* (pp. 93–100). Cambridge: Cambridge University Press.

Gardner, R. (2010) *Motivation and Second Language Acquisition: The Socio-Educational Model*. New York: Peter Lang.

Gardner, R. and Lambert, W. (1959) Motivational variables in second language acquisition. *Canadian Journal of Psychology* 13, 266–272.

Gardner, R. and Lambert, W. (1972) *Attitudes and Motivation in Second Language Learning*. Rowley, MA: Newbury House.

Gordon, L. (2008) Writing and good language learners. In C. Griffiths (ed.) *Lessons from Good Language Learners* (pp. 83–98). Cambridge: Cambridge University Press.

Grabe, W. (2009) *Reading in a Second Language: Moving from Theory to Practice*. Cambridge: Cambridge University Press.

Graham, S. (1997) *Effective Language Learning: Positive Strategies for Advanced Level Language Learning*. Clevedon: Multilingual Matters.

Griffiths, C. (2008) Strategies and good language learners. In C. Griffiths (ed.) *Lessons from Good Language Learners* (pp. 83–98). Cambridge: Cambridge University Press.

Holec, H. (1981) *Autonomy in Foreign Language Learning*. Oxford: Pergamon.

Hughes, R. (2002) *Teaching and Researching Speaking*. London: Pearson.

Hyland, K. (2003) *Second Language Writing*. Cambridge: Cambridge University Press.

Interagency Language Roundtable (ILR) (2014) ILR Skill Level Descriptions. See www.govtilr.org (accessed 7 July 2015).

Kumaravadivelu, B. (1994) The postmethod condition: (E)merging strategies for second/foreign language teaching. *TESOL Quarterly* 28 (1), 27–48.

Larsen-Freeman, D. (2010) Having and doing: Learning from a complexity theory perspective. In P. Seedhouse, S. Walsh and C. Jenks (eds) *Conceptualising 'Learning' in Applied Linguistics* (pp. 52–68). London: Palgrave Macmillan.

Little, D. (1997) Responding authentically to authentic texts: A problem for self-access language learning? In P. Benson and P. Voller (eds) *Autonomy and Independence in Language Learning* (pp. 225–236). London/New York: Longman.

Littlewood, W. (1997) Self-access: Why do we want it and what can it do? In P. Benson and P. Voller (eds) *Autonomy and Independence in Language Learning* (pp. 79–92). London/New York: Longman.

Long, M. (1991) Focus on form: A design feature in language teaching methodology. In K. De Bot, R. Ginsberg and C. Kramsch (eds) *Foreign Language Research in Cross-Cultural Perspective* (pp. 39–52). Amsterdam/Philadelphia, PA: John Benjamins.

Long, M. and Robinson, P. (1998) Focus on form: Theory, research and practice. In C. Doughty and J. Williams (eds) *Focus on Form in Classroom Second Language Acquisition* (pp. 15–41). Cambridge: Cambridge University Press.

Lynch, T. (2009) *Teaching Second Language Listening.* Oxford: Oxford University Press.

Markus, H. and Nurius, P. (1986) Possible Selves. *American Psychologist* 41, 954–969.

Nation, I.S.P. (2001) *Learning Vocabulary in Another Language.* Cambridge: Cambridge University Press.

Nation, I.S.P. (2007) The four strands. *Innovation in Language Learning and Teaching* 1, 1–12.

Noels, K.A. (2001) New orientations in language learning motivation: Towards a model of intrinsic, extrinsic, and integrative orientations and motivation. In Z. Dörnyei and R. Schmidt (eds) *Motivation and Second Language Acquisition* (pp. 43–68). Mānoa, HI: University of Hawaii Press.

Norton, B. (1995) Social identity, investment and language learning. *TESOL Quarterly* 29, 9–31.

Norton, B. (1997) Language, identity, and the ownership of English. *TESOL Quarterly* 31, 409–429.

Nunan, D. (1997) Designing and adapting materials to encourage learner autonomy. In P. Benson and P. Voller (eds) *Autonomy and Independence in Language Learning* (pp. 192–203). London/New York: Longman.

Ochs, E. (1979) Planned and unplanned discourse. In T. Givón (ed.) *Syntax and Semantics 12: Discourse and Syntax* (pp. 51–80). New York: Academic Press.

O'Malley, J. and Chamot, A. (1990) *Learning Strategies in Second Language Acquisition.* Cambridge: Cambridge University Press.

Oxford, R. (1990) *Language Learning Strategies: What Every Teacher Should Know.* New York: Newbury House.

Oxford, R. (2011) *Teaching and Researching Language Learning Strategies.* London: Pearson.

Oxford, R. and Shearin, J. (1994) Language learning motivation: Expanding the theoretical framework. *Modern Language Journal* 78, 12–28.

Oxford, R. and Leaver, B. (1996) A synthesis of strategy instruction for language learners. In R. Oxford (ed.) *Language Learning Strategies Around the World: Cross-cultural Perspectives* (pp. 227–246). Mānoa, HI: University of Hawaii Press.

Richards, J. (1983) Listening comprehension: Approach, design, procedure. *TESOL Quarterly* 17, 219–239.

Rowsell, L.V. and Libben, G. (1994) The sound of one hand clapping: How to succeed in independent language learning. *Canadian Modern Language Review* 50 (4), 668–688.

Rubin, J. (1975) What the 'good language learner' can teach us. *TESOL Quarterly* 9 (1), 41–51.

Samuda, V. (2001) Guiding relationships between form and meaning during task performance: The role of the teacher. In M. Bygate, P. Skehan and M. Swain (eds) *Researching Pedagogic Tasks: Second Language Learning, Teaching and Testing* (pp. 119–140). Harlow: Pearson.

Schachter, J. (1974) An error in error analysis. *Language Learning* 24 (2), 205–214.

Schumann, J. (2001) Learning as foraging. In Z. Dörnyei and R. Schmidt (eds) *Motivation and Second Language Acquisition* (pp. 21–28). Mānoa, HI: University of Hawaii Press.

Scollon, R. and Wong-Scollon, S. (1991) Topic confusion in English-Asian discourse. *World Englishes* 10 (2), 113–125.

Sheerin, S. (1997) An explanation of the relationship between self-access and independent learning. In P. Benson and P. Voller (eds) *Autonomy and Independence in Language Learning* (pp. 54–65). London/New York: Longman.

Sherman, J. (1998) Independent vocabulary learning. *IATEFL Issues* June–July, 14–15.

Skehan, P. (1996) A framework for the implementation of task-based instruction. *Applied Linguistics* 17 (1), 38–62.

Swain, M. (1985) Communicative competence: Some roles of comprehensible input and comprehensible output in its development. In S. Gass and C. Madden (eds) *Input in Second Language Acquisition* (pp. 235–256). New York: Newbury House.

Syverson, M.A. (2014) The learning record. See www.learningrecord.org (accessed 20 July 2014).

Wenden, A.L. (1991) *Learner Strategies for Learner Autonomy*. Hemel Hempstead: Prentice Hall.

Williams, J. (2005) *Teaching Writing in Second and Foreign Language Classrooms*. New York: McGraw Hill.

Willing, K. (1989) *Teaching How to Learn: Learning Strategies in ESL*. Sydney: National Centre for English Language Teaching and Research.

5 Maximizing Oral Proficiency Development via Telecollaborative Partnerships in the Portuguese Flagship Program

Victoria Hasko, Robert Moser, Fernanda Guida, Mary Elizabeth Hayes and Viviane Klen Alves

Introduction

The Language Flagship program's ambitious goal of enabling students to attain a minimum oral proficiency level of Interagency Language Roundtable (ILR) 2 (Appendix A), to prepare them for extended study abroad (usually 9–12 months) and attainment of ILR 3 proficiency, presents major challenges to US universities (Murphy *et al.*, this volume). In a typical non-immersion US foreign language (FL) program, learners typically stall below the American Council on the Teaching of Foreign Languages (ACTFL) Advanced (ILR 2) level of proficiency (the phenomenon referred to as the 'ceiling effect', Rifkin, 2005). These findings seem to hold not only for undergraduate language majors in a four-year language program but even for pre-service language teacher candidates (Moeller, 2013).

The findings regarding the typical FL proficiency attainments of US learners reflect common curricular challenges faced by universities hosting Language Flagship programs. A limited number of contact hours (three to four hours of classroom instruction per week), limited active participation (i.e. speaking) time per student and scarce opportunities for individualized feedback in a typical North American FL university classroom are widely documented (Eaton, 2012; Maxwell & Garrett, 2002). The additional requirement of preparing students for year-long overseas cultural immersion in academic and professional settings requires sophisticated understanding of and comfort with pragmatic, discursive, cultural and strategic competencies underlying various functional roles that the students are to fulfill abroad (see Davidson *et al.*, this volume). These high expectations present a formidable task, given that US FL classes are often isolated from authentic second language (L2) use outside of the classroom, and US language programs often present 'limited opportunities for committed and consequential communicative engagement' (Thorne, 2010: 139) with communities of L2 practice.

Given the numerous common curricular and instructional limitations, the challenge of meeting the ambitious goals of the Language Flagship (Nugent & Slater, this volume) requires thoughtful, systematic and committed instructional solutions and experimentation with new models of language learning that transcend the traditional boundaries of FL classrooms. In this chapter, we contribute to such efforts by exploring how digitally based pedagogy can bolster FL students' oral proficiency development.

The notion that telecollaborative, digitally supported learning has the potential to play a significant role in the push for innovation in FL instruction has been voiced by numerous scholars advocating for international institutional partnerships in which language partners make use of affordable and accessible technologies to simulate immersion experiences, intercultural dialogue and reciprocal peer-to-peer feedback (for recent arguments, see Chun, 2015; Dooly, 2015; Tcherepashenets, 2015). Yet, empirical investigations into the efficacy of multimodal (i.e. audio-video-textual), synchronous telecollaborative projects built into FL curricula are still fairly scarce and vary greatly in their choice of languages, levels of proficiency, objects of inquiry, tasks and goals. The present study fits into the line of research on digitally supported communicative language teaching by seeking to illuminate how bilingual telecollaborative partnerships built into a FL course may facilitate oral proficiency development, specifically in the context of a Language Flagship program. This study analyzes a synchronous video-audio telecollaborative project carried out between the University of Georgia and the State University of São Paulo, Brazil (Universidade Estadual Paulista – UNESP) during which the participating FL (Portuguese and English, respectively) students engaged in an open-ended task of collaborative dialoguing in bilingual tandem teams. The project was integrated into a custom-designed intermediate-level Portuguese course designated as a site for pedagogical innovation research by and for the University of Georgia Portuguese Flagship program.

Telecollaboration as a Promising Pedagogical Avenue

Telecollaboration is defined as a shared teaching and learning experience facilitated through internet or other network-based technologies between distanced partners in institutional settings in order to provide language learners with opportunities for social interaction, dialogue, debate and intercultural exchange in their language of study, and for collaborative construction of knowledge in the form of various virtual artifacts and practices (Belz, 2003; Dooly, 2008; Guth & Helm, 2012). Digitally based communication tools used for these purposes have included written interactions via email, videoconferencing, social networking sites, mobile phone applications, chat, forum boards, blogging sites, virtual worlds, online gaming environments and mobile apps. The list is ever expanding.

Bilingualism, learner autonomy and reciprocity are among the central principles underlying successful FL telecollaborative partnerships. For example, in a telecollaboration where US learners of Portuguese are partnered with Brazilian students learning English, the participants are responsible for balancing their language use in English and Portuguese. The proponents of telecollaborative learning argue that because each partner is practicing the FL and serving as a language model and tutor of his or her native language, this pedagogical arrangement creates an inherently autonomous, reciprocal and collaborative learning context (Telles & Vassalo, 2006). Such 'alchemy' of internet-mediated communication tools and FL instruction has the potential to bolster FL instruction by engaging university students in plurilingual communication and literacy practices, cultivating their abilities 'to make collectively relevant meanings in the inherently intercultural contexts of everyday life' (Thorne, 2006: 23).

The conceptualization of FL learning that embraces online literacies and emphasizes the connection between relevant lifelong learning, language, communication and communities is in line with both the *World-Readiness Standards for Learning Languages* (National Standards in Foreign Language Education Project, 2015) and the *Common European Framework of Reference for Languages* (Council of Europe, 2014). A review of recent collections (Dooly & O'Dowd, 2012; Guth & Helm, 2012; Thomas *et al.*, 2013) containing vignettes of rich educational exchanges demonstrates the inspiring goals, thoughtful design and curricular innovation made possible by telecollaborative technologies. Yet, Dooly (2015) admits that robust examples of carefully orchestrated telecollaborative learning opportunities are still scant on a global level, and that there is still a gap between awareness of the need for such practices and effective integration of technology into collaborative practices in FL classrooms.

Furthermore, our knowledge with regard to the effectiveness of telecollaboration for specific FL goals is quite limited. A recent review of over 350 studies (Golonka *et al.*, 2014), which included but was not limited to network-based social computing, revealed that 'in spite of an abundance of publications available on the topic of technology use in FL learning and teaching, evidence of efficacy is limited' (Golonka *et al.*, 2014: 70) and that the state of the relevant literature 'leaves much to be desired in terms of a unified research agenda' (Golonka *et al.*, 2014: 71) as well as 'durable, validated findings' (Golonka *et al.*, 2014: 71; see also Felix, 2005). In reference to the goal of oral proficiency development, reports of the empirically established efficacy of computer-mediated communication studies versus traditional face-to-face environments are not conclusive.

A recent meta-analysis of 25 relevant studies (Lin, 2015) reveals that communication mediated by computer technologies can produce a moderate positive effect on L2 learners' oral proficiency, including pronunciation and the lexical and syntactic levels of oral production; at the same time, the author reports a (counterintuitive and unexplained) negative effect on fluency and accuracy. While many believe that real-time synchronous speaking should be the holy grail of effective FL instruction, another meta-analysis of 59 primary investigations examining the impact of computer-mediated communication on L2 learning outcomes offers a conflicting conclusion that 'studies employing synchronous communication for speaking generated both the largest positive...and the largest negative effect sizes' (Lin, 2014: 132).

The promise of peer feedback presumed to result from the reciprocal nature of telecollaboration is another under-researched area. While many educators may be drawn to telecollaboration due to its potential for individualized peer-to-peer assistance, questions of how frequently or effectively peer-to-peer error correction and feedback actually occur in telecollaborative environments appear not to have been sufficiently explored in reference to synchronous oral exchanges, possibly because oral interactions do not result in readily available texts or transcripts. Countering the assumption that telecollaborative environments naturally facilitate peer correction, recent studies have instead discovered only negligible evidence of error correction in the transcripts of oral telecollaborative sessions (e.g. Ware & O'Dowd, 2008).

Following this line of inquiry, and in the search for effective and empirically informed pedagogical solutions for students in our intermediate-level Portuguese Flagship Program, this study seeks to understand the potential of bilingual telecollaborative communication for L2 oral proficiency development.

Theoretical Framework

The theoretical framework for the study is dually informed by a cognitive approach drawing on a series of psychologically oriented measures of FL gains (complexity, accuracy, fluency) as well as a socially informed interpretive approach to understanding oral skills development through the lens of sociocultural theory (Lantolf & Thorne, 2006; Vygotsky, 1978) and dynamic usage-based interpretations of language learning (de Bot *et al.*, 2013; Larsen-Freeman, 2014). The duality of the adopted theoretical framework allows us to document and interpret FL learners' oral proficiency development in the context of their socioeducational histories as well as the affordances for language development as they sequentially emerge moment-to-moment in the ecology of telecollaborative dialoguing between learners.

The idea that mediated social activity is the key both to learning and to cognitive development is predicated on the work of Vygotsky (1978) and is captured in his two key concepts, the *Zone of Actual Development* (ZAD) and the *Zone of Proximal Development* (ZPD). The two notions juxtapose what the learner can achieve independently and those functions still in the process of maturation that can emerge under the guidance of more capable collaborators (Vygotsky, 1978). The distinguishing characteristic of this approach is that it 'places mediation, either by other or self, at the core of development and use' (Lantolf, 2011: 24).

While most studies of computer-mediated communication have focused on *other* mediation (i.e. peer feedback), other types of mediation not to be overlooked include self-regulation and tool/artifact/sign/ task mediation (Karpov, 2005; Lawrence & Valsiner, 2003). Speech or language itself is seen to play a dual role as a primary meditating means (a semiotic system) and a mediated function (Damianova & Sullivan, 2011). Thus, Swain (2006: 98) coined the term *languaging* to refer to 'the process of making meaning and shaping knowledge and experience through language'. The argument is that 'through the use of language to intentionally organize and control their mental processes during the performance of cognitively complex tasks, [L2 learners] discover meanings and connections that were unknown to them prior to the act of languaging' (Knouzi *et al.*, 2010: 24).

The environment of telecollaborative interactions abounds in cognitive and social affordances for languaging in an FL classroom. To understand how the potential for the development of oral skills emerges during telecollaboration, we detail instances of peer-to-peer interactions during which microscopic changes on various sublevels of linguistic abilities may occur. The approach of documenting moment-to-moment emergence of higher levels of linguistic knowledge in (tele)collaborative activity is referred to as *microgenesis* (Gutierrez, 2007). The intense focus on developmental processes of short duration informs our broader understanding of the development and reconstruction of higher mental capacities as a consequence of their formation during sociocultural and sociogenetic mental activity.

Motivated by the above theoretical considerations, our study sought answers to the following research questions:

(1) How did the profile of the learners' oral proficiency change from before to after the telecollaborative project?
(2) What types of microgenetic episodes did the context of telecollaborative dialoguing generate? How was collaborative assistance within these episodes solicited, offered and appropriated by the learners?

Methodology

Pedagogical site

The Portuguese Program at the University of Georgia, one of the largest in the nation, offers a wide range of language and literature courses and degrees at both the undergraduate and graduate levels. It first implemented telecollaborative learning in conjunction with UNESP in spring 2011, as part of UNESP's well-established instructional and research-based Teletandem project (UNESP, n.d.). The study reported here focuses on a high-intermediate Portuguese course required for Flagship candidates, which served as a pedagogical site for the telecollaborative exchange.

The course is designed to enable students to achieve high levels of conversational Portuguese; thus it provided a fitting platform for a pedagogical project focused on oral proficiency development. The telecollaborative sessions were built into the University of Georgia Portuguese course as a series of unstructured peer-to-peer conversations between University of Georgia learners of Portuguese and UNESP students studying English as an FL. These telecollaborative sessions took place weekly for 50 minutes, with a total of eight meetings over the course of one semester. We refer to the activity that ensued during the telecollaborative sessions as *telecollaborative dialoguing* to acknowledge the reciprocal nature of joint communication construction inherent and unique to computer-mediated telecollaborative learning.

Each of the bilingual sessions occurred half in English and half in Portuguese, with students controlling the language balance autonomously in paired tandem partnerships. The students also assumed authority for selecting the topics of their interactions, choosing from personal, social, cultural, academic or political issues. While an instructor was present during the telecollaborative sessions, her role was that of an observer and general facilitator rather than a teacher in the traditional sense.

Participants

Eleven telecollaborative pairs participated in the semester-long project. In our effort to carry out a close, in-depth analysis of the dynamics of oral proficiency development embedded in telecollaboration, we selected three focal learners of Portuguese of several different acquisitional profiles, including those with and without immersive experiences as well as heritage versus non-heritage speakers of Spanish.

Sources of data

Pre- and post-telecollaboration oral proficiency interviews (OPIs)

To assess the effects of telecollaborative interactions on the participants' development of oral proficiency, we collected their oral speech samples before and after the telecollaboration by using a truncated version of the OPI developed for local institutional purposes. The Truncated Institutional OPI tests[1] used for this study (hereafter, TIOPI) were administered on campus by a native Portuguese speaker who was undergoing training for OPI certification.

TIOPI tests were not administered with the purpose of determining the learners' level corresponding to the official ACTFL proficiency scale per se. Rather, we were interested in collecting the transcripts of the students' performance to study any developmental shifts in their ability to carry out spontaneous oral production tasks within the context of the TIOPIs conducted before and after telecollaborative dialoguing.

Video recordings of telecollaborative dialoguing

Given the relatively short duration of the project, we chose two maximally distant measurement points to gauge and understand the microgenetic dynamics of learners' oral proficiency, i.e. the first and the last (eighth) sessions. The video recordings of the TIOPI and telecollaborative sessions of the three focal learners were transcribed by one of the co-authors and checked for accuracy by at least one more co-author. Only the Portuguese-language half of the session was used for the present study.

The language learning history questionnaire

To gain a more informed, emic-oriented understanding of the learners' diverse experiences with FL learning, intercultural interactions and patterns of language socialization, we designed and administered a *Language Learning History Questionnaire*. The questionnaire additionally included an element of self-assessment of learners' speaking, listening, reading and writing skills in each of their languages to allow us an additional level of appraisal of the learners' capabilities in all of their languages and the complex relationships among such competencies.

Analytical foci

Cognitive measures of oral proficiency development

The construct of oral proficiency in an FL is multicomponential. Traditionally, the most prominent descriptors of oral proficiency, as well as the largely accepted measures of L2 development, have included complexity, accuracy and fluency (Housen & Kuiken, 2009). In this study, we prioritize fluency and complexity over accuracy due to space constraints, but also following Brumfit (1984), who posited that fluency is associated with open-ended activities that foster spontaneous oral communication, which aligns well with our study design; accuracy, on the other hand, prioritizes controlled production of grammatically correct linguistic structures, which was not our focus.

Definitions of *fluency* typically underscore ease and smoothness of delivery. Recent research studies have empirically determined several factors that contribute to perceptions of fluency in FL speech (see Housen & Kuiken, 2009 for an overview): these factors include speed fluency and speech disfluencies such as self-repairs and false starts. Accordingly, in our study we offer a twofold assessment of fluency: *speed fluency*, measured as the number of words per minute (wpm), and *repair fluency*, defined as the rate of occurrence of false starts, self-repairs and hesitation markers per 100 words.

Complexity is captured in our study through the lens of syntactic complexity, which can be defined as 'progressively more elaborate language' (Foster & Skehan, 1996: 303). Here, we measure syntactic complexity by calculating AS-units (Analysis of Speech Units) in learner speech. AS-units include utterances consisting of an independent clause or a subclausal unit, plus any subordinate clause(s) associated with it (Foster *et al.*, 2000). AS-units are commonly used as markers of syntactic sophistication of oral language, although admittedly they measure the length of surface syntactic structures rather than variation.

While we see considerable value in investigating L2 oral proficiency by measuring increases in learner fluency and expansion of their syntactic complexity repertoires, we also side with the scholars who believe that reducing our interpretation of learner development to a quantitative presentation of select measures is not sufficient. Thus, we additionally put forth our qualitative interpretation of the fluency and complexity measures, which is grounded in the learners' socioeducational histories as detailed in the questionnaire responses, to contextualize and inform our interpretation of the cognitive measures vis-à-vis the unique experiences that the learners may bring with them to the telecollaborative project.

Sociointeractional analysis of oral proficiency development

We now turn to the telecollaborative sessions to understand the unique nature of affordances for oral proficiency development embedded in the sociocultural activity of telecollaborative dialoguing. To answer the research question (Q #2) related to the types of assistance offered and used by the participants, language-related episodes (LREs) were used as a unit of microgenetic analysis. Swain and Lapkin (1998: 326) define LREs as 'any part of a dialogue where the students talk about the language they are producing, question their language use, or correct themselves or others'. Foster and Ohta (2005) specify that LREs can lead to modifications in learner language that result from peer feedback but may also assume the form of self-initiated self-repair or elaborations prompted by such nuanced types of peer assistance as expression of interest, encouragement or surprise. Here, we define microgenetic LREs as any part of the conversation in which participants mediate each other's L2 oral development by questioning language use, soliciting or offering help, engaging in meta-talk about the language, encouraging each other to continue speaking or self-mediating their own performance while engaged in telecollaborative dialoguing. Accordingly, we identified the instances of interactions in our data that included: the focal learners asking their peers for specific assistance (e.g. help with answering their question on lexicon or grammar); Brazilian peers taking the initiative to provide unsolicited feedback (instantiated as an explicit correction or an implicit recast); metalinguistic discussion initiated by either the US learners or their Brazilian peers interrogating the language used and episodes of affective mediation offered by the Brazilian peers in encouragement of the learners' talk (*affective continuers*). We additionally coded for whether or not the identified LREs led to observable modifications in learner speech following these episodes. These LRE types are summarized in Table 5.1.

Table 5.1 LRE types

LRE types	Coding for subsequent modifications
Request for specific assistance	+/- appropriation of provided language models in learner speech
Peer-initiated assistance	+/- appropriation of provided language models in learner speech
Metalinguistic discussion about language use	
Affective continuers	

Analysis

We start our analysis from the narrative presentation of the participants' socioeducational profiles, based on the results of the *Language Learning History Questionnaire*. The cognitive measures and sociogenetic data stemming from the analysis of the LREs are presented quantitatively, followed by a qualitative discussion and interpretation of all the data types.

Participants' socioeducational profiles

Brian's socioeducational profile

Brian (all names are pseudonyms) was a junior majoring in International Affairs. According to the *Language Learning History Questionnaire*, he had taken some Spanish in high school and Mandarin at the University of Georgia but deemed his knowledge of Spanish below minimal. He self-assessed his proficiency as rather low (2 on a 5-point Likert scale for listening and speaking, and 1 for reading and writing, where 1 stood for 'minimal' and 5 for 'native-like'). By the time of the telecollaboration project, Brian had studied Portuguese for one year: two consecutive academic semesters at the University of Georgia and one summer at a rigorous Portuguese immersion program at a prestigious US liberal arts college immediately thereafter. He was emerging from just one year of Portuguese studies as a confident and determined language learner; he self-assessed his proficiency in Portuguese as intermediate (3 for listening, speaking and reading, and 2 for writing). He intended to continue taking Portuguese and to travel to Brazil for the Flagship capstone overseas program.

Veronica's socioeducational profile

Veronica, a junior majoring in Environmental Health Sciences, started studying Portuguese at the University of Georgia as a novice and was enrolled in her fifth consecutive Portuguese course at the time of the project. Veronica's *Language Learning History Questionnaire* paints a picture of rather exclusive world travels and extensive immersive experiences in some of the most plurilingual and pluricultural communities in the world throughout her childhood: she attended a Dutch-language elementary school in Amsterdam while residing there for four years with her family, and then an English-language K-12 international middle school in Geneva, where she studied French as an FL. She continued to study French again in the United States for four years in high school. Curiously, however, when self-rating her proficiency in FLs, Veronica rated her Portuguese the highest (4 on the 5-point Likert scale in speaking; 3 in listening, reading and writing), followed by French (3 in all four skills) and Dutch (3 in speaking and listening; 2 in reading and writing). Veronica deemed Portuguese helpful for her future career but clarified that studying the language was her personal choice rather than a requirement.

Andrea's socioeducational profile

Andrea was a junior majoring in International Affairs and Romance Languages who had completed two semesters of Portuguese prior to the semester during which the telecollaborative project took place. Born in Bolivia to a Bolivian father and a Californian mother, Andrea moved with her family to the United States at the age of one. She grew up speaking both English and Spanish, thus acquiring Spanish as a heritage language in addition to studying it formally at school and at the university. She self-rated her proficiency in English and Spanish for all four skills as native-like but admitted that she rarely read or wrote in Spanish outside of class. Andrea additionally shared that her motivation to study Portuguese was supported by her rapid progress with the language; indeed, only in her third semester of Portuguese, she self-rated her proficiency in listening and reading as a 4 (on the 5-point Likert scale) and as a 3 in speaking and writing.

Brazilian peers

The Brazilian learners who partnered with the students under examination were all female undergraduate students at UNESP in Brazil pursuing an educational degree in teaching English as an FL. In addition to English, they were also proficient in Spanish.

Results from cognitive measures

The dynamics of the cognitive indices of oral proficiency development for each of the focal learners are represented graphically in Figures 5.1 through 5.4. The figures illustrate that the participants' initial oral proficiency profiles and the dynamics of the growth trajectories under analysis reveal some common trends but are also characterized by considerable inter-learner and intra-learner variability. With regard to *speed fluency* (Figure 5.1), Brian outperformed Veronica and Andrea on TIOPI 1, exhibiting a highly impressive rate of speech at 103 wpm in comparison to a much lower count of 40 and 61 wpm recorded for Veronica's and Andrea's speed fluency, respectively.

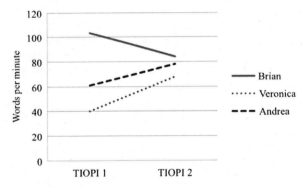

Figure 5.1 Dynamics of speed fluency

If we consider the dynamics of changes from before to after the project, both Veronica's and Andrea's speed fluency grew substantially to reach 68 and 78 wpm, respectively, on TIOPI 2, while Brian's rate of speech dropped to 84 wpm. Notwithstanding this slowing of speech rate, Brian still showed the highest speech rate among the focal group on both the initial and final assessment interview.

The results of *repair fluency* counts (Figure 5.2), defined and measured here in terms of the instances of such types of disfluency as false starts, self-correction and hesitation markers, align with and add some depth to the matrix of speed fluency performance outcomes: Brian's initial interview contained the lowest number of disfluencies (10 per 100 words) within the group, but TIOPI 2 was characterized by a higher level of repairs and hesitation markers in comparison to the first one (19 per 100 words). Veronica's and Andrea's performance, on the other hand, exhibited a marked improvement, with the ratio counts of various types of disfluencies decreasing in their speech from 23 to 16 per 100 words, and 26 to 8, respectively, from TIOPI 1 to 2. Andrea's improvement on this measure was the most drastic: overall, she emerged from the project as the learner whose delivery was marked by the lowest number of repairs and hesitation markers in TIOPI 2.

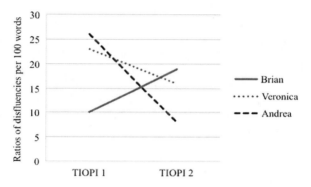

Figure 5.2 Dynamics of repair fluency

With regard to *syntactic complexity* (Figure 5.3), as measured by the average length of AS-units, all participants exhibited upward growth: Brian's performance on both TIOPI 1 and 2 was slightly superior at 9 and 12 words per AS-unit, respectively.

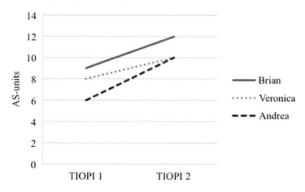

Figure 5.3 Dynamics of syntactic complexity

Veronica's and Andrea's syntactic complexity counts increased on average from 8 to 10 and 6 to 10 words per AS-unit, respectively. Note that Brian started out as the learner whose speech averaged the longest AS-units, and he also completed TIOPI 2 with the most syntactically complex responses among the focal group.

To highlight the magnitude of the growth patterns, we further transformed the number counts for each of the measures into percentages: the percentages of the recorded changes allowed us to gauge the extent to which the learners' performance shifted more readily from the TIOPI 1 to 2 assessment. As Figure 5.4 illustrates, although Brian's performance indicated a 19% decline in speed fluency with a 47% spike in disfluencies in TIOPI 2, his syntactic complexity grew by 25%. Veronica's performance was characterized by growth, most notably with regard to fluency (a 41% increase in speed fluency and a 30% drop in repair fluency); 20% of AS-units in her speech grew lengthier from TIOPI 1 to 2. The dynamics of Andrea's oral proficiency development, which also revealed a positive growth trend on all measures, are particularly impressive, with a 69% decrease in disfluencies and a 40% increase in syntactic complexity; her overall speed fluency grew by 22%.

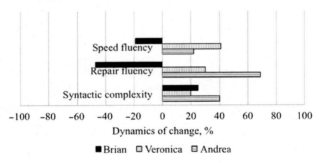

Figure 5.4 Dynamics of change in percentages

Sociogenetic interactions with the LREs

The second question of the study shifts the focus away from the oral proficiency tests to the transcripts of telecollaborative dialoguing in an effort to gain insights into the learners' development via the examination of languaging instances in Portuguese during the initial and final sessions between the participants and their Brazilian partners. We were interested in how the LREs were invoked during the sessions, and in how collaborative assistance within these episodes was solicited, offered and appropriated by the learners.

Table 5.2 Sociogenetic interactions within the LREs

	Session	Total LREs, count (% of total number of words per session)	Request for specific feedback, count (% per category)	Unsolicited peer feedback, count (% per category)	Metalinguistic discussion, count (% per category)	Affective mediation, count (% per category)
Brian	First	15 (35%)	10 (67%)	1 (7%)	2 (13%)	2 (13%)
	Last	2 (8%)	2 (100%)			
Veronica	First	10 (72%)	8 (80%)	1 (10%)		1 (10%)
	Last	10 (46%)	5 (50%)	3 (30%)	1 (10%)	1 (10%)
Andrea	First	17 (40%)	13 (76%)	1 (6%)	1 (6%)	2 (12%)
	Last	10 (47%)	8 (80%)	2 (20%)		

The results presented in Table 5.2 show that if we consider the total number of words produced per telecollaborative session, the LREs were quite prominent in the transcripts of both the initial and final telecollaborative sessions for each of the three pairs, albeit with some variability. Languaging exchanges during which LRE-involved interactions took place were highly frequent in the conversations between Veronica and her peer; they amounted to 72% of the speech produced during the initial session and 46% of all words in the final session. For Andrea and her peer, the numbers correspond to 40% and 47%, and for Brian and his partner to a more modest percentage of 35% and 8%, respectively. The number of *instances* of such episodes for the initial and final sessions includes 15 and 4 LREs in the interactions between Brian and his partner, 10 and 10 in Veronica's case and 17 and 10 LREs in Andrea's case. Given this inter-pair and intra-pair variability, averaging is not a perfect measure; yet, based on the data we have available, we can conclude that within a single telecollaborative dialoguing session (which amounted to fewer than 25 minutes per session in our project), an L2 learner may be expected to request and receive mediation with about 11 linguistic structures.

In terms of the types of sociogenetic interactions we ascertained within the LREs, the most frequent type included *participants' requests for specific assistance*: such requests accounted for 67% and 100%, respectively, of all types of the LREs in the initial and final telecollaborative session in Brian's case, 80% and 50% of the LREs for both sessions in Veronica's case and 76% and 80%, respectively, in Andrea's initial and final conversations with her partner. Consider Example 1, in which Brian is soliciting the lexical item he needs:

(Ex. 1) **B**: não sei como se disse em português las rochas? Escalamentar? É isso?

*I don't know how you say in Portuguese the cliffs? *To climb? Is that it?*
BP: Ah, escalar montanhas
Ah, to mountain climb

Unsolicited peer feedback was much less frequent and accounts only for 7% of the LREs occurring in the first session between Brian and his partner; no such instances were found in their final session. Veronica's and Andrea's partners also volunteered unsolicited assistance less frequently than they responded to requests for specific feedback: only 10% and 30% of the LREs ascertained in the respective initial and final telecollaborative interactions include evidence of unsolicited assistance from Veronica's Brazilian peer; the counts correspond to 6% and 20% of LREs in the transcripts of the latter pair. Example 2 illustrates a recast offered by Veronica's partner, in which she indicates understanding (uhum, sim) but also corrects Veronica's inappropriate use of the infinitive and supplies the proper noun:

(Ex. 2) **V**: Também é minha presente de formar
It's also my present for graduating
VP: Uh uhum de formatura, sim
Uh uh-hm for graduation, yes

Instances of *metalinguistic discussion* during which the participants engaged in languaging about the language structures in question constitute a small percentage of the LREs. As Table 5.2 shows, metalinguistic discussions account only for 13% of the LREs in conversations between Brian and his partner and 6% of the LREs between Andrea and her partner in the initial session, and 10% of the LREs in the transcripts of the final session between Veronica and her partner. Consider Example 3, in which Veronica and her partner reflect on the borrowing of the English word 'bullying' into Portuguese (followed by an intercultural discussion of this societal issue, which is beyond our analysis here):

(Ex. 3) **V**: É interessante ah porque em Brasil não tem uma palavra é de/ de bullying usa a palavra inglês, mas porque não **não não tem**?
*It's interesting ah because in Brazil there isn't a word, that is, of, *for bullying, you use the English word, but why isn't isn't isn't there one?*
VP: Ah, porque é um conceito que a gente não tinha no Brasil
Ah, because it's a concept that we didn't have in Brazil

We recorded several instances of *affective mediation* as well. In Brian's pair, affective continuers account for 13% of the LREs during the initial conversation. Veronica's partner volunteered an affective continuer in 10% of the LREs during the first and initial interaction, and Andrea's partner offered affective support in 12% of the LREs. To illustrate, in

Example 4 Andrea apologizes for resorting to Spanish, her heritage language, in narrating her story and receives enthusiastic feedback from her interlocutor:

(Ex. 4) **A**: um pouco de espanhol, eu sou de Bolíva
A little bit of Spanish, I'm from Bolivia
AP: Ahhh voce é daqui de pertinho do Brasil
Ahhh you are from here, close to Brazil
A: Sim
Yes
AP: Aa não tem problema! Eu adoro espanhol!
Ah, no problem! I love Spanish!

In terms of the linguistic content interrogated within the LREs, all of the requests for specific assistance made by the learners were of *lexico-grammatical nature*: in essence, the majority of them were requests for translation of words or phrases that the learners either could not access spontaneously or did not know, but at the same time, linguistic assistance provided by the Brazilian peers often automatically modeled appropriate morphosyntax (see Ex. 2).

We were additionally interested in examining to what extent the learners showed appropriation of the language models into their own speech following peer mediation, focusing on adjacent modifications in learner speech or lack thereof. Our results revealed that even when the learners solicited or received specific assistance, they capitalized on the assistance generated within these LREs dissimilarly (Table 5.3).

Table 5.3 Appropriation of assistance within LREs

	Appropriated peer feedback (%)	Did not appropriate peer feedback (%)	Self-regulation (%)
Brian	21	36	43
Veronica	61	39	
Andrea	54	33	13

The transcripts of Brian's telecollaborative dialoguing showed that he appropriated peer-presented language models in his speech (as in Ex. 1) in 21% of all episodes during which peer mediation was offered, but he chose to move on without explicitly incorporating the offered models in the adjacent turns 36% of the time. The largest percentage of the LREs during which mediation was provided reveal yet a different sequence: Brian's explicit requests for help were followed by episodes of successful self-regulation: his own resolution of the language problem, either overlapping with or ahead of his partner's verbal assistance (consider Ex. 5).

(Ex. 5) **B**: como se diz funny? Engraçado? Mas interessante para ver. Engraçado
> *How do you say* funny? *Funny? But interesting to see. Funny*
PB: Engraçado. Funny
Funny. Funny.

In Veronica's case, upon soliciting her partner's feedback, she incorporated it into her speech in 61% of all LREs; conversely, in 39% of the episodes during which language models were offered, we found no evidence of appropriation. Similarly to Veronica's transcripts, Andrea's language transcripts reveal appropriation of the new or corrected language supplied by her partner in the majority of the LREs during which peer mediation was provided: she did so in 54% of all LREs, albeit she did not immediately utilize this assistance in the adjacent turns in 33% of the cases when it was offered by her partner. She was additionally able to self-regulate her speech in 13% of the episodes during which she had initially requested peer assistance.

In the following section, we discuss the quantitative results presented above and reconsider the interactions of discourse that occurred during the telecollaborative dialoguing sessions in light of the learners' socioeducational profiles, with the goal of interpreting the quantitative outcomes and understanding the microgenetic processes associated with the attested oral proficiency development data.

Discussion

The present study was designed principally to investigate whether telecollaborative dialoguing fosters oral proficiency development and to obtain empirical guidance with regard to how telecollaboration can be utilized to maximize developmental outcomes for our Flagship candidates. The results obtained during the investigation lead us to the encouraging conclusion that the proponents of telecollaborative projects in L2 classrooms can take heart, as the pre- and post-telecollaboration measures of oral skills (specifically, speed fluency, repair fluency and syntactic complexity) indicate that *participation in telecollaborative dialoguing led the focal learners in our study to notable positive improvements in oral proficiency.* Comparison of the TIOPI 1 and TIOPI 2 assessments, the small number of participants notwithstanding, offers encouraging outcomes, especially given the relatively short time frame of a single academic semester during which the project unfolded. The study documents impressive upward growth of syntactic complexity for all three learners and increases in fluency for Veronica and Andrea.

At the same time, despite the generally reassuring oral skills development trend, the review of the focal learners' TIOPI outcomes does not present a picture of uniform or even unidirectional (in Brian's case) growth vectors for the measures of fluency and complexity and reveals notable inter- and intra-learner variability. The attested variability parallels the outcomes of several recent second language acquisition case studies. Larsen-Freeman's (2006) statistically sophisticated investigation demonstrates that when longitudinal group data are disaggregated, many paths to development are revealed even within a structured classroom environment in which all learners follow the same syllabus and tasks. Investigation of L2 study abroad programs have similarly documented that study abroad immersive experiences lead to the development of communicative competence in general but result in considerable individual variation. Thus, in addressing inter-learner variability outcomes in study abroad, Kinginger (2008: 53) comes to the conclusion that 'no doubt some part of the variation in the scores can be attributed to the proficiency that students bring with them to the experience'. The distinct dynamics of progress with regard to each of the measures of oral proficiency among the participants in our study may be taken to reflect the level of readiness for participating in open-ended telecollaborative dialoguing: the variability in outcomes may be conceptualized as ZPDs of different sizes or as disparate distances that the participants had to traverse developmentally to be able to reap the gains from the affordances that the teletandem environment offers for fostering oral skills.

With regard to our data, the asymmetricity of the profiles becomes much less surprising if we accept that institutionally defined levels of proficiency, which all learners in the same course should ideally share, are in fact extremely fuzzy measures of proficiency (Thewissen, 2013). The results of the TIOPI 1 reveal that although all participants in our study were enrolled in the same intermediate-level course, their oral proficiency profiles were considerably dissimilar from those at the onset of the project. The learners' pre-project diverse language learning must also be taken into account in considering the outcomes: Brian, Veronica and Andrea started the sequence of Portuguese courses at the University of Georgia together, yet all joined this course at the center of this study with varied experience in learning Portuguese and FL language use in general. Brian was the only participant who had undergone a rigorous academic immersion program prior to the project. Veronica had taken four and Andrea two Portuguese courses prior to the project. Both Veronica and Andrea had some competency in another closely related Romance language (French as an FL and Spanish as a heritage language, respectively).

We believe that Andrea's striking leaps on all measures can be attributed to her heritage learner status in Spanish, since Spanish and Portuguese are closely related. The importance of addressing the specific needs, advantages and challenges of Spanish-speaking learners of Portuguese has been underscored in recent scholarship. Unique features particularly relevant to this study include high proficiency in receptive skills, rapid stabilization of structural errors during early phases of learning/instruction, a flatter learning curve and the prevalence of both positive and negative transfer, for example, of lexicon (Carvalho et al., 2010; Simões et al., 2004). The faster learning process is indeed a critical factor: Wiedemann and Scaramucci (2011) argue that Spanish speakers learn Portuguese twice as fast, while others have reported that Spanish speakers with no previous knowledge of Portuguese comprehend spoken Portuguese at a rate of 50% (Jensen, 1999) and written Portuguese at an astonishing rate of 94% (Henriques, 2000). These findings are in line with recently reported evidence that heritage learners tend to outperform traditional FL learners in computer-mediated FL environments due to their more rapid progress in the acquisition of speaking skills (Blake & Zyzik, 2003; Blake et al., 2008).

In a program like the Language Flagship, where students need to reach advanced levels of proficiency in a relatively short period, faster developmental dynamics of speaking skills could prove to be key to a learner's overall participation and success. While it remains unclear whether a steep learning curve similar to that reported by Jensen (1999) for comprehension in Spanish-speaking learners of Portuguese can be drawn for oral production, Andrea's data would certainly support such an argument: recall that Andrea's TIOPI outcomes demonstrate a 40% increase in syntactic complexity and a 64% decrease in disfluency occurrences from the initial to the final assessment. Andrea herself lends support to the idea that Portuguese was relatively easy for her: in the *Language Learning History Questionnaire* she cited her rapid progress in Portuguese as the source of motivation for pursuing advanced courses.

Veronica's progress from TIOPI 1 to 2, while not as remarkable as Andrea's, is still impressive, particularly in light of her hesitant responses during the pre-telecollaboration interview, characterized by the lowest speech rate in the group, 40 wpm. In fact, at one point during TIOPI 1 she became so taxed and nervous that not only was her speech highly disfluent, but she was visibly trembling. Her performance on the final TIOPI was notably more confident, with her speech rate soaring by 41%, disfluency counts dropping by 30% and syntactic complexity increasing by 20%. We are inclined to attribute such progress to the state of maturation of her ZPD in oral production skills. Indeed, while Veronica had only taken four Portuguese courses prior to the project, she was a highly experienced FL learner: she had studied French (a Romance language) for eight years, including during an immersive residence in French-speaking communities abroad throughout her elementary and middle school years. We therefore believe that she had the developmental maturity to start practicing Portuguese extensively in unrehearsed communicative situations. She might not have had as many opportunities to do so, given the constraints of the traditional FL curriculum in a regular classroom, but the peer and task mediation afforded by the telecollaborative environment allowed her to make a notable developmental leap in oral communication from the ZPD to ZAD in a relatively short period of about eight weeks.

Brian's developmental profile represents different dynamics of fluency and complexity measures from those in Andrea's and Veronica's cases and is additionally characterized by intra-learner variability: namely, a significant drop in fluency measures from TIOPI 1 to 2 (lower speech rate and a higher number of false starts, self-repairs and repetitions) but an increase in syntactic complexity. If we conceptualize development in a traditional stepladder-like, linear fashion, these outcomes may be construed as mutually negating or lacking in evidence of noteworthy progress. Dynamic Systems Theory, however, offers an alternative account which posits that restructuring within one linguistic subsystem can cause drops within a different subsystem due to the accommodations that need to be made as development occurs, given limited cognitive resources (de Bot et al., 2013). A number of previous studies (e.g. Ahmadian, 2011; de Bot et al., 2013; Skehan, 2014) have reported that L2 learners at different proficiency levels sacrifice performance in one area of oral proficiency (the so-called 'trade-off effects' attributable to limited resources) while improving in another. The trade-off effects could explain drops in fluency and the proliferation of hesitation markers in Brian's speech in TIOPI 2 by the fact that he was attempting to formulate responses of greater syntactic complexity and to employ a more sophisticated and creative repertoire of syntactic choices in TIOPI 2. Brian's data show that L2 learners may temporarily grow more disfluent due to the cognitive accommodations that need to be made as they are expanding their repertoire of L2 lexis and appropriating more sophisticated syntax (Segalowitz, 2010). These outcomes lend support to the view that developmental change may be best construed 'not so much [as] the stage-like progression of new accomplishments [but] as the waxing and waning of patterns, some stable and adaptive and others fleeting and seen only under special conditions' (Thelen & Bates, 2003, cited by Larsen-Freeman, 2006: 615), and that L2 development is not linear or evenly paced but characterized by complex dynamics of inter- and intra-learner variability, fluctuation, plateaus and breakthroughs (Hasko, 2013). Unarguably, the fact that Brian had just completed an intensive summer immersion program at the start of the project could also explain the rapid pace of his oral performance on TIOPI 1 and the respective drop in TIOPI 2: it is possible that his fluency was decreasing due to the overall loss of oral practice time during a regular academic semester (even with the built-in telecollaborative practice) in comparison with the opportunities for communicative practices afforded by the full immersion program preceding the project.

But what were the exact affordances that we can trace by reviewing telecollaborative transcripts, and what types of sociogenetic LREs did the context of telecollaborative dialoguing generate? The most encouraging finding with regard to this question is that we were able to ascertain that languaging was bountiful during telecollaboration: LRE-involving turns average 41% of all words produced during the telecollaborative sessions. The high ratio of the LREs is particularly impressive given that the telecollaborative dialoguing sessions analyzed here stemmed from a communicative task prioritizing the focus on meaning over form. The transcripts reveal that while the participants explored a variety of communicative topics during the sessions, each of the pairs still spent an impressive amount of time engaging in the intentional use of language as a cognitive tool to mediate each other's and their own cognitive processes and performance during telecollaborative dialoguing. Even though the number of such episodes is not staggering and amounts to 11 interrogated language structures/foci per individual session on average, it is important to remember that we analyzed only the conversations that took place in Portuguese and excluded peer-editing sessions related to written essays; thus, our sociogenetic analysis does not in fact represent the full potential of peer mediation during the entire session that could be expected to occur within a 50-minute class.

Returning to the question of variability, the results of the sociogenetic interactions with the LREs, beyond the aforementioned common tendencies, reveal a somewhat different model of interactions for each of the pairs. This finding is hardly surprising if we posit that peer assistance (either the offering or solicitation thereof) is not an automatic characteristic of learner interaction but rather a variable dependent on the characteristics of the interpersonal relationship within each of the pairs (i.e. the level of comfort and trust, gender, personality match); the intercultural/inter-institutional differences in understanding what peer feedback is; peers' perceptions of each other's roles, tasks, goals and responsibilities within the project; and the boundaries of what each may believe to be useful or appropriate (Dooly, 2008, 2015; Li & Swanson, 2014). With regard to Brian, for example, it appears that his strategy included reliance on self-regulation rather than peer assistance, since he did not actually wait for peer responses when he posed questions to his partner. The task itself, the presence of the peer (as well as affective mediation and non-verbal confirmations of comprehension from the peer) and the use of the language as a cognitive tool in formulating his questions, appear to have provided enough mediation for him to be able to access and utilize less familiar vocabulary and structures. His prior participation in the immersion program, which demands a great degree of linguistic as well as social self-regulation and self-reliance, likely contributed to the interactional strategies he chose to rely on during the virtual conversations with his telecollaboration peer.

Veronica's and Andrea's sessions, on the other hand, show their orientation toward the reciprocal nature of telecollaborative dialoguing. The LRE-related turns account for a high percentage of their interactions with their peers, with both of them actively soliciting peer assistance, as well as appropriating the majority of the new structures. In reviewing the transcripts of the interactions between Veronica and Andrea and their peers, we noticed an additional meditational means used by both of them: code-switches to their more dominant languages. Nine percent of all language produced by Veronica in the initial session and 10% of the language in the final session included code-switches to English. While Andrea used very little English, she chose to code-switch to Spanish, her heritage language, in 6% and 3% in her final and initial conversations with her partner, respectively. In the context of FL education, the topic of the first language (L1) is usually focused on when, and to what extent, L1 is permissible in the classroom, as L1 is seen as an unwelcome communicative and cognitive crutch. This view has recently been challenged by scholars who argue that targeted and strategic use of L1 can facilitate acquisition of complex grammatical concepts and can lead to other learning benefits (e.g. Lee & Macaro, 2013). While the analysis of code-switching strategies by the learners is beyond the focus of the present study, it is possible that code-switching played an important mediational role in boosting Veronica's and Andrea's confidence in their oral production skills and may have contributed to their improved independent performance on TIOPI 2. Concurrently, it is also possible that the relatively high percentages of code-switching instances in Veronica's and Andrea's sessions, coupled with the relatively infrequent instances of unsolicited peer feedback (Table 5.2), are indicative of missed opportunities for constructive feedback and represent an area of telecollaborative dialoguing that would benefit from more structured peer mediation and the fostering of greater metalinguistic awareness for both the learners and their partners. The topic of how telecollaboration participants can be prepared to offer, formulate and respond to peer feedback – linguistically, interactionally, culturally and emotionally – warrants close pedagogical attention (cf. Ware & Kessler, 2013).

Conclusion

This study provided us with sufficient empirical evidence to support the hypothesis that synchronous telecollaborative dialoguing can serve as an effective means to support Portuguese instruction for our Flagship students who must meet the high standards of the program, especially in oral proficiency. We are encouraged both by the improvements from the pre- to post-project TIOPIs and by the amount of contextualized language-related interactions we discovered in the transcripts to argue that telecollaboration may not only improve oral proficiency outcomes, but may also prepare L2 learners for immersive experiences by boosting their confidence levels and preparing them for situations in which they may need to solicit specific assistance.

While the study provides us with important guideposts for enhancing learners' experiences within the curriculum of our Language Flagship program, we are well aware of its limitations. Our discussion here is limited to three case studies (hence, referential statistics) and only two assessment points during which we assessed the dynamics of partner interactions and the general characteristics of how peer feedback was requested, offered and appropriated. To trace the exact trajectory of L2 development with regard to specific lexico-grammatical structures and their emergence in independent performance, a more extensive corpus-based study with closely spaced assessment points would be required. We acknowledge that the learners' gains discussed here cannot be attributed solely to their participation in the telecollaborative project, since their course activities additionally included non-telecollaborative components (such as reading and writing based on authentic Brazilian literary and mass media resources and engaging in associated communicative activities, as well as likely extra-curricular Portuguese language learning and use in their spare time).

Although our results cannot be generalized to all FL programs, or, in fact, even to all the Portuguese learners in the course under investigation, the insights we gain from the study highlight the importance of customizing learning activities for learners with various backgrounds, learning experiences and ZPDs in Portuguese programs. Particularly, the inclusion of the Spanish-speaking language learner allowed us to ascertain the potential for impressively rapid gains among such learners and, consequently, the need for differential pedagogical solutions that curriculum developers should consider in order to maximize such learners' outcomes, especially given the high number of heritage learners of Spanish seeking access to Portuguese courses.

Note

(1)   The TIOPIs included (a) an introductory warm-up prompt (self-representation in the present), (b) a question prompting narration in the past, (c) a role play prompt and (d) a wind down prompt (small talk in the future).

References

Ahmadian, J. (2011) The effect of 'massed' task repetitions on complexity, accuracy and fluency: Does it transfer to a new task? *The Language Learning Journal* 39 (3), 269–289.

Belz, J.A. (2003) Linguistic perspectives on the development of intercultural competence in telecollaboration. *Language Learning & Technology* 7 (2), 68–117.

Blake, J. and Zyzik, E. (2003) Who's helping whom? Learner/heritage-speaker networked discussions in Spanish. *Applied Linguistics* 24 (4), 519–544.

Blake, R., Wilson, N., Cetto, M. and Pardo-Ballester, C. (2008) Measuring oral proficiency in distance, face-to-face, and blended classrooms. *Language Learning & Technology* 12 (3), 114–127.

Brumfit, C.J. (1984) *Communicative Methodology in Language Teaching.* Cambridge: Cambridge University Press.

Carvalho, A.M., Freire, J.L. and Silva, A.J.B. (2010) Teaching Portuguese to Spanish speakers: A case for trilingualism. *Hispania* 93 (1), 70–75.

Chun, D.M. (2015) Language and culture learning in higher education via telecollaboration. *Pedagogies: An International Journal* 10, 1–17.

Council of Europe (2014) *Common European Framework of Reference for Languages.* See http://www.coe.int/lang-CEFR (accessed 17 June 2015).

Damianova, M.K. and Sullivan, G.B. (2011) Rereading Vygotsky's theses on types of internalization and verbal mediation. *Review of General Psychology* 15, 344–350.

de Bot, K., Lowie, W., Thorne, S.L. and Verspoor, M. (2013) Dynamic Systems Theory as a theory of second language development. In M. Mayo, M. Gutierrez-Mangado and M. Adrián (eds) *Contemporary Approaches to Second Language Acquisition* (pp. 199–220). Amsterdam: John Benjamins.

Dooly, M. (ed.) (2008) *Telecollaborative Language Learning: A Guidebook to Moderating Intercultural Collaboration Online.* Bern: Peter Lang.

Dooly, M. (2015) It takes research to build a community: Ongoing challenges for scholars in digitally-supported communicative language teaching. *CALICO Journal* 32 (1), 172–194.

Dooly, M. and O'Dowd, R. (eds) (2012) *Researching Online Interaction and Exchange in Foreign Language Education.* Bern/Wien: Peter Lang.

Eaton, S.E. (2012) How will Alberta's second language students ever achieve proficiency? ACTFL Proficiency Guidelines, the CEFR and the '10,000-hour rule' in relation to the Alberta K-12 language-learning context. *Notos* 12 (2), 2–12.

Felix, U. (2005) Analyzing recent CALL effectiveness research? Towards a common agenda. *Computer Assisted Language Learning* 18, 1–32.

Foster, P. and Skehan, P. (1996) The influence of planning and task type on second language performance. *Studies in Second Language Acquisition* 18 (3), 299–324.

Foster, P., Tonkyn, A. and Wigglesworth, J. (2000) Measuring spoken language: A unit for all reasons. *Applied Linguistics* 21 (3), 354–375.

Foster, P. and Ohta, A. (2005) Negotiation for meaning and peer assistance in second language classrooms. *Applied Linguistics* 26 (3), 402–430.

Golonka, E.M., Bowles, A.R., Frank, V.M., Richardson, D.L. and Freynik, S. (2014) Technologies for foreign language learning: A review of technology types and their effectiveness. *Computer Assisted Language Learning* 27 (1), 70–105.

Guth, S. and Helm, F. (2012) Developing multiliteracies in ELT through telecollaboration. *ELT Journal* 66 (1), 42–51.

Gutierrez, A.G. (2007) Microgenesis, method and object: A study of collaborative activity in a Spanish as a foreign language classroom. *Applied Linguistics* 29 (1), 120–148.

Hasko, V. (2013) Capturing the dynamics of second language development via learner corpus research: A very long engagement. *Modern Language Journal* 97 (1), 1–10.

Henriques, E.R. (2000) Intercompreensão de texto escrito por falantes nativos de português e de espanhol [Intercomprehension of written text by native speakers of Portuguese and Spanish]. *D.E.L.T.A.* 16 (2), 263–295.

Housen, A. and Kuiken, F. (2009) Complexity, accuracy, and fluency in second language acquisition. *Applied Linguistics* 30 (4), 461–473.

Interagency Language Roundtable (ILR) (2014) ILR Skill Level Descriptions. See http://www.govtilr.org (accessed 7 August 2015).

Jensen, J.B. (1999) Sociolinguistic variations in Portuguese: Challenge to Spanish speakers. Paper presented at the Annual Congress of the American Association of Teachers of Spanish and Portuguese, Denver, CO.

Karpov, Y. (2005) *The Neo-Vygotskian Approach to Child Development.* Cambridge: Cambridge University Press.

Kinginger, C. (2008) Language learning in study abroad: Case studies of Americans in France. *Modern Language Journal* 92, 1–124.

Knouzi, I., Swain, M., Lapkin, S. and Brooks, L. (2010) Self-scaffolding mediated by languaging: microgenetic analysis of high and low performers. *International Journal of Applied Linguistics* 20 (1), 23–49.

Lantolf, J. (2011) The sociocultural approach to second language acquisition: Sociocultural theory, second language acquisition, and artificial L2 development. In D. Atkinson (ed.) *Alternative Approaches to Second Language Acquisition* (pp. 24–47). New York: Routledge.

Lantolf, J. and Thorne, S.L. (2006) *Sociocultural Theory and the Genesis of Second Language Development.* New York: Oxford University Press.

Larsen-Freeman, D. (2006) The emergence of complexity, fluency, and accuracy in the oral and written production of five Chinese learners of English. *Applied Linguistics* 27 (4), 590–619.

Larsen-Freeman, D. (2014) Complexity theory. In B. VanPatten and J. Williams (eds) *Theories in Second Language Acquisition* (pp. 227–244). New York: Routledge.

Lawrence, J. and Valsiner, J. (2003) Making personal sense. An account of basic internalization and externalization processes. *Theory & Psychology* 13, 723–752.

Lee, J.H. and Macaro, E. (2013) Investigating age in the use of L1 or English-only instruction: Vocabulary acquisition by Korean EFL learners. *Modern Language Journal* 97 (4), 887–901.

Li, S.L. and Swanson, P. (2014) *Engaging Language Learners through Technology Integration: Theory, Applications, and Outcomes.* Hershey, PA: IGI Global.

Lin, H. (2014) Establishing an empirical link between computer-mediated communication (CMC) and SLA: A meta-analysis of the research. *Language Learning and Technology* 18 (3), 120–147.

Lin, H. (2015) Computer-mediated communication (CMC) in L2 oral proficiency development: A meta-analysis. *ReCALL* 1–27.

Maxwell, D. and Garrett, N. (2002) Meeting national needs: The challenge to language learning in higher education. *Change: The Magazine of Higher Learning* 34 (3), 23–29.

Moeller, A.J. (2013) Advanced low language proficiency: An achievable goal? *Modern Language Journal* 97 (2), 549–553.

National Standards in Foreign Language Education Project (2015) *World-Readiness Standards for Learning Languages.* Alexandria, VA: American Council on the Teaching of Foreign Languages.

Rifkin, B. (2005) A ceiling effect in traditional classroom foreign language instruction. Data from Russian. *Modern Language Journal* 89 (1), 3–18.

Segalowitz, N. (2010) *Cognitive Bases of Second Language Fluency.* New York: Routledge.

Simões, A.R.M., Carvalho, A.M. and Wiedemann, L. (2004) *Português para falantes de espanhol* [Portuguese for Spanish Speakers]. Campinas: Pontes Editores.

Skehan, P. (ed.) (2014) *Processing Perspectives on Task Performance.* Amsterdam: John Benjamins.

Swain, M. (2006) Languaging, agency and collaboration in advanced second language proficiency. In H. Byrnes (ed.) *Advanced Language Learning: The Contribution of Halliday and Vygotsky* (pp. 95–108). London: Continuum.

Swain, M. and Lapkin, S. (1998) Interaction and second language learning: Two adolescent French immersion students working together. *Modern Language Journal* 82, 320–337.

Tcherepashenets, N. (ed.) (2015) *Globalizing Online: Telecollaboration, Internationalization, and Social Justice*. Bern: Peter Lang.

Telles, J.A. and Vassalo, M.L. (2006) Foreign language learning in-tandem: Teletandem as an alternative proposal in CALLT. *The Especialist* 27 (2), 189–212.

Thelen, E. and Bates, E. (2003) Connectionism and dynamic systems: Are they really different? *Developmental Science* 6, 378–391.

Thewissen, J. (2013) Capturing L2 accuracy developmental patterns: Insights from an error-tagged EFL learner corpus. *Modern Language Journal* 97, 77–101.

Thomas, M., Reinders, H. and Warschauer, M. (eds) (2013) *Contemporary Computer-Assisted Language Learning*. London: Bloomsbury Academic.

Thorne, S.L. (2006) Pedagogical and praxiological lessons from internet-mediated intercultural foreign language education research. In J. Belz and S.L. Thorne (eds) *Internet-Mediated Intercultural Foreign Language Education* (pp. 2–30). Boston, MA: Thomson Heinle.

Thorne, S.L. (2010) The 'intercultural turn' and language learning in the crucible of new media. In F. Helm and S. Guth (eds) *Telecollaboration 2.0 for Language and Intercultural Learning* (pp. 139–164). Bern: Peter Lang.

UNESP (n.d.) *Teletandem Brasil*. See http://www.teletandembrasil.org (accessed 17 June 2015).

Vygotsky, L.S. (1978) *Mind in Society: The Development of Higher Psychological Processes*. Cambridge, MA: Harvard University Press.

Ware, P. and O'Dowd, R. (2008) Peer feedback on language form in telecollaboration. *Language Learning and Technology* 12 (1), 43–63.

Ware, P. and Kessler, G. (2013) Computer-assisted language learning and digital feedback. In M. Thomas, H. Reinders and M. Warschauer (eds) *Contemporary Computer-Assisted Language Learning* (pp. 323–340). London: Bloomsbury Academic.

Wiedemann, L. and Scaramucci, M.V.R. (2011) Português para falantes de espanhol: Ensino e aquisição (Portuguese for Spanish speakers: Teaching and acquisition). *Hispania* 94 (4), 772–774.

6 Creating Collaborative Communities through Online Cafés

Sharon Bain and Madeline K. Spring

Introduction

This chapter will describe the design and outcomes of two online collaborative-learning communities, or 'language Cafés', developed by instructors from Chinese and Russian Language Flagship Programs in cooperation with the National Foreign Language Resource Center (NFLRC) at the University of Hawai'i at Mānoa. These Cafés offered American Council on the Teaching of Foreign Languages (ACTFL)-Advanced (Appendix A) learners and native speakers of Chinese and Russian opportunities to correspond with each other about their respective cultures in the target language (TL) of the Flagship programs, to make observations and request clarifications about each other's posts and to compare authentic media and print materials through guided discussions in the TL. The chief objective of the Café project since its inception in 2011 and throughout its development in subsequent years was to prepare US students of Chinese and Russian for direct enrollment at overseas Flagship institutions by increasing their ability to perceive, understand, tolerate and appreciate cultural differences through discovery processes facilitated in an online environment. The need for increasing students' cultural competency was born out of decades of research on the role of cultural knowledge in second language (L2) learning (Lange & Paige, 2003).

This chapter begins by describing the use of online technology for language learning and the Massachusetts Institute of Technology's (MIT) *Cultura* Project (Furstenberg & Levet, 2014; Furstenberg *et al.*, 2001), an innovative model for enhancing deep understanding of TL cultures, which served as the inspiration for the Chinese and Russian online Cafés. The chapter then traces the development of the Chinese and Russian Cafés and describes the ways the development teams modified the *Cultura* model to align it with the proficiency goals of ACTFL Advanced-level language courses in the domestic Chinese and Russian

Flagship Programs. Finally, this chapter provides examples of cultural prompts and learners' responses, as well as preliminary evaluations of the effectiveness of the Cafés in promoting cultural understanding and communication in the TL.

For most language learners in US universities, the classroom serves as their primary learning community and the instructor is the sole representative of the TL's culture. Online technology can expand a learning community beyond the immediate classroom, allowing learners to explore another culture and communicate directly with speakers of the language in communities outside of the classroom. Research on TL participation in internet chat rooms has revealed a number of benefits of online communities in language learning, including increased participation by TL learners and the opportunity for learners to express genuine thoughts and opinions, to express themselves without interruption and to receive immediate feedback regarding linguistic errors (Kelm, 1992; Kern, 1995; Warschauer, 1996). Although language learners have demonstrated nuanced language use in cross-cultural negotiation of meaning in chat rooms (Tudini, 2007), they can still avoid subjects that lack familiarity or are difficult, given their current proficiency level, and can limit their interactions to short, syntactically simple utterances, including text-speech (e.g. LOL, OMG) and emoticons. The positive social benefits of internet chat rooms notwithstanding, learners in an internet chat environment may not necessarily be challenged to push the boundaries of their current proficiency level toward the acquisition of advanced- and superior-level language skills. Given proper guidance through collaborative online activities, however, learners can apply what they are learning in the classroom in interactive online spaces by practicing their language skills, while exploring the linguistic, social and aesthetic aspects of the TL culture.

To that end, the *Cultura* Project developed at MIT by Gilberte Furstenberg, Sabine Levet, Kathryn English and Katherine Maillet (2001) used a comparative approach in the teaching and learning of culture. This approach prompts learners from the home-language and TL communities to analyze materials from their respective cultures and to engage in dialogue in an effort to understand the similarities and differences they have observed. These virtual dialogues take place 'with the ultimate goal of getting an insider's view of the other culture' (Furstenberg & Levet, 2010: 308). In the *Cultura* model, the role of the instructor is to provide content that serves as a scaffold for learners' observations and discussions. However, the learners themselves are the primary conduits of input for each and the online Café is the social setting in which they construct their perceptions of each other's cultures. This way, the content is merely a springboard for discussion, and the learners function as experts of their respective cultures in the scaffolded environment and provide information, correction and affirmation to each other, in keeping with collaborative educational approaches (Donato, 1994; Kramsch, 2003; Paige *et al.*, 2003).

To date, interactive online language and culture learning programs such as *Cultura* have been developed mainly for beginning and intermediate learners of more commonly taught languages in the United States such as French, German and Spanish (Bauer *et al.*, 2006; Blyth, 2012; Garcia *et al.*, 2007). This chapter describes a collaborative project of Flagship programs in Chinese and Russian to develop interactive programs for students at the ACTFL Advanced-level of proficiency, in accordance with Flagship's proficiency goals, in the languages taught in Flagship programs. The project was based on the shared understanding among participating faculty that language learners must also acquire cultural knowledge. The following sections will provide a detailed overview of each Flagship Language Café and its challenges, successes and general outcomes.

Genesis and Pedagogical Foundations of the Chinese and Russian Online Cafés

When the Language Flagship was first established in 2002, it funded pilot programs in Arabic, Chinese and Korean, with Russian to follow a few years later. These programs existed solely at the graduate or advanced undergraduate level, the primary aim being to prepare students who had already reached Advanced-level proficiency for Flagship capstone overseas programs. In light of this narrow academic structure, many Flagship programs developed their own units on TL culture to prepare Flagship students for the capstone overseas program. As the numbers of Flagship students increased, more options within the capstone were introduced. For example, Chinese Flagship students could start their capstone year either in the fall or in the spring and could choose between two overseas sites. For students of Russian, the variety of professional internship opportunities on the capstone greatly increased, giving students more options to gain professional experience in their fields of interest. Over the course of a decade, the Flagship program grew from a few graduate-level programs to 27 undergraduate Language Flagship programs as of this writing. With this conversion of pilot programs into full undergraduate programs, combined with Flagship students' increased interaction in professional domains overseas, Flagship directors recognized the importance of more explicitly addressing culture learning in the pre-capstone curriculum, as well as the potential for interactive online learning through internet chat to familiarize students with formal and informal cultural norms, behaviors and beliefs of the cultures in which the TLs are spoken.

To that end, in July 2011, Flagship faculty from several US universities representing the Chinese and Russian Flagship Programs attended the Online Learning Communities for Less Commonly Taught Languages Summer Institute at the University of Hawai'i at Mānoa, where they created a series of Language Flagship Online Cafés in conjunction with the NFLRC. Following the *Cultura* model, the Chinese and Russian Flagship teams created online environments where advanced-level learners and TL native speakers could learn from each other through written posts, photos and videos. The resulting online communities comprised domestic and overseas groups. The Russian Flagship Café, for example, included US students of Russian in domestic Russian Flagship Programs interacting with each other and with Russian students of English from a university in Russia. Likewise, the Chinese Flagship Café offered exciting options for students to interact with speakers of Chinese in the People's Republic of China as well as with other Flagship students of Chinese in the United States. These communities created a new platform that fostered language use and culture learning beyond the classroom.

The Flagship Cafés utilized an open-source courseware system, BRIX, developed at the NFLRC with the support of several grants from federally funded Language Resource Centers. This platform featured customized tools allowing participants 'to co-construct word banks, communicate asynchronously via threaded discussions with voice recordings and engage in multi-draft process writing with peer editing' (University of Hawai'i at Mānoa, Center for Language and Technology). In light of the NFLRC's efforts to disseminate BRIX to institutions that wished to create their own language Cafés, the Chinese and Russian Flagship Programs became interested in trying this approach in some of their own advanced-level language courses. The BRIX software appealed to the Chinese and Russian Flagship projects, because it served as a hub that supported interactions among students at different universities. It would have been difficult to use courseware systems in place at individual campuses, where providing online access to outsiders was not always feasible.

As they experimented with the functionality of BRIX, the Chinese and Russian Café developers agreed that communication in the Cafés would occur asynchronously, so that participants would have time to think and revise statements before posting them, and given the time differences and conflicting academic schedules among the US, Chinese and Russian institutions, real-time discussions were difficult or impossible to schedule. All US-based participants would be expected to post only in their respective TLs – an aspect of the Café that would be modified in a later version of the program – and they would also be encouraged to post personal photos and videos to illustrate their views. The curriculum developers chose to incorporate the Cafés into Advanced-level Flagship courses taught in the TL on the students' home campuses in the United States, in order to prepare students for the Flagship capstone overseas program. In this way, students could consult with their instructors and with each other during regular face-to-face class meetings to check their comprehension of posts, to review unfamiliar vocabulary and syntax encountered in the Café and to consider their own written responses to the views expressed by their peers at other Flagship institutions and overseas. The Cafés took place over a period of six to eight weeks during a regular semester course or as a co-curricular activity.

The Cafés were designed not only to provide opportunities for Flagship students to engage in meaningful written communication with other speakers of Chinese and Russian, but also to challenge students to question their assumptions about their own and other cultures and to formulate new hypotheses, or modify previous ones, based on their interactions with their peer interlocutors. The teams chose to focus discussions on themes such as family and education that were relevant to all students. The topics for the Cafés were chosen according to the principle that they should represent an integral part of the participants' lives, and that they should be sufficiently multifaceted to allow participants to branch easily into related subtopics. Given the political climates and strict monitoring of social media sites in China and Russia, the teams were careful to choose neutral topics and to avoid overtly political ones that might result in putting overseas participants at risk, should they make statements considered by their respective political authorities to be provocative or anti-government.

The participating faculty developed activities and prompts geared toward the Advanced level on the ACTFL scale for students to respond to in writing, but the students themselves were expected to steer the discussion, as they might in a neighborhood coffee shop. Having decided on discussion topics, the Chinese and Russian teams debated which language(s) should be used in the Cafés for what purposes. In the original *Cultura* model, in which online activities were designed for ACTFL Intermediate-level learners, participants in the United States and France posted in their respective native languages, so that US learners read posts in French but may respond in English, and French learners read posts in English but may respond in French. At first, the developers of the Chinese and Russian Cafés agreed that all online activities and all communication should be in the TL of the Flagship program. The rationale behind this decision was rooted in the proficiency goals of Flagship, which aims to 'create global professionals' who can communicate in the TL at the ACTFL Superior level. In the end, the Chinese and Russian Café developers decided to modify their decisions about the language of communication, but did so in different ways and for different purposes, which will be discussed in the following section.

Chinese and Russian Cafés

Participants and language of communication

Prior to the NFLRC 2011 workshop, the Chinese Flagship Program at Arizona State University ran a pilot project to gain some familiarity with the BRIX software and the *Cultura* model. Three groups of students were involved in this initial project, which will be referred to as Chinese Café 1. Participants included students in a fourth-year Chinese Flagship course and students in a fourth-year Chinese non-Flagship course at two universities in different regions of the United States, as well as graduate students in a Teaching Chinese as a Foreign Language (TCFL) MA program at a university in southwestern China.

When the Chinese team piloted Chinese Café 1, they required that all communication be conducted in Chinese. However, they found that this requirement shifted the main goal of the Café from a cultural exchange into a writing exercise. The added emphasis on producing written Chinese reduced potential gains in cultural understanding, as the US learners found that the added pressure of having potential teachers of Chinese examining their posts as examples of US student writing in Chinese focused their attention away from content and thus detracted from the project's goal. Due to their concerns about L2 usage, the undergraduate learners limited their language production; as a result, their responses appeared inauthentic. Consequently, the Chinese team modified their Café model to include only Flagship students from several Chinese Flagship Programs in the United States and a group of undergraduate students from a well-known university in Beijing. For the subsequent Chinese Café, the team reverted to the original *Cultura* model, in which students could opt to write in their first language (L1) and read the L2. These changes sparked more observations and exchanges about Chinese and US cultures, and, according to instructors, students seemed more willing to express themselves while still receiving L2 input from their interlocutors. Interestingly, some of the Flagship students began responding to Chinese posts in Chinese, and no mention of the language switch (or comments about the students' language proficiency) ensued.

In a pilot for the Russian Café, as well as in subsequent Russian Cafés, US learners of Russian from four US Russian Flagship Programs interacted with Russian learners of English at the Linguistics University of Nizhny Novgorod (LUNN) over an eight-week period (Russian Café 1) and then, in two subsequent Cafés, over a six-week period. During the design phase of Russian Café 1, the development team concluded that the LUNN students would lose motivation to participate in the Café if all communication was conducted in Russian, as the language-learning aspects of the project would benefit only the US participants. As a result, the team decided that the language of communication should alternate between English and Russian every week or two, in order to place participants on an equal footing. By alternating the language of communication between Russian and English, students took turns modeling authentic language use for each other.

All Cafés shared these pedagogical goals, but they took different approaches to reach them. The following sections describe the individual Cafés in terms of their content before returning to a general discussion of their outcomes.

Chinese Café Activities

As mentioned above, participants in all Cafés were provided with topics and activities centered on familiar themes such as family, education, food and the local environment. The first Chinese Café asked participants to examine multiculturalism in three vastly different locations: the southwestern United States; Sichuan Province, China and the US state of Hawai'i. Through their interactions in small groups of six students (two from each location), students shared perceptions of food, religion and environmental conditions. An assessment component was also integrated into the Café. The assessment included a pre- and post-program essay, which was designed to document learning gains in intercultural perceptions, as well as linguistic gains that came from the interactions within the Café.

In order to begin generating discussion about the similarities and differences in family relationships in America and China, Chinese Café 1 participants completed a word association exercise for which they were given a list of topics related to multiculturalism (e.g. food, environment and local cultural practices) and were asked to write one to three words that first came to mind in response to each prompt. US participants responded to a list in English, and Chinese participants responded to a list in Chinese. The results were posted as tag clouds, which are 'text-based visual depiction(s) of tags (or words), typically used to display the relative tag frequency, popularity, or importance by font size' (Lee *et al.*, 2010: 1182). The manipulation of tag clouds has been explored through work at the NFLRC. This system of 'knowledge management... generate(s) flexible presentations of data through visual constructions', which can be manipulated by instructors and/or online community participants (Tschudi *et al.*, 2011). Participants then worked in small groups online to discuss their observations. This word association exercise and the ensuing discussions were the main focus of the activities in this Café pilot.

Like Chinese Café 1, the subsequent Chinese Café[1] began by asking students to give brief self-introductions. Rather than including the word association exercise in this Café, the developers offered activities requiring participants to watch three sets of commercials produced in

China and Taiwan, as well as corresponding US advertisements on the same topics. The first set of commercials depicted relationships between mothers and sons, the second set showed adults who were struggling to decide how to care for their aging parents and the third dealt with young adults who were embarking on new careers. Chinese Café participants were divided into small groups, for the purpose of facilitating discussion. The groups were made up of students from two different Flagship universities and one class of Chinese undergraduate students in Beijing. Participants were asked to observe whether any differences between the parent–child relationships reflected distinctions between Chinese and US cultural values. Keeping in mind that the discussion prompts were advertisements, Café participants were also asked to comment on whether the relationships in the advertisements were realistically portrayed, if they idealized cultural values or if they reinforced stereotypes within each country (Table 6.1).

Table 6.1 Overview of Chinese Café activities

	Chinese Café 1 (Spring 2011)	*Chinese Café 3 (Spring 2013)*
Week 0	Participants familiarized themselves with Café site.	Same as previous Café.
Week 1	Café participants uploaded audio files introducing themselves in Chinese. Students also posted photographs to personalize their introductions.	Café participants introduced themselves and became acquainted with each other in their respective languages.
Week 2	Participants were prompted to consider the question 'What is diversity?' and to post a short essay (for instructors' eyes only) explaining their thoughts. Students were urged to find census data, survey data, web sites, etc. to support their definition of diversity.	Participants were asked to watch two advertisements, one in English and one in Chinese, which portray parent–child (mother–son) relationships. Participants were prompted to make general observations about the clips.
Week 3	Participants met in small groups at their own institutions to complete a word association 'tag cloud' activity. Each group was given a different focus: food, personal identity, values, social class and leisure.	Participants were prompted to find their own example of an advertisement or video clip portraying a Chinese or US family and to make hypotheses, to explain their observations and to clarify any ambiguous comments they made about the cultural depictions in each other's clips in English or Chinese.

Week 4	Responses to each prompt were collected into tag clouds and grouped by cohort. Participants manipulated tag clouds to form visual representations of word associations that are co-constructed in virtual space.	Participants were asked to watch two new advertisements, one in English and one in Chinese, that portray another dimension of parent–child relationships, i.e. how families deal with aging parents. Participants were prompted to make general observations about the clips, to discuss whether they portray parent–child relationships realistically and to explain what they might reveal about Chinese and US culture.
Week 5	Participants at each site worked in small groups to produce an 'interpretation' of the juxtaposed collection of words.	Participants were asked to watch two advertisements, one that takes place in the US and one in Taiwan, which portray young business professionals, and were prompted to make observations about how professional identity is depicted.
Week 6	Each group's work was shared in the 'Tag Cloud Gallery'. Students participated in a discussion thread to compare and contrast tag clouds in the gallery and discuss results.	Participants were asked to read and think about all the posts on professional identity, to request clarification for things they did not understand, and to respond to questions from others.
Week 7	Students participated in personal reflection through an online post-Café survey. Is there evidence of gains in intercultural competence and awareness of linguistic aspects of exchanges?	Participants were prompted to find their own example of an advertisement or video clip that portrays young professionals in the US and in Taiwan and to make hypotheses, to explain their observations and to clarify any ambiguous comments they made about the cultural depictions in each other's clips in English or in Chinese.
Week 8	Reflection of Café organizers and site leaders at each institution: Which directions are indicated for future development of the tag cloud tool and the design of tasks that use it? Discussion of future possibilities for improving Café model and implementation.	Participants were asked to select an advertisement posted by another student and to respond to that student's explanation of the clip. Students were again encouraged to make observations, to hypothesize and to clarify any ambiguous comments.

Russian Café Activities

The Russian Café developers created three 'rooms' on their site: a casual chat room, a room to discuss current events and a room for the 'Education Forum'. The Russian team recognized that the student participants, as peers, needed to spend some time in the Café engaging in less formal, unstructured activities to develop their sense of community as a learning group. The designated chat room space provided an area where participants could go to discuss movies, television shows, music or current events, as well as to post personal photographs or to share a YouTube video that was going viral. The Russian Café developers also understood that awareness about current events plays a role in a learner's growing understanding of different cultures. To that end, the team dedicated a virtual room in which faculty posted news items and discussion questions about current events. The informal interactions in the chat room, combined with the more formal, guided discussions on education and current events, were designed to prompt Russian Café participants to make observations about the interactional norms of both cultures, to reflect on their own culture, to hypothesize about the TL culture and to draw conclusions, if possible, about Russian and US cultural values.

In Russian Café 1's Education Forum, participants were provided with discussion prompts and activities about US and Russian educational systems over the course of eight weeks. Participants were asked to engage in individual as well as small-group work on the Café site; these activities were organized so that individual work was connected to small-group activities. For example, during the second week of Café activities, participants completed a word association exercise, similar to the one in the Chinese Café, for which they responded to a list of words related to education in their respective languages. After the Café administrator tallied and posted the results, participants then worked in small groups online to discuss their findings. Participants were assigned to groups to ensure representation from each of the five participating institutions in the United States and Russia, and each group was provided its own virtual space in the Café for discussion. While many participants made a number of insightful comments (discussed later in this chapter), student evaluations revealed that they found the asynchronous communication cumbersome for a small-group setting. Participation in some small groups dropped off quickly, and many students became mere observers after a few students shared their reflections about the word association exercise. In the end, some groups had long threads of discussion, while others had no more than two or three posts between two participants in their small-group space. It is unclear whether participants would have engaged in more discussion by working in pairs instead of in small groups, but it was clear to the design team that small-group activities with asynchronous communication were not the best way to elicit communication from all participants. The small-group activity was eliminated from the Café's second run the following year.

During Russian Café 1, it became apparent to the language instructors that participants often perceived activities as assignments to be completed before a deadline, rather than as opportunities for interaction, because many participants posted at the last minute, apparently for the sake of completing an assigned task. Moreover, not all participating institutions graded the activity, so students from institutions where participation was voluntary seemed to treat assignments as optional. As a result, participants did not interact with each other in the ways the instructors anticipated. Some instructors and students complained that because many students waited until the end of the week to post their analyses or reflections, those who logged onto the site earlier in the week simply posted their thoughts and did not return to the site to read other posts. Alternatively, students who decided to wait until others posted first – which did not occur until the end of the week –had little or no time to read and reflect on what others wrote. In response to this finding, the design team shifted the ownership of discussion moderation to the participants themselves for the revised six-week Russian Café 2. The participants were expected to prompt and steer discussions centered on US and Russian educational systems, and deadlines were broken down to indicate midweek and end-week goals. Because five different institutions were involved in Café activities, each week a different student group was assigned to moderate discussion. Making the students themselves responsible for initiating and moderating discussion in the Café worked well, and participants generated compelling discussion topics; however, the topics they offered did not always generate discussion about cultural similarities and differences. In Russian Café 3, student groups still took turns moderating discussions, but the faculty provided initial discussion prompts to keep students focused on culture, as reflected in the Russian and US education systems. The structure of Russian Café 3 was nearly identical to that of Café 2, with the exception that the dedicated space for current events was eliminated to allow participants more time to do activities in the Education Forum (Table 6.2).

Table 6.2 Overview of Russian Café activities

	Russian Café 1 (Spring 2012) 8 weeks	Russian Café 2 (Fall 2012) 6 weeks	Russian Café 3 (Fall 2013) 6 weeks
Week 0	Participants familiarized themselves with Café site.	Same as previous Café.	Same as previous Café.
Week 1	Discussion prompt in English: Tell us about yourself. Who are you? Where are you from? What is your family like? What are your hobbies and interests?	Student offered discussion prompt in English about student life and how Café participants balance academic work with leisure activities.	Discussion prompt from faculty (in English): Same as Café 1
Week 2	Word association exercise in Russian and English.	Student offered discussion prompt in Russian asking to discuss the idea of a 'campus' as conceptualized in the US and Russia.	Discussion prompt in Russian: Tell us about your university, its location and size. What is it known for? What are the application and enrollment procedures? What is required to be accepted into a university?
Week 3	Students worked online in small groups to discuss and summarize their conclusions about the word association exercise. Virtual space was allotted in the Café to each group for their discussions conducted in Russian.	Student offered discussion prompt in English asking about standardized testing in the US and Russia and whether Café participants think it predicts future success in academics and career.	Discussion prompt in English: Tell us about your university life. Where and with whom do you live? Describe your daily schedule, classes and teachers. When do you have vacations and how do you spend them?
Week 4	Students were asked to tell a story in Russian about a memory or experience they had in school.	Student offered discussion prompt in Russian asking whether Café participants agree that BA degrees have lost their prestige, making it necessary to earn a master's degree in order to find good employment.	Discussion prompt in Russian: Tell us how you chose your major and about your plans for the future. Why did you choose this major? Which subjects are required for this major? What are your career plans?

Week 5	Students were asked to choose a personal story they read in the previous week and to write in English about the similarities and differences they observed.	Student offered discussion prompt in English asking how Café participants imagine the future of education in their respective countries, what the biggest problems are and their ideas for education reform.	Discussion prompt in English: Same as Café 2.
Week 6	Students were asked to listen to one Russian speech and one English speech on problems in the Russian and US educational systems and to discuss in English the similarities and differences between the concerns raised in the speeches.	Student offered discussion prompt in Russian asking whether the cost of higher education should be covered by the government or by students and their families.	Discussion prompt in Russian: Recall a conversation in the Café from the past six weeks and tell what you found most interesting. Did anything surprise you? Is there anything else you would like to ask or add?
Week 7	Students were asked to consider how they envision the future of education. Posts were written in Russian.		
Week 8	Café wrap-up and goodbyes written in Russian.		

Outcomes: Café Participants' Cultural Awareness

The number of students involved in the Cafés was too small to allow for any statistical analysis, but anecdotal data indicate that many of the domestic and overseas students who took part in the Café project offered analysis, constructed hypotheses, asked questions and demonstrated new or modified knowledge about the target culture. In both the pilot and revised runs of the Chinese and Russian Cafés, Flagship students offered astute analyses in their observations of their own cultures in comparison to the TL cultures:

> [In response to the word association prompt 'dormitory':] It was interesting that the most popular word for the Russian students was 'friends' (or friendship), but this word was not written once by the American students...For example, many Americans chose the words 'noise', 'small size' and 'uncomfortable', but Russian students chose happier words, like 'laughter', 'parties', 'friends' and 'merriment'. It seems this difference appeared because in America usually all students, especially in their first or second year, live in dormitories, and, as far as I know, Russian students usually live at home with their parents. (US Russian Flagship student [translated from Russian])

In this post about dormitories, the US student suggests that her Russian counterparts associated dormitories with 'happier words', thinking they do not have to live in noisy, 'uncomfortable' dormitories, but can live at home. Subsequent posts challenged this view and suggested that US students associated dormitories with buildings, whereas Russian students associated dormitories with relationships.

The US students also directly or indirectly requested feedback from their peers to confirm whether their understanding of the other culture was correct.

> It seems in Russia grades don't have as strong an influence on what happens after the completion of studies as it does for us in America. However, one of the Russian students noted that grades can predict a 'lower salary in the future'. Is this true? (US Russian Flagship student [translated from Russian])
>
> The majority of Americans feel that sending their parents to an assisted living facility is normal; there are some parents who even want to go live there. I think this might be related to the way that Americans raise their children. American parents instill in their children a sense of independence. So after the children reach adulthood they move away; thus there are very few parents and children who rely on each other. Therefore the children don't feel like they need to take care of their parents when they are elderly. To the contrary, they send them to an

assisted living facility – there are a lot of professionally trained workers who can take better care of them, so maybe it's a better choice. I don't know if what I said is right or not? (US Chinese university student participant [translated from Chinese])

In the above examples, students hypothesized about an aspect of the target culture and then sought confirmation by asking directly 'Is it true?' or by indirectly inviting their peers to respond by suggesting their own uncertainty ('I don't know if what I said is right or not?'). These requests for further information not only served as good communication strategies to keep the conversation moving forward, but they also challenged the other students either to question their own assumptions or to share their knowledge with the group. Although not all requests for information received responses, several participants freely offered explanations and clarifications in answer to others' comments and questions, as in the example below:

US student: It's interesting that I counted no fewer than 11 words on the English list which expressed purely negative associations with the word 'cheat sheet', but there weren't any on the Russian list. I've heard that a type of tradition exists in Russia, which we would call 'cheating' in English, but the understanding of that word is different in English and in Russian. How much of this is true, in your opinion?

Russian student: In Russia students very often use cheat sheets, although instructors don't allow them...I personally sometimes made a cheat sheet for geometry and used it in classes as a prompt. But for tests the use of cheat sheets for me is a sign of weakness...For Russian students cheat sheets don't have a negative association. Of course, cheat sheets are [a form of] deception for the teacher. But it's doubtful that many students perceive cheat sheets as a deception. In Russia the attitude toward cheat sheets is quite different from the one in Western Europe or America. (Interaction between Russian Flagship and Russian university student [translated from Russian])

In the above exchange, the US student receives a response to her question about cheat sheets; however, the Russian student is careful to distinguish her own practice ('But for tests the use of cheat sheets for me is a sign of weakness') from what she views as a common practice among Russian students in general ('For Russian students cheat sheets don't have a negative association'). She also attempts to parse the views of students and teachers as they relate to the deceptiveness of cheat sheets. For the purpose of classroom discussion outside of the Café, an instructor could use this exchange as a reminder that the question 'How much of this is true?' in the context of a conversation on culture cannot be given a quantifiable answer – observations about a culture are not generalizable.

In the end, the Chinese and Russian Cafés proved to be a rich resource for promoting intercultural awareness and competence, since participants were interacting with native speakers outside of the classroom in a real-world, albeit virtual, context. Instead of role-playing fictional dialogues with non-native-speaking peers in class, Café participants were responding to real conversation cues and negotiating meaning with their interlocutors.

Expectations versus Reality

As the Café projects proceeded, a number of unexpected developments occurred that underscored the need for careful long-term planning. Coordinating the Chinese and Russian Cafés required a much larger time commitment than expected, largely because the development teams and instructors – all in different time zones and following different academic calendars – had to balance their commitment to this project with the heavy demands of their existing academic responsibilities. They also needed to agree on activities that could be done in varied educational environments, as some instructors chose to embed the Café into a course, while others offered it as an extracurricular activity. In the end, the teams agreed that, if feasible, having one faculty or staff person serve as an activities coordinator for the whole project was the best approach from an organizational and communication standpoint; that person, however, would need to be compensated for the many hours required to coordinate the Café. Keeping in mind that the Chinese and Russian Cafés comprised multiple institutions and numerous personnel, a Café could very easily be scaled down to include students from only one US and one overseas institute, greatly reducing the time commitment to coordinate activities.

Another challenging aspect of the Café projects involved the amount of time it took participants to familiarize themselves with the BRIX platform in which the Cafés operated. When it was first developed in the early 2000s, BRIX was considered cutting edge; however, improvements to the BRIX technology to make it more user-friendly and to keep it on par with innovations in other social media platforms could not be implemented, due to limited resources. As a result, Café participants who had already become accustomed to social media platforms such as Facebook and Twitter, which require only a couple of steps to upload images, avoided posting photos and videos in the Cafés, since it took anywhere from 7 to 10 steps, depending on the type of media. Consequently, the absence of rich visual sources of cultural information, which serve as highly effective springboards for discussion, left participants relying on text alone to share their cross-cultural observations. Current plans at the Center for Technology at the University of Hawai'i at Mānoa are underway for updating the program to make it more user-friendly and easily adaptable to the needs of language instructors.

Regarding the pedagogical approach adopted by the Chinese and Russian Café development teams, classroom instructors involved in the Café projects were asked not to interfere with online exchanges, but to allow the students themselves to revise or clarify their posts in the context of online discussions. Given this independence, the development teams anticipated that some students would be eager to interact with TL speakers, while others might be intimidated but would nonetheless participate. Hence, creating and regularly using a separate forum for discussions within faculty teams is necessary, since communications through email correspondence proved awkward and at times disconnected.

As it turned out, personal motivation emerged as a factor determining the level of active student participation in the Chinese and Russian Cafés, and offering the opportunity to interact with TL speakers from the comfort of one's laptop turned out not to generate the amount of interest and activity the team anticipated. Some students posted often, while others remained passive observers and others stopped logging onto the site altogether. In the end, the Chinese and Russian Café faculty teams agreed that individual motivation needed to be coupled with an explicit academic impetus, with all online activities closely embedded in the curriculum and with buy-in from instructors involved with each student population. Students need to know that their participation in the online Cafés is being assessed, although the details of such assessment may vary depending on the educational environment. This is true both in the US communities and those in the TL country.

The team observed that students needed more guidance in ways to engage with and seek clarification from their interlocutors – especially non-native speakers of English – in an online environment. On the one hand, students did elicit discussion by directing responses to specific overseas counterparts, sometimes using shortcuts, such as '@Anya', or by affirming someone's viewpoint ('Thank you for your comment. I'm glad to see your perspective...'). On the other hand, sometimes students used sarcasm, slang or non-standard forms, some of them difficult to comprehend by their interlocutors, as was the case when a US Chinese Flagship student mentioned being 'ready to get outta dodge [sic]'. Instead of requesting an explanation or clarification of such expressions, students often did not respond to these posts; this resulted in a breakdown of discussion. Some literary and historical references also went unrecognized. In the discussion of the Chinese advertisement that showed how dealing with an aging mother affected the dynamics between a husband and wife, a student in China alluded to China's long tradition of tension between mothers-in-law and daughters-in-law by mentioning the 'Ballad of the Peacock Flying South' (孔雀东南飞), a well-known long narrative poem that dates back to the Han dynasty (206 BCE–220 ADE). In the same way, Russians are likely to understand a reference to Pushkin, 'Ballad of the Peacock Flying South' is readily understood by Chinese audiences, as the poem has been retold for centuries in Chinese opera, drama, film and song. In this case, however, the US student clearly did not understand the comment and simply broke off communication.

These situations provide language instructors with teaching points that can be addressed in their face-to-face class sessions. For example, instructors can encourage their students to return to the Café and ask for more information about someone's post. They can also remind students to remember their audience – that in the same way that US learners would have difficulty comprehending non-standard speech or subtle literary references in a TL, so too might L2 users of English have difficulty understanding non-standard English lexicon and syntax. Ideally, providing explicit instruction in intercultural communication draws attention to these types of differences in cross-cultural discourse and helps students learn how to negotiate meaning to keep the conversation going. It also generates in students a heightened awareness of their own language norms and prompts them to monitor their language use by adjusting their word choices, tone or register as they communicate with overseas participants. Admittedly, there is value in studying non-standard forms of a TL; however, although one of the goals of the Cafés was to promote Superior-level discourse, their main goal was to promote discussion and intercultural understanding, so anything that halts discussion also halts the exchange of ideas.

Lessons Learned

Having conducted three rounds each of Chinese and Russian Cafés, the development teams offer the following advice to others who wish to replicate this project for their own language classes:

- It is not necessary to develop your own software platform, like BRIX. Work with your school's or university's IT staff to set up an online learning community using a Learning Management System (LMS) such as Moodle, Blackboard or Canvas, and to set up access to participants outside of your institution. Using your university's LMS will ensure better control over online security than would using public social media platforms like Facebook.
- Instructors creating a scaled-down version of a Café involving one US and one overseas institution can combine asynchronous communication with opportunities for live interaction via synchronous communication tools such as Skype. Adding a live chat component to Café projects involving more than three or four institutions in different time zones becomes difficult to manage.

- In soliciting overseas participants, it is best to work with someone you or a colleague already knows and trusts. Likewise, overseas institutions might be reluctant to work with someone they do not already know. In the case of the Russian Café, the Flagship director at Portland State University had a long-term professional relationship with two language instructors at LUNN: their mutual trust and respect played a valuable role in securing their participation in the Russian Café. If you do not already have any overseas connections, network among colleagues who can help make introductions.
- Allow your Café participants ample time to familiarize themselves with the technological platform and interface prior to starting Café activities. Some LMSs will allow you to set up a separate 'sandbox' where teachers and students can experiment with different aspects of the technology.
- Plan and pilot your entire online curriculum with the instructors from your partner institution(s) prior to launching your Café. Once the Café is launched, it is much easier to modify existing plans if something is not working out than to make things up as you go along.
- Finally, talk to participants about the importance of thinking through their posts before posting. Could anything potentially be construed as insensitive or even offensive to other participants? Given the ever-changing political climates in some countries overseas, students should be mindful about what is and is not appropriate to post. Urging students to think about the content of their posts prior to posting also raises their awareness of cross-cultural issues.

Logistical and pragmatic challenges aside, the participating faculty felt that the Chinese and Russian Café projects were a worthwhile endeavor that helped students notice similarities and differences of their TL cultures. The immediate goal of the Cafés was to prompt US Flagship students to notice how their Chinese and Russian counterparts perceive their own and US cultures in relation to the specific topics of family and education. The overarching goal was to train students to be aware that all people, themselves included, interpret the world through a cultural framework, and, as such, noticing is a skill to be practiced and honed – and to practice in a relatively low-stakes environment allows them to learn from mistakes before entering a more high-stakes professional domain. The ability to notice nuances in language and behavior, and to draw balanced conclusions about them in an intercultural context, is a necessary skill for those who wish to navigate professional domains in an L2 culture successfully and to build strong relationships with friends and colleagues overseas.

Note

(1)   Chinese Café 2 was planned but never executed. Chinese Café 3 was a revised version of Café 2 and launched the following year.

References

American Council on the Teaching of Foreign Languages (ACTFL) (2012) *ACTFL Proficiency Guidelines 2012*. See http://www.actfl.org/sites/default/files/pdfs/public/ACTFLProficiencyGuidelines2012_FINAL.pdf (accessed 15 June 2015).

Bauer, B., deBenedette, L., Furstenberg, G., Levet, S. and Waryn, S. (2006) Internet-mediated intercultural foreign language education: The *Cultura* project. In J.A. Belz and S.T. Thorne (eds) *Internet-Mediated Intercultural Foreign Language Education* (pp. 31–62). Boston, MA: Thomson, Heinle.

Blyth, C. (2012) Cross-cultural stances in online discussions: Pragmatic variation in French and American ways of expressing opinions. In J.C. Félix-Brasdefer and D.A. Koike (eds) *Pragmatic Variation in First and Second Language Contexts* (pp. 49–79). Amsterdam: John Benjamins.

Donato, R. (1994) Collective scaffolding in second language learning. In J.P. Lantolf and G. Appel (eds) *Vygotskian Approaches to Second Language Research* (pp. 33–56). Norwood, NJ: Ablex.

Furstenberg, G., Levet, S., English, K. and Maillet, K. (2001) Giving a virtual voice to the silent language of culture: The *Cultura* project. *Language Learning and Technology* 5 (1), 55–102.

Furstenberg, G. and Levet, S. (2010) Integrating telecollaboration into the language classroom: Some insights. In S. Guth and F. Helm (eds) *Telecollaboration 2.0 for Language and Intercultural Learning in the 21st Century* (pp. 305–336). New York: Peter Lang Publishing Group.

Furstenberg, G. and Levet, S. (2014) Cultura: From then to now. Its origins, key features, methodology, and how it has evolved. Reflections on the past and musings on the future. In D.M. Chun (ed.) *Cultura-Inspired Intercultural Exchanges: Focus on Asian and Pacific Languages* (pp. xi–xx). Honolulu, HI: National Foreign Language Resource Center.

Garcia, J.S. and Crapotta, J. (2007) Models of telecollaboration: Cultura. In R. O'Dowd (ed.) *Online Intercultural Exchange: An Introduction for Foreign Language Teachers* (pp. 62–84). Clevedon: Multilingual Matters.

Kelm, O. (1992) The use of synchronous computer networks in second language instruction: A preliminary report. *Foreign Language Annals* 25 (5), 441–454.

Kern, R. (1995) Restructuring classroom interaction with networked computers: Effects on quantity and characteristics of language production. *Modern Language Journal* 79 (4), 457–476.

Kramsch, C. (2003) Teaching along the cultural faultline. In D.L. Lange and R.M. Paige (eds) *Culture as the Core: Perspectives on Culture in Second Language Learning* (pp. 19–36). Greenwich, CT: Information Age Publishing, Inc.

Lange, D.L. and Paige, R.M. (eds) (2003) *Culture as the Core: Perspectives on Culture in Second Language Learning*. Greenwich, CT: Information Age Publishing, Inc.

Lee, B., Riche, N. Karlson, A., and Carpendale, S. (2010) HYPERLINK "http://research.microsoft.com/en-us/um/people/nath/docs/sparkclouds_infovis2010.pdf" \t "_blank" SparkClouds: Visualizing trends in tag clouds. *IEEE Transactions on Visualization and Computer Graphics* 16 (6), 1182–1189

Paige, R.M., Jorstad, H.L., Siaya, L., Klein, F. and Colby, J. (2003) Culture learning in language education: A review of the literature. In D.L. Lange and R.M. Paige (eds) *Culture as the Core: Perspectives on Culture in Second Language Learning* (pp. 173–236). Greenwich, CT: Information Age Publishing, Inc.

Tschudi, S.L, Medina, R. and Hiple, D. (2011) Interactive tag clouds: A tool supporting new possibilities for dialog in online language learning. Presented at CALICO Conference. University of Victoria, British Columbia.

Tudini, V. (2007) Negotiation and intercultural learning in Italian native speaker chat rooms. *Modern Language Journal* 91 (4), 577–601.

University of Hawai'i at Mānoa, Center for Language and Technology. BRIX open-source course management system. See https://clt.manoa.hawaii.edu/online-teaching-tools/brix-2/ (accessed 27 August 2014).

Warschauer, M. (1996) Comparing face-to-face discussion and electronic communication in the second-language classroom. *CALICO Journal* 13 (2), 7–26.

7 Heritage Language Learners in Flagship Programs: Motivation, Language Proficiency and Intercultural Communicative Competence

Olga Kagan and Cynthia Martin

Introduction: Heritage Language Learners in Language Flagship Domestic and Overseas Programs

This chapter describes heritage language learners (HLLs) in Language Flagship programs and provides some recommendations regarding how to increase the motivation for improving their language proficiency. One of our goals is to explore why more heritage speakers do not enroll in Flagship programs and to offer some thoughts on how more heritage speakers can be attracted to such programs.

When the Flagship programs were first established in 2002–2003, there was an expectation that many of the students enrolling in the programs would be heritage speakers, i.e. students who grow up speaking a language other than English at home, and that for some programs heritage speakers might even comprise the majority of Flagship students. These potential students were thought of as a 'national resource' (Brecht & Ingold, 2002) that merely awaited discovery. Ten years later, these predictions have clearly not been borne out in most programs: according to the survey of students conducted by University of Texas at Austin Arabic Flagship Program in 2010–2011, in Flagship programs between 10% and 17% of all Flagship students are of heritage background (Al-Batal & Glakas, this volume). The overwhelming majority of students in Flagship programs are foreign language (L2) learners whose first exposure to the language was in formal instructional environments. The largest numbers of heritage speakers enrolled in Flagship programs appear to be in Chinese and Korean Flagship Programs.

While '[t]he knowledge possessed by heritage speakers puts them years ahead of anyone studying the language from scratch' (Benmamoun *et al.*, 2010: 83), these students still have to work diligently to reach high levels of proficiency (Kagan, 2005; Kagan & Dillon, 2004; Martin *et al.*, 2013; Swender *et al.*, 2014). Those who choose to complete the Flagship program have demonstrated that they have an excellent chance of succeeding and of exceeding expectations, reaching not only a superior, but even a distinguished level of proficiency: Davidson and Lekic (2013) show that heritage learners who complete the year-long Russian Flagship capstone overseas program tend to graduate with American Council on the Teaching of Foreign Languages (ACTFL) Distinguished (ILR 4; Appendix A) more frequently than non-heritage learners, indicating that heritage speakers may indeed have an advantage over L2 learners, who typically reach a Superior level of proficiency during the same amount of time spent abroad. But what does it take for this advantage to be realized? This chapter attempts to provide a very preliminary answer to that question. The preliminary nature is due to the small numbers of HLLs enrolled in Flagship programs. This in itself, however, may lead to a discussion of how the Language Flagship Program, or other language programs whose goal is high-level proficiency, may be made more attractive to HLLs. As one of the Flagship directors wrote, 'It is always good to attract a variety of students to the program, including heritage speakers who already have a background in… language and cultural knowledge'.

The definition of HLLs used in this chapter was offered by Polinsky and Kagan (2007), who propose both a narrow and a broad understanding of heritage speakers. The narrow definition embraces those students who have been exposed to a particular language in childhood in their homes but did not learn the home language to full capacity because another language became dominant. Students who fit the broad definition have been raised with a strong cultural connection to a particular language but may not have any measurable proficiency; therefore, they may require the same curriculum as foreign language learners.

Typically, speakers of the narrow definition belong to the 1.5 or second generation, i.e. they either immigrated with their families at an early age (Kasinitz *et al.* [2008] put that age at 12 or below) or were born in the United States, and are therefore either simultaneous or sequential bilinguals. Most of them speak the home language until the age of five, when they start school (Carreira & Kagan, 2011), and then gradually switch to English as the dominant language while continuing to use their home language in limited circumstances, for example with family or in the community. Carreira and Kagan (2011) find that the majority of their respondents use their home language to speak to parents, watch videos or attend community events. However, areas of language use differ depending on the particular language community. For example, while community events figure prominently in the lives of Korean speakers in the United States, they do not play the same role in the life of Russian speakers.

Depending on the language and the reasons for migration, some heritage speakers continue to travel to their country of origin regularly, while others do not. For example, a very small percentage of Russian HLLs in the survey conducted by the National Heritage Language Resource Center (NHLRC) (Carreira & Kagan, 2011) travelled to Russia, while a comparatively large percentage of Chinese and Korean speakers travel to their country of origin almost every year.

Relatively few HLLs in the United States elect to study in the country of their origin for a long period of time, and therefore there are few, if any, studies that provide data on this topic. Davidson and Lekic (2013: 88) observe that 'while the heritage learner within the domestic language learning context is relatively well represented in the literature, relatively little research has been devoted to the acquisition experiences of heritage learners engaged in overseas immersion study (re-learning) of their home language'. Additionally, in general, little research has been dedicated to the study of HLLs achieving high levels of proficiency. The next section presents a summary of such research.

Heritage Speakers at High Levels of Proficiency: A Review of Past Research

Not much has been written about US language learners, either L2 learners or heritage speakers, achieving ACTFL Superior or higher levels of proficiency. The first volume to address this issue was edited by Leaver and Shekhtman (2002), and the papers in the volume made it very clear that this was new territory for the language teaching profession. As Malone *et al.* (2004: 67) note when discussing the needs of high-level speakers of multiple languages, 'if relatively few individuals in the United States learn languages other than English, even fewer learn them to achieve a high levels of proficiency'. Byrnes and Maxim (2004) and Byrnes *et al.* (2006) also address this phenomenon. Overall, most of the publications on language teaching address instruction and performance at lower levels. Leaver and Shekhtman (2002), however, do offer some suggestions regarding the needs of students who strive to reach higher levels of language proficiency. The authors isolate a number of components that need to be put in place in a program that aims to enable the attainment of high-level proficiency. Their findings, which remain relevant today, are summarized below.

The first component in the Leaver–Shekhtman paradigm is linguistic competence that includes a strong grammatical base, a sophistication and accuracy of structure, an understanding of genre, a high level of competence in discourse organization and a precision of lexicon and stylistic register leading to an overall appropriateness of expression. Classroom instruction on its own, however, is not sufficient to attain these goals; students also need to possess a high degree of learner autonomy that, according to the authors, includes emotional and learning competence consisting of motivation and the ability to cope with interactions both inside the classroom and beyond. These factors allow students to learn outside of the classroom and not to be completely dependent on their teachers and study materials. Finally, students should also possess social competence and be willing to engage with native speakers of the target language.

If we analyze these competencies from the point of view of heritage speakers, several of these components are particularly significant. As a rule, heritage speakers do not have a strong grammatical base and do not understand the need to be precise in their expression, including the need to pay attention to register. This is easily explained by the language context in which they learned to communicate, one that typically exposes them only to informal registers. Finally, as Karapetian (2014) notes, when interacting with native speakers, heritage speakers may face identity issues and even experience shame because of the inadequacies of their language. All of these components may need to be addressed in order to engage HLLs effectively and to facilitate their path to high-level proficiency. In the subsequent section that includes Flagship directors' comments about their students, we will see that some directors report that they believe that some of their heritage learners feel very uncertain about their knowledge of the language, resulting in some learners' inability to progress beyond ACTFL Intermediate High.

In an attempt to understand what may hold heritage speakers back from achieving high levels of language proficiency and what kind of instruction may better facilitate their learning, the 2013 Summer Heritage Language Research Institute, sponsored by the Title VI-funded NHLRC, was dedicated to this issue and combined papers on both linguistic and pedagogical themes. The Institute was funded in part by the Language Flagship in recognition of the need to understand how HLLs can reach ACTFL Superior or higher proficiency. A special issue of the *Heritage Language Journal* (Volume 10, Number 2, 2013) summed up the Institute's discussions, focusing specifically on the linguistic and pedagogical issues that stand in the way of such achievement. One of the contributors writes that, at present, 'the vast majority of linguistic and psycholinguistic studies have investigated the lower end of the proficiency spectrum, characterizing the non-target-like linguistic abilities of heritage speakers as the products of incomplete acquisition and/or attrition' (Montrul, 2013: 153). Montrul (2013: 157) continues that 'because of their early experience with the language', heritage speakers show 'a much higher incidence of native ability in morphosyntactic and lexical aspects of language, areas that are extremely hard for L2 learners to master at native levels'. On the basis of her earlier studies, Montrul (2013: 172) concludes that 'heritage speakers are quite native when it comes to implicit knowledge and production of gender, a very difficult aspect to master at native-like levels by L2 learners'. She points out that the time has come to stop focusing on what issues and errors keep heritage speakers from gaining full proficiency, and to start exploring what makes heritage speakers more native-like than their non-heritage counterparts.

As Martin *et al.* (2013) demonstrate in the same issue of the journal and Swender *et al.* (2014) confirm, HLLs appear to have a better chance of reaching ACTFL Superior/Interagency Language Roundtable (ILR) Level 3 proficiency within a formal educational environment. We do not yet know, however, how many hours on task it would take an average HLL to move from the ACTFL Intermediate to the Advanced level, though we do have some data to demonstrate what kind of exposure is required to move from the ACTFL Advanced to the ACTFL Superior or higher (Davidson & Lekic, 2013). Further study is needed to determine how many hours may be required for heritage learners who start at the ACTFL Intermediate level to reach Advanced-level proficiency. At the same time, this number would be meaningful only if there is also an efficient and well-tested curriculum design that would make such an achievement possible. The available data on the number of hours required by L2 learners to reach certain proficiency levels (Liskin-Gasparro, 1982; McGinnis, 1994) can provide a useful comparison once such a study has been accomplished.

Survey of Flagship Program Directors

Reflecting upon both available literature and classroom experience, we propose that in order to understand the place of HLLs in Flagship programs, we need to look at least at two factors: motivation and curriculum design. In an attempt to get a brief overview of HLLs in Flagship programs, the authors conducted a survey of directors of Flagship programs in the United States. Program directors and other faculty of 15 Flagship programs around the United States responded to a short questionnaire (Appendix 7.1). Responses were received from three Arabic programs, four Chinese programs, three Russian programs, the Korean program, the Persian program, the Portuguese program, the Hindi/Urdu program and the Turkish program. Other Flagship programs were approached but were either too new or did not have any HLLs.

Motivation

There is no question that motivation plays a primary role in learning a language (Csizér & Dörnyei, 2005; Dörnyei, 1994; Dörnyei & Ushioda, 2009; Gardner, 1985, 2001; Gardner & Lambert, 1972; for HLLs' motivation, see Carreira & Kagan, 2011; Comanaru & Noels, 2009; Geisherik, 2004; Le, 2004; Lee, 2005; Lee & Shin, 2008; Li & Duff, 2008; Noels, 2005; Rueda & Chen, 2005; Wen, 2011). The data collected from the 15 Flagship programs show that faculty believe that most heritage students in Flagship programs are indeed interested in the business or career opportunities afforded by better knowledge of the language, but they were also interested in gaining an in-depth understanding of their heritage culture. For example, according to one Flagship program director, heritage students constantly underscore that:

> they want to be able to connect to their heritage language and culture at a deeper, more sophisticated level, connect to their family members [overseas] much better and even be able to attend lectures at universities or do internships if they ever get a chance to go [abroad] for visits. Parents also seem to encourage them to continue learning the language at a professional level, particularly if they have received some instruction through Saturday/community schools, i.e. schools run by community members or churches. These schools are outside of the formal educational system but provide access to heritage languages to thousands of students in heritage communities.

For their part, Russian-speaking students seemed to indicate an interest in content courses, thus confirming a finding by Kagan and Dillon (2001) that the main motivator for Russian families in maintaining Russian was to develop an appreciation of Russian literature or culture. One of the Russian Flagship directors wrote that the opportunity 'to take content classes plus the focus on applicability (career development) seems to be the greatest motivator'.

According to one of the directors of a Chinese Flagship, the Chinese HLLs were motivated by the desire to 'reconnect with their roots and be more competitive in the job market'. The motivation for Korean HLLs included 'searching for self or ethnic identity, interest in parents' language and culture, meeting family expectations, communication with first-generation family members', as well as an interest in 'Korea-related companies' such as IT companies doing business in the United States. According to respondents, heritage speakers of Portuguese join the Flagship 'to acquire a job in which they will use the language, and because they perceive Brazil to be a place that is fun and culturally rich'. In other words, most of the students seem to display combined integrative and instrumental motivations for studying their heritage language (Gardner, 1985, 2001; Gardner & Lambert, 1972).

A number of students in the Portuguese Flagship Program are heritage speakers of Spanish. In the Turkish Flagship Program, there were no heritage speakers of Turkish at the time the survey was conducted, but there are students who are speakers of Uzbek or Uygur, or possibly other Turkic languages. The Turkish Flagship staff mentioned that these students hope that studying Turkish will make them more marketable than speakers of just Uzbek/Uyghur/etc., they have career aspirations in the Turkic-speaking world, and/or learning Turkish is easier for them than other languages due to its relationship to their native Central Asian language(s).

Of course, attitudes both vary among individuals and depend on the language-specific background. For example, the staff of the Hindi/Urdu Flagship did not believe that either HLLs or their parents saw reaching a high level of proficiency in Hindi/Urdu as desirable or career enhancing. Some Flagship directors believe that some parents and students, particularly of Arabic and Hindi/Urdu, did not consider language study or study abroad advantageous. Respondents reported that Arabic-speaking parents in particular may actively discourage language study.

Russian program directors also mentioned that some parents do not want their children to study in Russia, which may be partially explained by the reasons for the parents' emigration: Kasinitz *et al.* (2008: 37) noted that 'Russian families generally make a "clean break" with the former Soviet Union'. Some parents of Hindi/Urdu-, Arabic- and Russian-speaking students are also concerned that Flagship courses will not allow students to graduate on time.

Several directors of the Flagship programs believe that HLLs are motivated by a desire to connect to the home culture (Carreira & Kagan, 2011). Their interest in acquiring high-level language proficiency may be secondary to their desire 'to connect'. A Russian-speaking student at the University of Wisconsin joined the Flagship because of a 'strong Russian identity/affiliation'. The student had a desire to learn to better 'balance being a Russian and an American'. An interest in political science and in a possible career promoting better US–Russia relations – for example, working for a non-governmental organization – also played a role.

The comment by one of the Flagship directors that heritage students may regard the Flagship program as a way to gain more in-depth knowledge of language and culture may be significant, and we may want to rethink how to appeal to heritage language students. Would a more intensive focus on cultural understanding through language be attractive to this group of students? We will address the importance and intricacies of intercultural communication later in the chapter.

Heritage language students as learners

The Flagship directors' comments reflect their belief that some HLLs may not appreciate why they should want to improve their language proficiency; moreover, they may not be willing to make the effort, because they feel they can already communicate effectively in the language. For example, one director wrote:

HLLs already have some basic knowledge of the (target) language and culture. Sometimes, some of them don't make the effort to learn something new. When they have two undergraduate majors (i.e. dual major or concurrent degree), they tend to spend more time on their first major. They think (the target language) is a little easy for them to study.

A director of an Arabic Flagship explained that 'The heritage students, most of them...will say, well, why do I need it, I speak this language and if I want to do business, I have the language, I can speak it so I don't need to go and take advanced-level courses'. One of the Russian directors mentioned that HLLs

combine deceptive fluency (sound like a native speaker!) with deficiencies in just about every linguistic area you can name. They struggle in traditional foreign-language classes and sometimes skate by on prior knowledge (hard to break old habits) in classes conducted in Russian.

A similar comment was made by a director of a Chinese Flagship, who stated that many HLLs' proficiency level 'stayed at Intermediate High/1+. No significant improvement after reaching Intermediate High'.

This summary of the directors' comments indicates several questions whose answers may be pursued in order to understand the needs of HLLs in Flagship programs: (1) What would motivate HLLs to participate in Language Flagship programs in greater numbers and to complete the programs? (2) Should the programs try to invest more energy in recruiting heritage speakers? (3) What kind of curriculum is needed to take heritage speakers to higher levels of proficiency? It is apparent that while HLLs have the potential to reach high levels of proficiency (Davidson & Lekic, 2013), they are not able to do so unless they are motivated to expend considerable time and effort on the study of their heritage language. While some individuals are willing and motivated to devote this time, these students are unfortunately in the minority in most Flagship programs. The only program that appears to send mostly HLLs on the capstone is the Korean program at the University of Hawai'i at Mānoa. So what does it take for HLLs to reach higher levels of proficiency?

In order to answer this question and also to make some recommendations regarding HLLs in heritage programs, we will analyze the results of a study conducted by the NHLRC and ACTFL (Martin et al., 2013; Swender et al., 2014). While the study investigated the proficiencies only of Spanish and Russian speakers, we believe that its conclusions may serve as recommendations for other languages as well. A study of Chinese heritage speakers also conducted by ACTFL and the NHLRC is underway.

Results of Oral Proficiency Interviews[1]

In 2010–2011, the NHLRC and ACTFL collaborated on a project mentioned in the previous section (Martin *et al.*, 2013; Swender *et al.*, 2014) with the aim of gaining an understanding of the linguistic, exposure and experiential factors that contribute to the speaking proficiency of HLLs. In particular, the project was designed to analyze the profiles of heritage speakers of Russian and Spanish who had received official ratings of Intermediate or Advanced according to the ACTFL scale, in order to determine which factors are most responsible for limiting the proficiency of these speakers. The goals of the study were also to contribute to our understanding of the instructional needs of these speakers and to enhance ACTFL Oral Proficiency Interview (OPI) tester training so that testers are able to assess more accurately the unique profiles of heritage speakers while simultaneously applying the same assessment criteria to all speakers, regardless of how, where or when they acquired the language. The project also aimed to produce a set of annotated descriptors of the ACTFL Proficiency Guidelines (2012) that would relate specifically to typical heritage profiles at each level. An additional aim of the study was to draw on the resulting detailed analysis of heritage profiles to inform instructional practices that target the typical linguistic strengths and weaknesses of this group. For this study, heritage speakers were defined as those who grew up speaking a home language other than English but who switched to English as their dominant language at an early age; those who received the majority of their education in an English-speaking school; those who were at least 18 years old; and those who were enrolled in school at the post-secondary level, either as an undergraduate or graduate student. Participants were first prescreened using a brief questionnaire about whether they were born in the United States, and if not, at what age they moved to the United States; their current age; the context in which their heritage language is used; and whether they had formally studied the language. The prescreening tool also contained a self-assessment of language proficiency. Select participants were then invited to take a more detailed qualification survey designed to gather demographic data, as well as more detailed information about their heritage language exposure and use, such as whether they could read or write, whether they had traveled or do travel to a country in which the heritage language is spoken, whether they had any formal instruction in the language and in which contexts they currently use their heritage language. Initially, Russian and Spanish were selected for this study, with other languages to be added. A total of 53 Russian and 41 Spanish heritage learners participated in the full study. Currently, Chinese samples are being analyzed.

Once the participants were selected, they took an Oral Proficiency Interview by computer (OPIc). All participants took the same form of the interview. The OPIcs were double-rated by certified ACTFL OPI raters. Raters were asked to complete evaluation forms on each OPIc that documented the rating rationale. Then, a team of researchers conducted a detailed linguistic analysis of each OPIc. The findings were analyzed in the aggregate to identify patterns of strengths and weaknesses for speakers with similar proficiency profiles (i.e. those who received the same rating), taking into account the demographic information provided by the participants. For a full discussion of the study, including examples of the analysis tools used, see Swender *et al.* (2014).

The main focus of the study was the factors that prevent HLLs from attaining higher levels of proficiency according to the ACTFL Proficiency Guidelines (American Council on the Teaching of Foreign Languages, 2012). The self-reported biographical data collected prior to the study helped identify factors accounting for the speakers' strengths. In both language groups, proficiency levels increased with more (self-reported) contact with the heritage culture, as well as greater use of either the heritage language or a mixture of the heritage language and English. A relationship can be seen between those who received ratings in the intermediate range on the OPIc and their self-reported use of more English than either the heritage language or a mix of the heritage language and English. Speakers of both languages who were rated Advanced or Superior (1) had either lived in a country or spent significant time in a country where the language is spoken and (2) reported having had formal instruction in the heritage language at the college level. There appears to be a strong connection between those who had formal, college-level instruction in the heritage language and those who reached higher proficiency levels. The data confirm that heritage speakers often have the common misperception that simply speaking the language at home and with friends is sufficient and automatically prepares them for using the language in more professional contexts, such as the workplace. This perception is likely linked to their tendency to over-assess their abilities and conclude that formal instruction is not necessary because they already speak the language. Understanding the reasons for over-assessing may help design strategies toward developing better self-assessment skills, which in turn could lead to higher levels of motivation among heritage learners to study the language in a more formal context, once they understand the expectations for professional language use, such as those described in the ACTFL Guidelines, as Superior. Based on the findings reported above, such explicit instruction should provide them with the necessary tools and practice to expand their lexical base to include more content areas that go beyond the familiar and autobiographical; to practice discussing a wide range of issues from an abstract, rather than a concrete, perspective; to practice producing cohesive, extended discourse in order to engage in extended discussions, support opinion and hypothesize; and to eliminate patterned structural errors that hinder communication at the higher levels.

Heritage Learners and Intercultural Competency

In view of heritage speakers' familiarity with the target language culture from home, it may be of interest to explore the new *Skill Level Descriptions for Competence in Intercultural Communication* (CIC), drafted by the ILR in 2012. The ILR is the standing volunteer committee composed of representatives of government organizations that require expertise in world languages and cultures. The *ILR Skill Level Descriptions for Speaking, Listening, Reading and Writing* have been used since the 1950s and are still used today as the primary assessment scale to evaluate the language competencies of Flagship learners. Considering that the ILR Descriptions are already in use to evaluate Flagship students, we suggest that the CIC Descriptions may be a useful tool when considering the intercultural competence of HLLs.

The CIC Descriptions define intercultural competency as 'the ability to take part effectively in a given social context by understanding what is being communicated and by employing appropriate language and behavior to convey an intended message' (ILR, 2012). We focus on ILR Levels 2 and 3, since most heritage learners exceed ILR Level 1, which targets the basic ability 'to participate in some everyday interactions, though not always acceptably' (ILR, 2012). At ILR Level 1, the learner recognizes that 'differences exist between behaviors, norms and values of the individual's own culture and those of the other culture, but shows little understanding of the significance or nature of these differences' (ILR, 2012). By the very nature of growing up in two cultures (Kagan, 2012), HLLs are implicitly aware of differences in behaviors, values and attitudes. A survey of heritage students in Flagship programs before their departure for the capstone (Kagan & Comstock, in preparation) confirms that Flagship heritage students are well aware of intercultural differences.

Ten pilot pre- and post-departure surveys and interviews with Flagship heritage students were conducted in order to understand the intercultural challenges they may face (Kagan & Comstock, in preparation). The study participants were Flagship students on the overseas programs in China, Korea, Russia, Egypt/Morocco and Nigeria. Students were contacted by email and asked to fill out questionnaires. The number of respondents was small, so these findings need to be treated as very tentative and highly preliminary. Nevertheless, the students' responses in view of the CIC Descriptions are illuminating. We are including some of the responses following the CIC Descriptions.

The CIC Descriptions describe 'Level 2 (Limited Working Competence)' (ILR, 2012) as follows:

- able to participate acceptably in many everyday social and work-related interactions;

- shows conscious awareness of significant differences between the individual's own culture and the other culture and attempts to adjust behavior accordingly, although not always successfully;
- can typically avoid taboos and adhere to basic social norms and rules of etiquette, such as in accepting and refusing invitations, offering and receiving gifts and requesting assistance;
- may sometimes misinterpret cultural cues or behave inappropriately for the culture, but is usually able to recognize and repair misunderstandings;
- understands the need to manage own attitudes and reactions to cultural dissonance, and is usually able to do so;
- normally functions as expected in predictable and commonly encountered situations, including public events and large gatherings, but may have difficulty when faced with less familiar circumstances;
- able to participate in various social media activities;
- in a work environment, can appropriately issue straightforward directions and instructions, give or receive orders, whether in person, on the telephone or in writing, and may be able to address some job-related problems. In some instances, demonstrates recognition of and makes appropriate reference to issues and topics that are customarily the subject of conversation, such as historical, cultural or current events.

If we analyze these features with a focus on heritage speakers, the second point, with its emphasis on the differences between the learners' 'own culture' and the 'other culture', needs to be reinterpreted. The home culture of the individual may also be based on a regional variant of the target language and culture or otherwise idiosyncratic (for example, based on a multicultural linguistic milieu), and it therefore needs to be juxtaposed with the dominant culture of the target country. The feature that addresses the individual's ability to 'accept and refuse invitations, offer and receive gifts', needs to be understood in terms of register, for while heritage speakers may be quite capable of carrying out these functions informally, any degree of formality may stump them.

Furthermore, reactions to cultural dissonance and discomfort may be more hurtful for heritage learners than for their L2 counterparts. Evidence of this point may be drawn from examples from the interviews conducted by Kagan and Comstock (in preparation). In one scenario, a student who had completed the Russian Flagship capstone overseas program said that most of her difficulties in interaction stemmed from the fact that people did not realize she was a foreigner and expected her to know how things worked. She added that there were moments when she thought she did not know Russian culture at all. Similarly, some Chinese heritage students in pre-departure interviews were concerned about 'adapting their "American" persona to fit Chinese norms'. Another Chinese heritage student reflected upon how her 'previous study abroad experiences had shaped her understanding of how she would be perceived to be different, contrary to her initial expectations to blend in'.

The following quotes from the interviews illustrate what heritage students think and what concerns them before their departure for the capstone.

> Socially, I hope to integrate myself in a part of the Arab world with which I am somewhat familiar. I do not believe full integration is possible, since I will always carry certain American mannerisms with which I have grown up.
>
> Unfortunately, I think I will always be considered as an outsider looking in when it comes to conversations about the Revolution, because I did not participate in the particular protests that many Egyptians are so proud of.
>
> Although I am ethnically the same, I know that the way I dress or my demeanor will show that I am not of the same land, culture and customs. Before my first time studying abroad, I thought I would blend in, because I am ethnically similar with my body features, but many locals could tell in a split second I was not of their kind. I identify myself as Chinese in America; however, when I am in Asia, I identify as an American
>
> I always knew that Eastern culture is quite different from the Western culture, and as much as I identify with both worlds, and prepare myself to be open-minded, there are certain standards and expectations that have already solidified within me. A big concern for me would be deciding when to let go or stand firm in my personal perceptions and standards to successfully complete this year in China.

One of the points in the CIC Descriptions discusses functioning in large gatherings. For heritage speakers who may not immediately be seen as foreigners, the success of an interaction can depend on the degree of formality of the gathering. It is hard to know which circumstances are more familiar to heritage speakers, as some of them, as Carreira and Kagan (2011) show, frequently attend community events (for example, speakers of Korean), while others do not (speakers of Russian). Finally, participating in the work environment may be fraught with frustrations. As Korean heritage speakers reported during the interviews:

> I am comfortable with the [Korean] school environment, but not so much for the work environment. It is different from the U.S., because as I mentioned before, the work culture is different. There are many things you have to look out for, because if you're not well prepared, then you could come off as rude and ill-mannered.

From my experience [in Korea] I think the one thing that us heritage language speakers are not familiar with is the work culture. So a special lecture on this topic would be useful, in my opinion: what actions are not looked greatly upon and what to look out for.

Similarly, some Chinese heritage students felt that the 'greatest concern [was] in making social connections', and expressed explicit awareness that their linguistic and cultural limitations might isolate them.

The CIC Descriptions may expand the HLLs' ability to overcome these limitations, as they will know better what to strive for. They need to be aware of such Level 3 recommendations as (1) 'transitioning smoothly from informal to formal styles of communication'; (2) producing appropriate 'non-verbal responses, such as gestures'; (3) having sufficient knowledge to 'discuss a variety of issues and subject matter that refer to...history, politics, literature and the arts' (ILR, 2012). Given that, according to Davidson and Lekic (2013), HLLs are able to achieve ACTFL Superior/Distinguished/ILR Level 3+/4 oral proficiency during the year-long capstone, these goals of intercultural communication seem to be within their reach. Of course, in order to use the CIC Descriptions effectively, programs will also need to develop ways to assess intercultural communicative competency. This may be the next step in developing more precise assessment instruments for the Language Flagship (Martin, in preparation).

Conclusions and Recommendations

While HLLs have the potential to reach high levels of proficiency, they do not currently flock to Flagship programs. Among the reasons for this lack of enrollment is some parents' reluctance to have their children spend a year in the country of their origin, as well as the fear that participation might delay graduation. While some parents and families encourage their children to become competent in their heritage language, other parents may not think that studying the home language is a worthwhile pursuit. We can only speculate as to whether this belief may be connected with the original reasons for emigration and the desire, or lack thereof, of families to stay connected to the country of origin. We should also remember that immigrants from some countries cannot travel back for various political reasons.

Another reason why more heritage speakers do not sign up for Flagship programs appears to be students' satisfaction with their current level of language proficiency. Some students who can manage adequately at the ACTFL Intermediate/Advanced level may not see why they should expend additional effort on developing their language ability rather than focusing on a major that, in their perception, will lead directly to a career. If jobs that reward high language proficiency were plentiful, however, this attitude would undoubtedly change. Even when jobs are available, students may not be aware of such opportunities. More easily accessible information about jobs may make heritage students more carefully consider studying their home language to a professional degree of proficiency.

What can be recommended to programs that have HLLs and find it difficult to move them beyond ACTFL Intermediate High/ILR Level 1+, as explained by one of the Chinese Flagship directors? First of all, grammatical accuracy and range of expression need to be stressed at all times. Emphasis on grammatical precision and vocabulary development is a must for heritage speakers, as they need to unlearn fossilized patterns and automatize newly learned structures and expressions in order to gain higher proficiency. Second, the curriculum for all students, and for heritage learners in particular, should combine language proficiency and intercultural competency. The CIC Descriptions delineate factors underlying high-level cultural competency, thus supplementing the ACTFL and ILR proficiency guidelines that focus on linguistic proficiency. Specifically, before their departure for the capstone, heritage students should understand that they may actually have a more difficult time in the country of their family's origin because of their 'looking like everyone else' or initially 'sounding like everyone else', as they may not be able to behave according to the accepted and expected conventions. The CIC Descriptions may serve as a roadmap to developing cultural competency. Making heritage learners aware of the framework of the CIC Descriptions may improve their potential for reaching the highest possible levels of proficiency, both linguistic and cultural.

Finally, there is some anecdotal evidence that some instructors may feel that they have contributed less to the achievements of HLLs in their program than they have to the achievements of L2 students who start from zero. This attitude may not even be conscious, and once it is recognized, we may want to rethink it. It is not easy for HLLs to reach ACTFL Superior proficiency; though their pathway may be faster than for L2 learners, the struggles of HLLs are different and are real. They cannot accomplish high-level proficiency without instructional help, i.e. without teachers. If HLLs do achieve high-level proficiency, educators should feel as proud as we do when our non-HLLs manage it. As one of the Chinese heritage speakers said,

> I think many people (or even themselves) perceive heritage language speakers as having a "head start" or an advantage (maybe in the foundation of the language), but as a heritage language speaker, the way I master a second language and my approach to studying abroad is no different than a non-heritage language learner.

Even if this may not be entirely correct, this student is clearly aware that bringing one's home language to a high level of proficiency is very hard work.

In light of some parents' unwillingness to send their children to the country of origin for a long period of time and their concerns about students not graduating on time, we would like to suggest that a track for heritage speakers in Flagship programs could be shortened, and that their time in the home country be shortened as well. Not only might this option attract more heritage speakers to Flagship programs, but if such special tracks were intentionally designed to be the most efficient for HLLs, it might contribute to the shared goal of increasing our national capacity in critical languages. Some flexibility in the curriculum for those students who are capable of reaching ACTFL Superior proficiency faster and by somewhat different routes may pay real dividends in the long run.

Note

(1)   This section of the chapter was reprinted with permission of the *Heritage Language Journal* (Martin *et al.*, 2013).

References

American Council on the Teaching of Foreign Languages (ACTFL) (2012) *ACTFL Proficiency Guidelines 2012*. See http://www.actfl.org/sites/default/files/pdfs/public/ACTFLProficiencyGuidelines2012_FINAL.pdf (accessed 15 June 2015).

Benmamoun, E., Montrul, S. and Polinsky, M. (2010) White paper: Prolegomena to heritage linguistics. *Heritage Linguistics*. See http://nhlrc.ucla.edu/nhlrc/resources/article/122865 (accessed 22 January 2015).

Brecht, R.D. and Ingold, C.W. (2002) *Tapping a National Resource: Heritage Languages in the United States*. Washington, DC: ERIC Clearinghouse on Languages and Linguistics.

Byrnes, H. and Maxim, H.H. (2004) *Advanced Foreign Language Learning: A Challenge to College Programs. Issues in Language Program Direction*. Boston, MA: Heinle.

Byrnes, H., Weger-Guntharp, H.D. and Sprang, K.A. (2006) *Educating for Advanced Foreign Language Capacities: Constructs, Curriculum, Instruction, Assessment*. Washington, DC: Georgetown University Press.

Carreira, M. and Kagan, O. (2011) The results of the National Heritage Language Survey: Implications for teaching, curriculum design, and professional development. *Foreign Language Annals* 44 (1), 40–64.

Comanaru, R. and Noels, K.A. (2009) Self-determination, motivation, and the learning of Chinese as a heritage language. *Canadian Modern Language Review/La Revue canadienne des langues vivantes* 66 (1), 131–158.

Csizér, K. and Dörnyei, Z. (2005) Language learners' motivational profiles and their motivated learning behavior. *Language Learning* 55 (4), 613–659.

Davidson, D.E. and Lekic, M.D. (2013) The heritage and non-heritage learner in the overseas immersion context: Comparing learning outcomes and target-language utilization in the Russian Flagship. *Heritage Language Journal* 10 (2), 88–114.

Dörnyei, Z. (1994) Motivation and motivating in the foreign language classroom. *Modern Language Journal* 78 (3), 273–284.

Dörnyei, Z. and Ushioda, E. (eds) (2009) *Motivation, Language Identity and the L2 Self*. Bristol: Multilingual Matters.

Gardner, R.C. (1985) *Social Psychology and Second Language Learning: The Role of Attitudes and Motivation*. London: Edward Arnold.

Gardner, R.C. (2001) Integrative motivation and second language acquisition. In Z. Dörnyei and R. Schmidt (eds) *Motivation and Second Language Acquisition* (pp. 1–19). Mānoa, HI: University of Hawaii Press.

Gardner, R.C. and Lambert, W.E. (1972) *Attitudes and Motivation in Second-Language Learning.* Rowley, MA: Newbury House Publishers.

Geisherik, A. (2004) The role of motivation among heritage and non-heritage learners of Russian. *Canadian Slavonic Papers/Revue Canadienne des Slavistes* 46 (1–2), 9–22.

Interagency Language Roundtable (ILR) (2012) *Interagency Language Roundtable Skill Level Descriptions for Competence in Intercultural Communication.* See http://www.govtilr.org/Skills/Competence.htm (accessed 16 June 2015).

Interagency Language Roundtable (ILR) *Interagency Language Roundtable Skill Level Descriptions.* See http://www.govtilr.org (accessed 16 June 2015).

Kagan, O. (2005) In support of a proficiency-based definition of heritage language learners: The case of Russian. *International Journal of Bilingual Education and Bilingualism* 8 (2–3), 213–221.

Kagan, O. (2012) Intercultural competence of heritage language learners: Motivation, identity, language attitudes, and the curriculum. In B. Dupuy and L. Waugh (eds) *Proceedings of the Third International Conference on the Development and Assessment of Intercultural Competence* (pp. 72–84). Tucson, AZ: University of Arizona: Center for Educational Resources in Culture, Language and Literacy.

Kagan, O. and Dillon, K. (2001) A new perspective on teaching Russian: Focus on the heritage learner. *Slavic and East European Journal* 45 (3), 507–518. Reprinted in *Heritage Language Journal* 1 (1), 76–90.

Kagan, O. and Dillon, K. (2004) Heritage speakers' potential for high-level language proficiency. In H. Byrnes and H. Maxim (eds) *Advanced Foreign Language Learning: A Challenge to College Programs. Issues in Language Program Direction* (pp. 99–112). Boston, MA: Heinle.

Kagan, O. and Comstock, L. (in preparation) Intercultural competencies of heritage language learners.

Karapetian, S. (2014) 'How Do I Teach My Kids My Broken Armenian?': A Study of Eastern Armenian Heritage Language Speakers in Los Angeles. PhD dissertation, The University of California, Los Angeles.

Kasinitz, P., Mollenkopf, J.H., Waters, M.C. and Holdaway, J. (2008) *Inheriting the City: The Children of Immigrants Come of Age.* New York: Russell Sage Foundation.

Le, J. (2004) Affective Characteristics of American Students Studying Chinese in China: A Study of Heritage and Non-heritage Learners' Beliefs and Foreign Language Anxiety. PhD Dissertation, The University of Texas at Austin.

Leaver, B.L. and Shekhtman, B. (2002) Principles and practices in teaching superior-level language skills: Not just more of the same. In B.L. Leaver and B. Shekhtman (eds) *Developing Professional-Level Language Proficiency* (pp. 3–33). Cambridge: Cambridge University Press.

Lee, J.S. (2005) Through the learners' eyes: Reconceptualizing the heritage and non-heritage learner of the less commonly taught languages. *Foreign Language Annals* 38 (4), 554–563.

Lee, J.S. and Shin, S.J. (2008) Korean heritage language education in the United States: The current state, opportunities, and possibilities. *Heritage Language Journal* 6 (2), 153–172.

Li, D. and Duff, P. (2008) Issues in Chinese heritage language education and research at the postsecondary level. In A.W. He and Y. Xiao (eds) *Chinese as a Heritage Language: Fostering Rooted World Citizenry* (pp. 13–36). Honolulu, HI: University of Hawai'i at Mānoa: National Foreign Language Resource Center.

Liskin-Gasparro, J.E. (1982) *ETS Oral Proficiency Testing Manual*. Princeton, NJ: Educational Testing Service.

Malone, M.E., Rifkin, B., Christian, D. and Johnson, D.E. (2004) Attaining high levels of proficiency: Challenges for language education in the United States. *Journal for Distinguished Language Studies* 2, 67–88.

Martin, C.L. (in preparation) Assessing intercultural communication.

Martin, C.L., Swender, E. and Rivera-Martinez, M. (2013) Assessing the oral proficiency of heritage speakers according to the ACTFL Proficiency Guidelines 2012 – Speaking. *Heritage Language Journal* 10 (2), 73–87.

McGinnis, S. (1994) The less common alternative: A report from the task force for teacher training in the less commonly taught languages. *ADFL Bulletin* 25 (2), 17–22.

Montrul, S. (2013) How 'native' are heritage speakers? *Heritage Language Journal* 10 (2), 153–177.

Noels, K.A. (2005) Orientations to learning German: Heritage language learning and motivational substrates. *Canadian Modern Language Review/La Revue canadienne des langues vivantes* 62 (2), 285–312.

Polinsky, M. and Kagan, O. (2007) Heritage languages: In the 'wild' and in the classroom. *Language and Linguistics Compass* 1 (5), 368–395.

Rueda, R. and Chen, C.Y.B. (2005) Assessing motivational factors in foreign language learning: Cultural variation in key constructs. *Educational Assessment* 10 (3), 209–229.

Swender, E., Martin, C.L., Rivera-Martinez, M. and Kagan, O. (2014) Exploring oral proficiency profiles of heritage speakers of Russian and Spanish. *Foreign Language Annals* 47 (3), 423–446.

Wen, X. (2011) Chinese language learning motivation: A comparative study of heritage and non-heritage learners. *Heritage Language Journal* 8 (3), 41–66.

Appendix 7.1

Questions sent to the directors of the Flagship programs:

(1) What percentage of students in your program are HLLs?
(2) How many of them continue all the way through the program? If they don't continue, why not?
(3) How many go on the summer program?
(4) How many go on the capstone?
(5) What are their motivations for studying their heritage language?
(6) What is their initial proficiency?
(7) What proficiency do they reach if they go on the capstone program?
(8) Are there any difficulties you encounter in teaching them?
(9) Do you think it is a good idea to try and attract more of them to the program?

8 Assessing Language Proficiency and Intercultural Development in the Overseas Immersion Context

Dan E. Davidson, Nadra Garas and Maria D. Lekic

Introduction

Among intercultural competencies, language plays a critical role, central to the perception and interpretation of external reality, the construction and transfer of meaning and the projections of self. Contemporary information technologies have done much to minimize geographical and temporal barriers to global communication, but native language(s), local culture and regional context strongly influence all modes and modalities of intercultural communication, particularly where the establishment or maintenance of mutual understanding, personal trust and professional collaboration are concerned. For that reason, overseas language immersion is an obligatory component of all Language Flagship programs, as well as of many other international programs today. Second language (L2) gain within the context of well-designed immersion study is extensively documented in the literature, as is the need for the overseas sojourner to comprehend and engage effectively with the host culture (Davidson, 2015).

Alumni of successful overseas immersion learning programs such as the Flagship are able to consciously adjust cognitive perspectives and adapt to different cultural environments, utilizing appropriate sociolinguistic and intercultural communication strategies. These abilities are what is meant by *intercultural competence* (IC), as reflected in Deardorff's (2004) widely recognized 'consensus definition'. IC comprises both internal (cognitive and attitudinal) and interactional components for an adaptable and nuanced ethno-relative capacity to interpret contexts and function effectively across cultural divides (Deardorff, 2006; King & Baxter Magolda, 2005). The interrelationship of second language acquisition (SLA) and intercultural development in the study abroad (SA) context, while often acknowledged as relevant, has remained largely unspecified. One recent study, for example, found that pre-program intercultural development scores appear to predict ultimate L2 proficiency outcomes (Baker-Smemoe *et al.*, 2014), while other researchers have observed parallel development of IC and L2 proficiency (Paige *et al.*, 2004; Watson *et al.*, 2013). Most existing research on IC and SA, however, has been limited to the examination of IC measurements of consecutive groups of SA populations who are at roughly the same stage in their learning careers and, typically, in connection with a first academic sojourn abroad, whether for a summer, semester or academic year. It is difficult in most cases to account for the differential effects of language proficiency, intercultural orientation and academic background on the overall outcome of the immersion experience.

The Intercultural Development Continuum (IDC) (Hammer, 2007, 2012; Hammer & Bennett, 1998, 2002), based on the intercultural sensitivity model first elaborated by Bennett (1986, 1993, 2004), characterizes orientations to cultural difference. Hammer (2012; Appendix 8.1) adapted the IDC to five measureable orientation ranges assessed by the Intercultural Development Inventory (IDI). The score produced by the IDI places each individual or group along a continuum ranging from monocultural perspectives to more intercultural/global mindsets: Denial, Polarization, Minimization, Acceptance and Adaptation.

A number of studies have used the IDI to examine the impact of SA programs. Vande Berg *et al.* (2004) employed the IDI to compare gains in intercultural development by SA students with gains of those students who had remained on the home campus over the same period, observing that the SA group generally exhibited more growth in intercultural development as well as some competence in an L2 in comparison with those who did not go abroad. Paige *et al.* (2004) studied the impact of the SA experience and curriculum intervention on students' intercultural development, SLA and employment of learning strategies related to language and culture, noting overall gains in intercultural sensitivity. Engle and Engle (2004) identified higher intercultural gains among SA students whose programs also included a cultural mentoring component as well as direct contact with the host culture.

Paige *et al.* (2004) and Engle and Engle (2004) examined SA language learning programs and intercultural sensitivity, concluding that those students who spent a year overseas showed gains in intercultural sensitivity, while those engaging in shorter-term programs were less likely to exhibit gains in IDI. A study by Medina-Lopez-Portillo (2004) also found little support for significant gains over short programs (seven weeks to one semester). However, Anderson *et al.* (2006) found that students who participated in two- and four-week SA programs showed small gains in intercultural sensitivity, compared with no gains for those students who spent that same time enrolled in courses at their home universities. Patterson (2006) examined the impact of short-term SA programs (two- or four-week programs) and concluded that those students who engaged in SA showed small improvements in intercultural effectiveness compared with those who spent that time in the classroom. Rexeisen *et al.* (2008) concluded that SA programs have a positive short-term effect on intercultural development, but noted that assessment of the long-term impact required further investigation. Anderson and Lawton (2011) argue that SA exerted a positive change on the intercultural development of students, as supported by the results of the pre-post administration of IDI to undergraduate students who spent a one-semester SA program in London.

Paige *et al.* (2004) and Vande Berg (2009) conclude that students studying abroad show gains in intercultural learning, using IDI scores to compare the impact of various curricular strategies adopted by SA programs on their students' IC. The Georgetown Consortium multi-year study showed that students in SA made small gains, but that these were tempered by the duration or length of the SA program and the extent to which the program offered guided learning. In some cases, the study revealed no significant difference between SA students and those who stayed at their home universities (Vande Berg *et al.*, 2009). Similarly, Pedersen (2010) concludes that guided learning is central to intercultural development and learning experience and that having students spend time overseas is not sufficient to foster effective global citizenship.

Among studies linking SA and intercultural development, Salisbury's (2011) large-scale (*N*=1593) longitudinal examination is of particular note. Drawing on data collected in 2006 for the Wabash Study of Liberal Arts Education, Salisbury (2011: 92) establishes, under rigorous analytic conditions, a statistically significant positive effect for SA on IC, 'an effect that appears to be general, rather than conditional'. While establishing that SA influences students' diversity of contact, the study was unable to establish statistically significant effects on participants' relativistic appreciation of cultural differences or comfort with diversity (Salisbury, 2011). The Salisbury study does not control for duration of immersion, study designs or engagement by participants in language or area studies.

Watson *et al.* (2013) assess change in intercultural development (using the IDI), language proficiency (oral proficiency interview [OPI]) and area knowledge (ARK/GRANT)[1] in a large-scale (*N*=498) longitudinal examination of third- and fourth-year-level US Military Academy cadets who studied one of seven different languages for a semester in 14 overseas study locations. The study reports multimodal proficiency gains at the unit level (e.g. American Council on the Teaching of Foreign Languages [ACTFL] Intermediate Low to Intermediate Mid) and 49% at the threshold level (e.g. Intermediate to Advanced) along with modest IDI growth across groups for semester-long cohorts placed for language study in China, Eastern Europe, Western Europe, Latin America and the Middle East (Watson *et al.*, 2013). The study also reports mean IDI gains in developmental orientation ranging from 2.5 to 5.1 points (87.2–92.3) over the four consecutive years for which data were collected. These changes are consistent with others reported in the literature for US undergraduate SA (Hammer, 2012; Vande Berg, 2009).

Baker-Smemoe *et al.* (2014) present data for approximately 100 summer and semester-long SA university students with initial measured proficiency levels largely in the ACTFL Intermediate range in six world languages. In comparing those whose proficiency increased over the course of the SA program with those who did not register gains, the authors report a positive correlation between pre-program IDI developmental orientation scores and ultimate gain (or no gain) across all SA groups under study. Among those variables assessed, pre-program IDI was shown to have the largest predictive value for language gain.

Research Questions

The construct underlying the assessment of intercultural competencies comprises a mix of traits related to the learner's background knowledge, critical thinking abilities, attitudes, executive functioning and interpersonal skills. The present study hypothesizes that language proficiency both influences and is influenced by the learner's level of intercultural development. Building on existing research on language gain and taking into consideration the range of evidence that has appeared regarding learning in the overseas immersion context, the present study poses the following research questions:

(1) How does OPI change differ across the immersion programs focused on early, mid and advanced levels of training and what, if any, relationships obtain between different levels of language proficiency and measured levels of intercultural development, as reflected by the IDI?
(2) To what extent do pre-program IDI scores predict ultimate L2 attainment of SA participants?
(3) What is the effect of lower, mid-range and advanced L2 proficiency on change in IDI during SA?

While the 'language barrier' is popularly cited as the most challenging factor to successful interactions across cultures, the present study seeks to better understand the role of proficiency in an L2 and the learner's own intercultural development of language as a potential barrier and as a potential mediator of interculturality.

Methodology

The study will first report and provide statistical comparisons of pre- and post-program OPI and IDI scores of students of various foreign languages who have undertaken formal language and cultural immersion training in countries where those languages are spoken. Change (positive and negative) in pre- to post-program OPI and IDI ratings will be noted and significant relationships highlighted. Significant sub-score effects, where observed, will also be reported.

The OPI is widely used in the United States today to measure speaking proficiency, based either on the government Interagency Language Roundtable (ILR) scale or on the ACTFL scale (Appendix A). The IDI is an online instrument which assesses intercultural development orientation (DO), perceived intercultural orientation (PO) and the orientation gap (OG: the gap between DO and PO) along a scale ranging from monocultural mindsets (Denial) up to and including a level of intercultural awareness and sensitivity sufficient for functional integration into the host culture (Adaptation; Appendix 8.1). The 50-item IDI generates a profile and a set of numerical scores and sub-scores for each test taker, placing the test taker on the IDI continuum. Movement along the continuum in either direction is possible. The IDI is available commercially and is used widely in government, industry and higher education today.

Subject Groups

Participants in the present study (N=305) consist of US high school and university students selected for participation in 2013 and 2014 for four federally supported overseas language immersion programs: Flagship capstone overseas program students (N=44), Russian Language and Areas Studies (RLASP) semester-long participants (N=104), National Security Language Initiative for Youth (NSLI-Y) (N=132) and outbound Kennedy Lugar Youth Exchange and Study Abroad program (YES) (N=25). YES and NSLI-Y students are comparable in age, selection, background and duration of overseas immersion (one year). The first three groups are engaged in formal language study. YES students are not engaged primarily in language study, but enjoy similar kinds of in-country support provided by English-speaking hosts. The NSLI-Y participants took part in year-long programs in China, India, Korea, Moldova, Morocco and Taiwan. The RLASP students participated in semester-long programs in various urban university locations in Russia; the Flagship capstone students participated in year-long programs in China, Kazakhstan, Morocco and Turkey and the YES students participated in year-long programs in Bosnia-Herzegovina, Ghana, Indonesia, Jordan, Macedonia, Morocco, Oman, Turkey and South Africa, residing with English-speaking families of recently returned inbound YES exchange students to the United States. Full demographic information is provided in Table 8.1.

Table 8.1 Demographic information

	All programs	L-2 programs*	NSLI-Y	RLASP	All Flagship programs		YES program
						(ROF only)	
N = 305		280	132	104	44	(19)	25
Age							
17 and under		21 (7.5%)	21 (15.9%)	–	–	–		21 (84%)
18–21		202 (72.1%)	111 (84.1%)	86 (82.7%)	5 (11.4%)	1 (5.3%)	4 (16%)
22–30		56 (20%)	–	18 (17.3%)	38 (86.4%)	17 (89.5%)	–
31–40		1 (0.4%)	–	–	1 (2.3%)	1 (5.3%)	–
Gender							
Male		117 (41.8%)	53 (40.2%)	40 (38.5%)	24 (54.5%)	11 (57.9%)	4 (16%)
Female		163 (58.2%)	79 (59.8%)	64 (61.5%)	20 (45.5%)	8 (42.1%)	1 (84%)

* L2 programs (N=280) are Flagship. NSLI-Y and RLASP. Russian Overseas Flagship (ROF) is a subset of Flagship. The YES outbound program (N=25) does not require previous language study.

The limitations of the participant samples should be clearly noted from the outset. The participants cannot be said to represent the US population more generally, or US high school or university students for that matter, due to the impossibility within the context of four competitive federal programs of controlling for selection effects or producing a randomized study of treatment or control groups. To the extent, however, that all four cohorts were selected for participation using widely accepted standardized criteria that did *not* consider IDI scores or consideration of the student's financial situation, and that participants represent a very broad range of public and private institutions, they may be regarded as typical of US students who currently study overseas at some point in their high school or university careers. In that sense, the results of this study should be useful for academic planning, policy and SLA research purposes.

Analysis[2]

Pre- and post-program OPI results

Figures 8.1 through 8.3 present pre- and post-program OPI results of the three programs in question. NSLI-Y accepts some students with no prior study of the language in question, whereas RLASP and Flagship have specific qualifying levels for entering participants of ILR 1 and ILR 2 proficiency, respectively.

Within the NSLI-Y cohort for 2014, 61% of participants completed the program at ACTFL Advanced (ILR 2) or higher, while an additional 23% scored at Intermediate High (IH), which is at or near the threshold of ILR 2 (Figure 8.1).

RLASP programs are of one-semester duration. It is noteworthy that 50% of the 2014 RLASP cohort completed the program at ILR 2, with an additional 24% of the program at IH, at or near the threshold of ILR 2 (Figure 8.2).

Language Flagship overseas programs accept students from US domestic Flagship programs who have attained ILR 2 proficiency in two modalities and who have devoted a minimum of eight weeks of prior formal academic study in the target country at the time of application. It should be noted, however, that within the present cohort, 10% of the total group were rated ACTFL IH rather than Advanced on the pre-program OPI. For the 2014 cohort represented in the study, 70% of students achieved ILR 3 (or higher) in speaking on the post-program OPI, while 23% were rated ACTFL AH, i.e. at or near the ILR 3 threshold (Figure 8.3).

The Russian Overseas Flagship (ROF) in 2014–2015 was shifted from St. Petersburg State University (Russia) to Al-Farabi Kazakh National

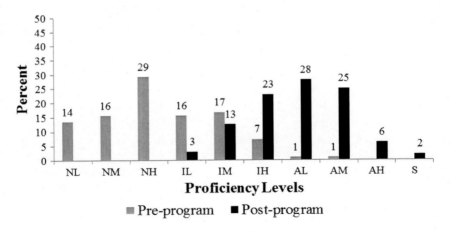

Figure 8.1 NSLI-Y programs pre- and post-program OPI levels (*N*=96)

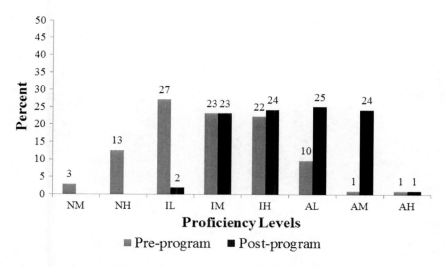

Figure 8.2 RLASP program pre- and post-program OPI levels (*N*=103)

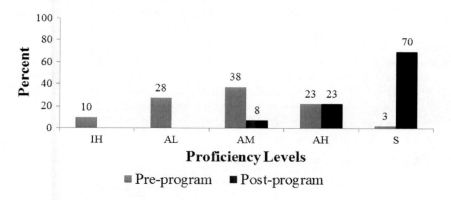

Figure 8.3 All Overseas Flagship programs pre- and post-program OPI levels (*N*=40)

University in Almaty (Kazakhstan). While still very much a part of the Russophone world, Kazakhstan is a bilingual nation in the heart of Central Asia, creating a tri-cultural experience for the 2014–2015 ROF cohort. For that reason, the ROF results are reviewed separately in Figure 8.4.

Analyzing OPI change across the three programs

The effects of the three language immersion programs on OPI growth were examined with a mixed linear model. The fit statistics for a series of related models varying in complexity are given in Table 8.2.

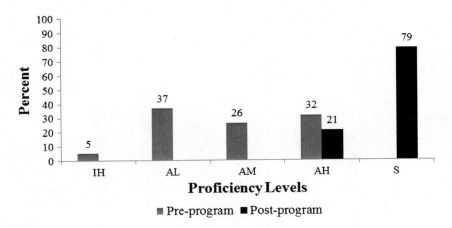

Figure 8.4 Russian Overseas Flagship Program pre- and post-program OPI levels (*N*=19)

The model in Table 8.2 is the best-fitting linear model of pre- and post-program OPIs. It indicates that the fixed-effect interactions between growth (f1) and program type are significant. While OPI change differences exist across the three programs, the average OPI change is approximately the same across all three programs. Language Flagship students attain comparable growth as lower- and middle-range-proficiency learners, but they produce these gains in the upper ranges of functional proficiency (ILR 3). The NSLI-Y group starts with the lowest performance (of 7.80–4.46=3.34) and demonstrates the largest improvement (of 1.83+1.63=3.46). These interaction effects are several times larger than their standard errors and thus highly significant.[3]

Table 8.2 A mixed linear model of OPI growth

Model	AIC	DIC	Deviance	Resid (SD)
1. Between Subjects Only	2262.7	2251.3	2254.0	2.00
2. Between Subjects+Growth	1958.4	1939.3	1944.8	1.08
3. Between Subjects+Program	2095.6	2073.7	2079.6	1.83
4. Between Subjects+Program+Growth	1762.6	1731.2	1740.9	1.09
5. Between Subjects+Program*Growth	**1672.8**	**1630.9**	**1643.9**	**0.89**

Pre- and post-program IDI scores

Table 8.3 presents the results of IDI data collected before and after participation by students in the three language-based immersion programs, as well as for the YES program. The DO score is the basal score produced by the IDI, against which a PO score (based on the same scale) is juxtaposed. The 'gap' measurement, the difference between DO and PO, is also a part of the IDI profile and is a significant finding in the present study.

Table 8.3 IDI pre- and post-mean developmental orientation scores

Program name	Mean pre	SD pre	Mean post	SD post	Mean difference
ROF program only (N=19)	97.11	16.34	102.26	14.11	5.15
OPI ILR 3 and above	97.92	16.47	103.05	14.13	5.14
All Flagship programs (N=42)	97.95	15.41	99.08	13.13	1.13
RLASP program (N=103)	95.53	12.78	97.84	14.91	2.31
NSLI-Y program (N=131)	92.66	13.73	93.94	13.85	1.28
YES program (N=25)	95.32	12.02	95.48	14.32	0.16

Group-level DO scores increased in every group taking part in the overseas immersion study, with the smallest mean difference between pre- and post-program score of 0.16 registered for the non-language YES cohort and the largest mean difference of 5.14 reported for the Russian Overseas Flagship Program. It is worth noting that the YES group entered the program with mean IDI scores of 95.32, a relatively high mean pre-program level in comparison with others reported in the literature for SA students in general. DO scores show large within-group-by-occasion standard deviations of 14–16, and together with a small group size (19) for ROF make several effects more difficult to detect. Analysis of variance (ANOVA) comparisons did not indicate any group differences before ($F=2.405$, df=[2, 277], $p=0.09$) or after ($F=2.88$, df=[2, 277], $p=0.06$) program participation. RLASP shows a detectable change from 96 to 98 (difference=2.31, $t=1.99$, df=103, $p=0.048$). The data also indicate an increase of the DO scores among the ROF students, but because of the small group size ($N=19$), additional data will have to be collected to affirm this trend. For the current ROF data, (pre=96, post=101, diff=4.83; $t=1.975$, df=18, $p=0.06$).

PO scores are scaled similarly as DO. Pre-program group means vary between 122 and 124; the post-program means vary between 123 and 124. The program groups do not show any detectable mean differences either before ($F=1.81$, df=[2, 277], $p=0.17$) or after ($F=1.203$, df=[2, 277], $p=0.30$) program participation. Across all programs, the PO scores show an increase from 123 to 124 (diff=1.08, $t=3.599$, df=279, $p<0.001$). Within individual programs, NSLI-Y shows a significant increase from 122 to 123 (diff=1.049, $t=240$, df=131, $p=0.018$) and RLASP from 123 to 124 (diff=1.357, $t=2.939$, df=103, $p=0.004$).

OG is defined as the difference between PO and developmental scores. Means and standard deviations of these data are different from the DO and PO scores from which they are derived – the group-by-occasion means range between 26 and 29, while the associated standard deviations range between 8 and 10. Pre-program means range between 26 and 29 and there is no systematic difference between the groups (F=2.829, df=[2, 277], p=0.06). The largest OG pre-program mean (29) is found for the NSLI-Y group. Post-program OG means range between 26 and 29, and significant differences are apparent (F=4.002, df=[2, 277], p=0.019). The RLASP and Flagship groups have the smallest post-program means of 26, while the NSLI-Y program shows an overall post-program mean of 29. The ROF program, taken separately, shows a drop of 3.26, from 27 to 24. The significance of this difference is indicated by t=−2.166, df=18, p=0.04.

The IDI profile also includes sub-scores for specific measureable traits, two of which revealed significant results in the current study (Table 8.4).

Pre-program *cognitive frame shifting* (Cog) scores range from 3.6 to 3.8 but are not statistically different (F=2.593, df=[2, 277], p=0.08). The post-program Cog scores, however, do show some differences, with the YES score of 4.32, the NSLI-Y score (3.95) the highest and the RLASP scores the lowest (3.70) (F=5.379, df=[2, 277], p=0.005). Although this difference is in the decimal figures (0.37), it reflects one quarter of the within-group-by-occasion standard deviation. There is also a significant Cog score increase across all data (diff=0.17, t=4.293, df=279, p=0.000). This increase can be detected in both the NSLI-Y (diff=0.20, t=3.502, df=131, p<0.001) and RLASP (diff=0.13, t=2.014, df=103, p=0.047) programs, but currently not with Flagship.

Table 8.4 Paired sample *t*-tests for YES program (*N*=24)

Variable	Mean pre	SD pre	Mean post	SD post	Mean difference	t	p
Cognitive frame shifting (Cog)	3.72	0.68	4.32	0.56	0.60	3.928	0.001
Behavioral code shifting (Beh)	3.96	0.61	4.44	0.65	0.48	3.361	0.003

Pre-program group mean scores of *behavioral code shifting* (Beh) show systematic differences (F=13.28, df=[2, 277], p<0.001). RLASP shows the smallest pre-program mean (3.57), Flagship the largest mean (4.02) and the means of YES and NSLI-Y fall in between (3.96 and 3.95, respectively). The post-program group means also differ significantly (F=9.861, df=[2, 277], p<0.001). RLASP again has the smallest mean (3.77), YES and NSLI-Y show the largest post-program mean (4.44 and 4.11, respectively) and the Flagship programs fall in between (3.97).

Beh scores increase significantly across all programs (diff=0.15, t=4.710, df=279, p=0.000). The increase is detectable for YES and NSLI-Y students (diff=0.19, t=4.149, df=131, p=0.000) and RLASP students (diff=0.20, t=3.711, df=103, p<0.001) but not among the Flagship students (Table 8.5).

Table 8.5 Paired sample *t*-tests for NSLI-Y program (*N*=131)

Variable	Mean pre	SD pre	Mean post	SD post	Mean difference	t	p
Acceptance	3.839	(0.717)	4.218	0.654	0.379	4.688	0.000
Adaptation	3.836	(0.530)	4.056	0.540	0.220	3.257	0.002
Cognitive frame shifting	3.701	(0.703)	3.947	0.645	0.246	2.658	0.010
Behavioral code shifting	3.945	(0.546)	4.142	0.551	0.197	2.899	0.005

Modeling the interrelationship of OPI and IDI

The trellis plots in Figures 8.5 through 8.7 represent regressions performed on NSLI-Y, RLASP and Flagship pre- and post-program values plotted against OPI or IDI by program type. (The YES program is not included in this portion of the analysis.) Figure 8.5 models the relative power of pre-program OPI ratings to predict post-program developmental orientation score. Numbers corresponding to proficiency levels (0 to 10, where 10=Superior) form the horizontal axis, while the vertical axis reflects the post-DO IDI score range. The NSLI-Y OPI values are centered primarily in the two left quadrants of the box graph, representing pre-program proficiency levels in the 0 to ACTFL Intermediate range, while the undergraduate RLASP scores are distributed along both sides of the central axis, representing pre-program OPIs in the ACTFL Intermediate range, annotated here as 3–7 on the horizontal axis. The Flagship box with scores concentrated in the two right-hand quadrants represents pre-program proficiencies in the ACTFL Advanced range (6–10). As is readily evident

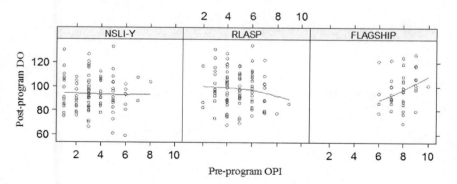

Figure 8.5 Post-program developmental orientation versus pre-program oral proficiency

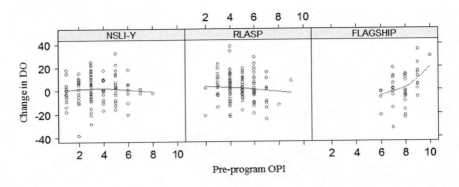

Figure 8.6 Change in developmental orientation versus pre-program oral proficiency

from the slopes of the three regression plots, NSLI-Y and RLASP pre-program OPI scores do not correlate with DO growth, whereas Flagship pre-program OPI scores are correlated with DO gain.

An IDI-DO 'change' variable was then created to assist in further analyzing developmental trends in IDI performances across programs. The vertical axis in Figure 8.6 represents change (either positive or negative), while the horizontal axis marks pre-program OPI, as in Figure 8.5. The positive relationship between OPI and DO gain is evident in the upper right-hand quadrant of the Flagship panel in Figure 8.6.

Figure 8.7 compares pre-program DO with post-program OPI outcomes for the 280 language-immersion participants at each of the three levels of study represented by NSLI-Y, RLASP and Flagship. As is evident from all three panels, no relationship between pre-DO and post-program OPI was detectable. A further negative finding was produced when pre-DO and a post-program OPI gain variable was tested. The finding proposed recently by Baker-Smemoe *et al.* (2014) could, therefore, not be replicated in the present study.

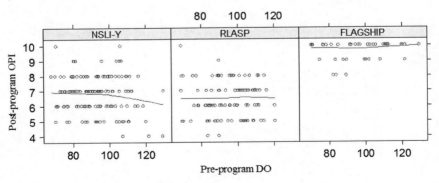

Figure 8.7 Post-program oral proficiency versus pre-program developmental orientation

Discussion

The powerful impact of structured immersion training on L2 gain has been reported in earlier studies (Davidson, 2015; Davidson & Lekic, 2012). These data and the accompanying analyses of OPI gain across levels of study and different languages are entirely new and reported here for the first time. They are consistent with earlier reports on these federal programs.

In addition to providing a comparative analysis of L2 gains in early, middle and upper ranges of proficiency of several critical languages, the present analysis also focused on the relationship between L2 gain at each level and the development of intercultural competencies within an overseas structured immersion context. In order to do this, it has made use of two widely recognized assessment tools, the ACTFL OPI and the IDI, and collected pre- and post-program data ($N=305$) using both instruments for groups of learners of different languages from a broad range of US institutions, who are at the early, middle or later stages of formal study of the language while engaged in year-long or semester-long structured L2 immersion programs overseas. In addition, we have reported on a further cohort of US SA students (students on the YES program), whose overseas study time was not focused on the formal study of language. The overall developmental orientation levels presented here, as reflected by IDI scores along the continuum, fall generally within the Minimization orientation (Appendix 8.1). As noted, mean IDI scores showed a positive change, from 92.11 to 103.05 across all cohorts, which indicates growth both within a single (Minimization) range, or, in some cases, post-program placement at the Acceptance orientation. The negative change in the OG (from 29.58 to 23.75) indicates a clear movement toward narrowing the gap between participants' perceived sense of intercultural sensitivity and their overall sensitivity as measured by the IDI. The heightened and more accurate level of intercultural self-awareness reported here is reminiscent of the increasingly accurate levels of oral proficiency self-assessment that has been observed among L2 speakers at or near ILR 3 and above (Freed *et al.*, 2004).

These results point to a significant change for all participants in the levels of Acceptance and Adaptation measured by the IDI. As noted, results of the sample *t*-test indicate a statistically significant change in the direction of growth for the IDI subscales of Acceptance and Adaptation, within the clusters of Cog and Beh. Moreover, mean scores on the Acceptance sub-score orientation among NSLI-Y participants changed from a pre-test score of 3.84 to a post-test score of 4.22 ($p \leq 0.05$). Within the Acceptance orientation, individuals recognize and appreciate not only similarities but, more critically, differences within cultures.

Overall, participants demonstrate increased cultural sensitivity and competence at the end of their SA program. All four programs facilitate and guide cultural learning through pedagogies and support structures that provide teacher and peer mentoring, monitored homestays, direct instruction and regular periods of self-reflection and self-assessment, interventions that are now widely recognized as best practices within the SA community. For example, students in one of the cohorts were asked to evaluate their own efforts to engage with the local population and context (on a scale of 1 to 10 where 10 was the highest rating) toward the end of their sojourn. Participants who had experienced notable growth in IC, as evidenced by the IDI scores, rated their own efforts to engage with the local context and population between 4 and 10, for an average of 6.6, while those showing more modest changes or negative growth rated these outreach efforts at 5.5 (ranging from 4 to 7). Two thirds of the participants who experienced positive gains on the IDI developmental orientation scores participated in extra-curricular activities offered at their host university. These activities were voluntary and distinct from the co-curricular program activities that are required for all participants and form an integral part of their capstone year. Participants chose to engage in a number of different activities such as discussion clubs, film club, English clubs with local students, music/singing, folk music instrument lessons and athletic events. Participants who developed close ties to host families and expanded their social network through attending events and activities gained more access to their host communities as well as more frequent exposure to local culture. Participants experiencing gains in IC reported significant contact with local individuals built through their networks of host families, other students at their host university and by introducing each other to those social group or groups that they were each able to join. These interactions occurred on a weekly basis, often taking place at least three times per week.

Conclusions

Several findings have emerged from this investigation, which are likely to be of interest to the field, as reflected in the research questions posed above.

(1) *How does OPI change differ across the immersion programs focused on early, mid and advanced levels of training and what, if any, relationships obtain between different levels of language proficiency and measured levels of intercultural development, as reflected by IDI?*

The present analysis has demonstrated that fixed-effect interactions between growth (f1) and program type are significant. While OPI change differences exist across the three programs, the average OPI change is approximately the same across all three programs. Language Flagship students attain growth comparable to that of lower- and middle-range-proficiency learners, but they produce these gains in the upper ranges of functional proficiency (ILR 3). The NSLI-Y group starts with the lowest performance (of 7.80−4.46=3.34) and demonstrates the largest improvement (of 1.83+1.63=3.46). These interaction effects are several times larger than their standard errors and thus highly significant.

This study found no statistically significant relationship between IDI scores and OPI ratings for students at the ACTFL Novice, Intermediate and Advanced levels, but did observe a correlation between Superior-level OPI and higher IDI scores, limited somewhat by a small sample size at that level (N=40). It was also observed that mean post-program IDI scores throughout tended to be higher for those groups who began their overseas study with higher levels of speaking proficiency.

Evidence is presented here that early- and middle-stage students of language in the immersion context demonstrate significant competencies in their abilities to shift cognitive frames and to switch behavioral codes in response to local cultural contexts. If replicated elsewhere, this finding may provide a major rationale for early-stage immersion, as the finding held for both the language-specific groups (NSLI-Y and RLASP) and the non-language-oriented group (YES).

The OG, defined as the numerical difference between one's self-perception of intercultural development and actual measured developmental orientation, was observed to narrow as a result of immersion study at any level, with the narrowest gap between perception and actual level associated with those participants commanding the highest levels of language proficiency.

(2) *To what extent do pre-program IDI scores predict ultimate L2 attainment of SA participants?*

Pre-program IDI was *not* found to be a predictor of L2 proficiency gain at ACTFL Novice to Intermediate, Intermediate to Advanced or Advanced to Superior. While there is no doubt that the combination of attitudes and attributes measured by IDI are relevant for intercultural adjustment and adaptation in the overseas study context, the present analysis found no positive correlation of pre-program IDI scores and post-program OPI outcomes for any of the three levels or languages under study.

(3) *What is the effect of lower, mid-range and advanced L2 proficiency on change in IDI during SA?*

The study presents abundant data to support the position that overseas immersion with or without language study, but undertaken within a properly structured curriculum, contributes to intercultural development. It also provides evidence supporting the power of more advanced levels of language study to maintain and continue developmental growth over the period of a longer learning career, regardless of the learner's initial IDI level. While Cog and Beh are associated with higher developmental orientations, early-stage immersion has, nonetheless, been shown to produce significant growth in these areas for learners who have not yet attained the Acceptance or Adaptation orientations.

The data presented here strongly suggest that students at middle and higher levels of cultural learning and language competence become increasingly aware of their own behavior and communication in cross-cultural settings as they experience daily life and manage their interactions with local communities through program activities and guided reflection. Finally, the issues raised here also point to the need for further research on the optimization of the L2 speaker's intercultural self-awareness in connection with the strengthening of the critical comprehension, flexibility of mind and interactional skills on which all interculturality is based. Intercultural competency at the professional level is the centerpiece of the transversal skills so valued in today's globalized workforce and the *sine qua non* for a generation prepared to live responsibly in today's rapidly changing and highly interconnected world.

Notes

(1) The Assessment of Regional Knowledge (ARK) and the General Regional Aptitude Network Test (GRANT) test instruments currently under development at the US Military Academy, as referenced in Watson *et al.* (2013).

(2) The authors are pleased to acknowledge support in the modeling and review of these analyses by Dr Werner Wothke and Saodat Bazarova, American Councils Assessment Department.

(3) >Model_Growth_times_Program_Interactions <- lmer(opi ~ 1 + (1 | id) + wave.f*prog.f)

```
> display(Model_Growth_times_Program_Interactions)
lmer(formula = opi ~ 1 + (1 | id) + wave.f * prog.f)
coef.est coef.se
(Intercept) 7.80 0.21
wave.f1 1.83 0.20
prog.f2 -4.46 0.24
prog.f3 -2.91 0.24
wave.f1:prog.f2 1.63 0.23
wave.f1:prog.f3 -0.19 0.23

Error terms:
 Groups Name Std.Dev.
 id (Intercept) 0.95
 Residual 0.89
 ---
number of obs: 514, groups: id, 275
AIC = 1672.8, DIC = 1630.9
deviance = 1643.9
```

Legend:

Wave.f0:	Pre-program	assessment
Wave.f1:	Post-program	assessment
Prog.F1:		Flagship
Prog.F2:		NSLI-Y
Prog.F3: RLASP		

References

Anderson, P.H., Lawton, L., Rexeisen, R.J. and Hubbard, A.C. (2006) Short-term study abroad and intercultural sensitivity: A pilot study. *International Journal of Intercultural Relations* 30, 457–469.

Anderson, P.H. and Lawton, L. (2011) Intercultural development: Study abroad vs. on-campus study. *Frontiers: The Interdisciplinary Journal of Study Abroad* 21, 86–108.

Baker-Smemoe, D., Dewey, D.P., Brown, J. and Martinsen, R.A. (2014) Variables affecting L2 gains during study abroad. *Foreign Language Annals* 47 (3), 464–486.

Bennett, M.J. (1986) A developmental approach to training for intercultural sensitivity. *International Journal of Intercultural Relations* 10 (2), 179–196.

Bennett, M.J. (1993) Towards ethnorelativism: A developmental model of intercultural sensitivity. In R.M. Paige (ed.) *Education for the Intercultural Experience* (pp. 21–71). Yarmouth, ME: Intercultural Press.

Bennett, M.J. (2004) Becoming interculturally competent. In J. Wurzel (ed.) *Toward Multiculturalism: A Reader in Multicultural Education* (2nd edn, pp. 62–77). Newton, MA: Intercultural Resource Corporation.

Davidson, D.E. (2015) The development of L2 proficiency and literacy within the context of the federally supported overseas language training programs for Americans. In T. Brown and J. Bown (eds) *To Advanced Proficiency and Beyond: Theory and Methods for Developing Superior Second-Language Ability* (pp. 117–150). Washington, DC: Georgetown University Press.

Davidson, D.E. and Lekic, M. (2012) The heritage and non-heritage learner in the overseas immersion context: Comparing learning outcomes and target-language utilization in the Russian flagship. *Russian Language Journal* 62, 47–77.

Deardorff, D.K. (2004) The identification and assessment of intercultural competence as a student outcome of international education at institutions of higher education in the United States (Unpublished doctoral dissertation). North Carolina State University.

Deardorff, D.K. (2006) Identification and assessment of intercultural competence as a student outcome of internationalization. *Journal of Studies in International Education* 10 (3), 241–266.

Engle, L. and Engle, J. (2004) Assessing language acquisition and intercultural sensitivity development in relation to study abroad program design. *Frontiers: The Interdisciplinary Journal of Study Abroad* 10, 219–236

Freed, B.F., Segalowitz, N. and Dewey, D.P. (2004) Context of learning and second language fluency in French: Comparing regular classroom, study abroad, and intensive domestic immersion programs. *Studies in Second Language Acquisition* 26 (2), 275–301.

Hammer, M.R. (2007) *Saving Lives: The S.A.F.E. Model for Negotiating Hostage and Crisis Incidents*. Westport, CT: Praeger International Security.

Hammer, M.R. (2012) The intercultural development inventory: A new frontier in assessment and development of intercultural competence. In M. Vande Berg, R.M. Paige and K.H. Lou (eds) *Student Learning Abroad* (pp. 115–136). Sterling, VA: Stylus Publishing.

Hammer, M.R. (2015) *A Resource Guide for Effectively Using the Intercultural Development Inventory (IDI)*. Berlin, MD: IDI, LLC.

Hammer, M.R., and Bennett, M.J. (1998) *The Intercultural Development Inventory (IDI) Manual*. Portland, OR: Intercultural Communication Institute.

Hammer, M.R. and Bennett, M.J. (2002) *The Intercultural Development Inventory Manual*. Portland, OR: Intercultural Communication Institute.

King, P.M. and Baxter Magolda, M. (2005) A developmental model of intercultural maturity. *Journal of College Student Development* 46, 571–592.

Medina-Lopez-Portillo, A. (2004) Intercultural learning assessment: The link between program duration and the development of intercultural sensitivity. *Frontiers: The Interdisciplinary Journal of Study Abroad* 10, 179–200.

Paige, R.M., Cohen, A.D. and Shively, R.L. (2004) Assessing the impact of a strategies-based curriculum on language and culture learning abroad. *Frontiers: The Interdisciplinary Journal of Study Abroad* 10, 253–276.

Patterson, P.K. (2006) Effect of study abroad on intercultural sensitivity (Unpublished doctoral dissertation). University of Missouri-Columbia.

Pedersen, P.J. (2010) Assessing intercultural effectiveness outcomes in a year-long study abroad program. *International Journal of Intercultural Relations* 34 (1), 70–80.

Rexeisen, R.J., Anderson, P., Lawton, L. and Hubbard, A. (2008) Study abroad and intercultural development: A longitudinal study. *Frontiers: The Interdisciplinary Journal of Study Abroad* 17, 1–20.

Salisbury, M.H. (2011) The effect of study abroad on intercultural competence among undergraduate college students (Unpublished doctoral dissertation). University of Iowa.

Vande Berg, M. (2009) Intervening in student learning abroad: A research-based inquiry. *Intercultural Education* 20 (1–2), 15–28.

Vande Berg, M., Balkcum, A., Scheid, M. and Whalen, B. (2004) A report at the half-way mark: The Georgetown University consortium project. *Frontiers: The Interdisciplinary Journal of Study Abroad* 10, 101–116.

Vande Berg, M., Connor-Linton, U.J. and Paige, M.R. (2009) The Georgetown consortium project: Interventions for student learning abroad. *Frontiers: The Interdisciplinary Journal of Study Abroad* 18, 1–75.

Watson, J.R., Siska, P. and Wolfel, R.L. (2013) Assessing gains in language proficiency, cross-cultural competence, and regional awareness during study abroad: A preliminary study. *Foreign Language Annals* 46 (1), 62–79.

Appendix 8.1: The Intercultural Development Continuum

This discussion of the IDI is adapted from Hammer (2015).

Denial: A Denial mindset reflects a more limited capability for understanding and appropriately responding to cultural differences in values, beliefs, perceptions, emotional responses and behaviors. Denial consists of a disinterest in other cultures and a more active avoidance of cultural difference. Individuals with a Denial orientation often do not see differences in perceptions and behavior as 'cultural'. A Denial orientation is characteristic of individuals who have limited experience with other cultural groups and therefore tend to operate with broad stereotypes and generalizations about the cultural 'other'. Those at Denial may also maintain a distance from other cultural groups and express little interest in learning about the cultural values and practices of diverse communities. This orientation tends to be associated more with members of a dominant culture as well as members of non-dominant groups who are relatively isolated from mainstream society, because both may have more opportunity to remain relatively isolated from cultural diversity. By contrast, members of non-dominant groups who are more actively engaged within the larger, mainstream society are less likely to maintain a Denial orientation, because they need to engage with cultural differences more often.

Polarization: Polarization is an evaluative mindset that views cultural differences from an 'us versus them' perspective. Polarization can take the form of defense ('My cultural practices are superior to other cultural practices') or reversal ('Other cultures are better than mine'). Within defense, cultural differences are often seen as divisive and threatening to one's own 'way of doing things'. Reversal is a mindset that values and may idealize other cultural practices while denigrating one's own culture group. Reversal may also support the 'cause' of an oppressed group, but this is done with little knowledge of what the 'cause' means to people from the oppressed community.

Minimization: Minimization is a transitional mindset between the more monocultural orientations of Denial and Polarization and the more intercultural/global worldviews of Acceptance and Adaptation. Minimization highlights commonalities in both human similarity (basic needs) and universalism (universal values and principles) that can mask a deeper understanding of cultural differences. Minimization can take one of two forms: (a) the highlighting of commonalities due to limited cultural self-understanding, which is more commonly experienced by dominant group members within a cultural community; or (b) the highlighting of commonalities as a strategy for navigating the values and practices largely determined by the dominant culture group, which is more often experienced by non-dominant group members within a larger cultural community. This latter strategy can have survival value for non-dominant culture members and often takes the form of 'go along to get along'.

Acceptance: Acceptance and Adaptation are intercultural/global mindsets. With an Acceptance orientation, individuals recognize and appreciate patterns of cultural difference and commonality in their own and other cultures. An Acceptance orientation is curious to learn how a cultural pattern of behavior makes sense within different cultural communities. This involves contrastive self-reflection between one's own culturally learned perceptions and behaviors and perceptions and practices of different cultural groups. While curious, individuals with an Acceptance mindset are not fully able to appropriately adapt to cultural difference. Someone with an Acceptance orientation may be challenged as well to make ethical or moral decisions across cultural groups. While a person within Acceptance embraces a deeper understanding of cultural differences, this can lead to the individual struggling with reconciling behavior in another cultural group that the person considers unethical or immoral from his or her own cultural viewpoint.

Adaptation: An Adaptation orientation consists of both Cog (shifting one's cultural perspective) and Beh (changing behavior in authentic and culturally appropriate ways). Adaptation enables deep cultural bridging across diverse communities using an increased repertoire of cultural frameworks and practices in navigating cultural commonalities and differences. An Adaptation mindset sees adaptation in performance (behavior). While people with an Adaptation mindset typically focus on learning adaptive strategies, problems can arise when people with Adaptation mindsets express little tolerance toward people who engage diversity from other developmental orientations. This can result in people with Adaptive capabilities being marginalized in their workplace.

9 Overseas Internships in Advanced to Professional-Level Language Acquisition

Samuel Eisen

Introduction

At the higher levels of foreign language proficiency (Interagency Language Roundtable [ILR] 2 and above [Appendix A]), a carefully designed professional internship provides a venue for language acquisition, cultural study and professional development to merge in a mutually reinforcing relationship. Through its overseas internships for US undergraduate students who have qualified for the overseas study year at ILR 2, the Language Flagship Program provides a laboratory for the integration of language and culture with professional development at the highest levels for US undergraduate students.

This chapter examines how overseas professional internships in the target language are associated with the interventions needed to achieve the highest results in foreign or second language acquisition (SLA). The chapter begins with a discussion of the dynamics of linking proficiency standards in higher education to professional goals, followed by an overview of SLA research on professional internships abroad. It then examines the structure and development of the model of the Language Flagship overseas internship, providing examples from Flagship programs in several languages. The chapter concludes with an analysis of elements of Flagship students' self-reflections on their overseas internship experiences that illustrate the interconnections between language acquisition at the highest levels, increasing cultural competence and professional growth.

Proficiency, Assessment and Professional Goals

The professional focus of the Language Flagship Program bridges the traditional gap between professional studies and foreign language, literature and culture education. Humanities and liberal arts educators have long viewed the encroachment of professional programs into the undergraduate curriculum as a dilution of the purity of the educational mission. The debate between the humanities and professional education advocates has been ongoing for hundreds of years (Harpham, 2011; Small, 2013). To take the British example, Small (2013: 61) observes that, 'The belief that the humanities, almost by definition, must be at odds with economic instrumentalism has been a potent strand in English thinking about the university, and about culture more broadly, running through Newman, Mill and Arnold'. In particular, with respect to foreign languages, professional programs and applied sciences have tended to increase expectations for coursework in technical fields at the expense of foreign language study on the assumption that English is now the global language (Berka & Grandin, 2014). Advanced foreign language education in the United States has been the exception rather than the rule, even for students specializing in fields such as international business, public administration and other disciplines with major international components.

There are, however, countervailing developments in higher education that demonstrate the effectiveness of combining science, technology, engineering and math (STEM) and professional studies with foreign language and culture study. The International Engineering Program (IEP) at the University of Rhode Island and the Humanities+ / +Humanities program at Brigham Young University (BYU) represent two innovative attempts to bridge the traditional gap between foreign language and cultural studies and professional preparation (Berka & Grandin, 2014; Brown, 2014). The IEP in particular has fostered unusually strong growth in the number of German and other foreign language majors by linking foreign language to professional goals and overseas internship opportunities. The number of German majors from an initially endangered department rose to 180, amid 600 foreign language majors overall at the University of Rhode Island (Berka & Grandin, 2014). The Language Flagship provides a similar stimulus for students with a social science, science or professional major to combine that by double (or triple) majoring in humanities fields (Eisen, 2014).

By integrating high assessment standards and an explicit professional dimension in foreign language and culture education, the Flagship addresses the national imperative in higher education to improve the language learning outcomes of US undergraduates and to expand the national capacity in languages other than English among students across disciplines. These elements were combined by design in the legislative authorization of the Flagship. The David L. Boren National Security Education Act of 1991 was unique in creating a partnership between government and higher education that explicitly links the mission to improve foreign language, area studies and international education with the mission to provide a pool of applicants for service in the federal government in national security fields. The legislation also mandates systematic assessment of language proficiency results (National Security Education Act 1991, as amended). The authorization of the Language Flagship Program in 2002 further specified that:

> Institutions of higher education shall establish, operate, or improve activities designed to train students in programs in a range of disciplines to achieve advanced levels of proficiency in those foreign languages that the Secretary identifies as being the most critical in the interests of the national security of the United States. (National Security Education Act, as amended)

Accordingly, the Flagship adopted ILR 2 in speaking and at least one other modality (i.e. listening, reading or writing) as a minimum qualification to participate in the capstone overseas programs required of students in all Flagship programs. The capstone combines academic and professional internship components with the goal of moving undergraduate students of all majors to the professional proficiency level (ILR 3) required for key diplomatic and analytical positions in US government service. The Flagship integrates assessment for the purposes of improving higher education and overseas immersion in a manner that advances the foreign language field and strengthens the international aspects of all fields while respecting the integrity of disciplines, both academic and professional. As Harpham (2011: 142) observed, 'If the liberal arts and professional education are to make common cause, both must be permitted to retain their integrity and their identity'.

The 2007 Modern Language Association (MLA) report (MLA Ad Hoc Committee on Foreign Languages) remains the major statement to date in the United States on strengthening the foreign language field. Significantly, the 2007 MLA report, while representing a major step forward in reaching out more broadly across higher education, also exemplifies the continuing difficulty in transforming and integrating foreign language study across US higher education. First, the MLA report resists defining specific assessment standards and stops short of suggesting incorporation of the American Council on the Teaching of Foreign Languages (ACTFL) guidelines for proficiency for the general student body. Moreover, the report defined dichotomies in the field, rather than proposing an integrated and fully collaborative model across fields:

> Freestanding language schools and some campus language-resource centers often embrace an instrumentalist focus to support the needs of the students they serve, whereas university and college foreign language departments tend to emphasize the constitutive aspect of language and its relation to cultural and literary traditions, cognitive structures, and historical knowledge. (MLA, 2007: 2)

The report implies that foreign language study for professional purposes tends to strip out the cultural and literary components that constitute the core of the discipline in the eyes of many foreign language and literature faculty. At higher levels (ILR 3+ and 4), however, the split between the 'instrumentalist' and 'constitutive' elements referred to in the 2007 MLA report falls away: the ability to progress in a professional capacity merges with acquisition of higher-level cultural and linguistic knowledge and vice versa.

Studies on developing professional-level language proficiency show that 'language and job performance are often intertwined at the Superior level' (Leaver & Shekhtman, 2002: 14). Referencing studies conducted at the Defense Language Institute Foreign Language Center, Leaver and Campbell (2015: 6) note that interviews with professionals who had achieved ILR 4 levels in language revealed that the experience of going to school with native speakers or 'holding a job abroad in the same capacity as a native speaker' is one of the core characteristics of learners able to achieve near-native proficiency. Leaver and Shekhtman cite the example of the training of Azerbaijani naval officers in Russian with a heavy infusion of Russian literature and culture into the professional language training. Similarly, the Beyond 3 initiative at the Foreign Service Institute at the US Department of State combined cultural and professional elements to move Russian-speaking US diplomats from the ILR 3 toward the ILR 4 level in response to work demands at the US Embassy in Moscow and the need to open additional embassies in the former Soviet space in the early 1990s (Ehrman, 2002: 246). Activities to reach ILR 4 in Russian at the Foreign Service Institute included both internship-like experiences with Russian émigrés and intensive reading of Russian novels, as well as other elements of Russian culture (Ehrman, 2002). Jackson (2015) recounts the case of a diplomat in the Beyond 3 Program at the Foreign Service Institute who studied jokes and political cartoons in order to better employ Thai humor in professional interactions with Thai audiences.

Resistance to assessment within academia is in part linked to the imposition of the terms of assessment from outside linked to political and economic objectives (Small, 2013). US university administrators are under increasing pressure to tie program assessment to specific results measures and professional outcomes. The proposed college ratings framework from the US Department of Education (2014) includes consideration of labor market success as a key component of future success measures in higher education. Considering proficiency-based outcomes for languages, the adoption of the standard of ACTFL Advanced Low for graduates of teacher education programs in Spanish, French and German by the National Council for Accreditation of Teacher Education (NCATE) provoked resistance and debate. Arguing against the NCATE position, Burke (2013: 531) voiced concern about 'a troubling era of accountability in U.S. education' and 'the ramifications certain top-down mandates will have on the language teaching profession in the future'. Despite admissions that the language teacher education system may be failing, the prospect of standards imposed from outside engenders resistance. Overall resistance to assessment and cross-disciplinary collaboration, still prominent in the US higher education community for language and literature studies, is counterproductive. In the long run, such resistance delays the development of a fully integrated model in which foreign language departments engaged in high-level cultural study will be considered an integral partner in global education across disciplines in the US university system.

SLA Research on Overseas Internships

Recently, Lafford (2013) set out an agenda for examining experiential language learning in domestic programs as well as in the study abroad/ work abroad setting. Lafford notes that, thus far, languages for special purposes (LSP) pedagogy and programs have concentrated on preparing students to use the language in US workplace settings (particularly Spanish for medical, legal or business purposes). However, Lafford indicates that no research has yet been done connecting internship programs to language learning outcomes. As Lafford (2013: 83) exclaims, 'This is the next frontier!' Although research on language acquisition in the study abroad context is fairly extensive, the literature specifically focused on language acquisition through internships is very limited. With few exceptions, the extant research 'displays many limitations in scope and design' (Kinginger, 2009: 213). Two recent studies at BYU have documented the impact of internship experiences at the Intermediate High to Advanced levels of proficiency. One study of BYU Russian language students ($N=61$) entering with Intermediate to Advanced proficiency documented sublevel and threshold gains into the Advanced and Superior levels by students who participated in a summer semester internship comprised of six hours per week of language courses and conducted in partnership with the Russian Presidential Academy of National Economy and Public Administration in Moscow (Brown, 2014). Brown notes that the BYU student participants had had 18 months' to two years' prior experience in Russia before entering BYU, indicating that the results may not be generalizable. Belnap and Abuamsha (2015) document that the introduction of a professional summer internship accompanied by two sessions per week of professional discussion and debate helped a group of five BYU students with no prior in-country experience with Arabic to progress to the Advanced-mid and Superior levels of language proficiency. Kinginger (2009: 5) mentions internships only in passing and does not analyze any major studies of language acquisition through experiential or service learning, although she does point out the many variables to consider in study abroad, including program elements in 'classrooms, homes, personal relationships, service learning or commercial interactions'.

Previous research has tended either to explore SLA in the academic study abroad context with little or no reference to experiential learning or professional internships or, conversely, to discuss work abroad experiences without examining language acquisition. Indeed, this is probably a fair reflection of the state of US study abroad and service or experiential learning: linguistic preparation has been minimal and study abroad programs have tended not to integrate all the elements needed to promote advanced language acquisition holistically. For example, a study of Dickinson College students participating in study abroad did not specify whether the overseas internships were conducted in English or the second language (L2) or whether the internships were in local or international organizations (Franklin, 2010).

In the study abroad literature, discussions of the benefits of service learning or work abroad experiences often portray competence in the foreign language as being a barrier or cause of frustration, rather than as an opportunity to deepen the students' cultural and professional experience (Hannigan, 2001; Tonkin & Quiroga, 2004). Neither Hannigan's study of work abroad and career development nor Tonkin and Quiroga's qualitative assessment of international service learning concluded that better language preparation would increase the value of the overseas experience; rather, Hannigan suggests that international educators should provide more extensive orientation to prepare students for the language-related barriers they may encounter, as well as other cultural differences they are likely to find abroad.

The Georgetown Consortium Project (Vande Berg et al., 2009), an ambitious and thorough study of the varied components related to language acquisition, stands out in its discussion of language learning and overseas internships. The project tracked gains in oral proficiency and intercultural development associated with overseas program variables such as duration, previous language study, academics, homestays, internships and mentoring. Although the study itself did not document gains associated with experiential learning, the authors concluded that to be effective in language acquisition and in developing intercultural understanding, internship elements would benefit from additional programmatic intervention from a cultural mentor to assist the student in processing the internship experience. The authors observe that just the experiential learning activity on its own, with no support interventions, may not greatly enhance student learning.

From a European Union (EU) perspective on residence abroad programs, one clear observation is that US students joining EU programs had lower target-language proficiency than the European students and had greater difficulty in communication (Coleman, 1998). Coleman (1998: 172) outlines the objectives of the Common European Framework with regard to language and culture, which includes the practical goal to 'improve working relations' among EU countries. The EU residence abroad programs are typically a full academic year in which students are placed alone or in small groups in a local institution, often after 8–10 years of prior classroom instruction in the local language (Coleman, 1998). Work placements constitute a significant portion of EU residence abroad programs: at the time, 21% of ERASMUS (European Community Action Scheme for the Mobility of University Students) exchange students included a work placement in the target country. Coleman expresses some skepticism that the studies of EU programs he reviews definitively tie language gains effectively to work abroad experiences; he cites as problematic student self-evaluation of proficiency gains, small sample sizes and selection bias. However, there are some indicative findings: Coleman (1998: 181) states that two thirds of European students surveyed found work placements 'more beneficial than study abroad'. He also cites evidence that students on work placements return 'more conscientious, venturesome and open-minded with an enhanced self-image' (Coleman, 1998: 184). Overall, the self-perception of students in work placements with regard to gains in speaking and listening in the target language were higher than those of students in academic study abroad programs.

A different strain of research conducted in the mid-1990s set the stage for the development of the Flagship overseas language immersion model. This research was complemented by the creation of the National Security Education Program (NSEP) as a significant source of study abroad funding that would increase the numbers of US students engaging in overseas immersion study outside of the traditional European locations (Freed, 1995). In this context, with federal legislation signaling a renewed interest in improving foreign language teaching and learning, the need to examine language learning in overseas immersion became a more pressing and practical concern.

This research included a focus on experiential learning as practiced in US government training programs. Specifically, research concerning the Peace Corps provided a study of language acquisition in a language training and work abroad immersion experience that also benefits from having Oral Proficiency Interview (OPI) proficiency data from the Foreign Service Institute at the US Department of State (Guntermann, 1995). While the Peace Corps goals and experience are very different from those of typical study abroad for undergraduates, Guntermann explicitly states that lessons drawn from the Peace Corps may inform the design of study abroad programs that could benefit by integrating some of the practices. One best practice for domestic or overseas language immersion programs is to engage in 'an intensive, ongoing process of program assessment and adjustment', as the Peace Corps has done since the 1960s (Guntermann, 1995: 151). Among the adjustments made by the Peace Corps to improve training results were the following: increasing training programs from 8–10 weeks to 11–12 weeks, integrating advanced students into guided independent study at worksites, centralized curricular guidance on essential language skills and topics for work-related skills, introducing a variety of assessments including the ACTFL OPI and self-reflective learner activities through language notebooks. Moreover, a clear proficiency training goal of ILR 1+ was set for those beginning full-time work at their Peace Corps site. Additional language training opportunities were provided, ranging from one weekend to two weeks. The nine subjects in Guntermann's study, who were learning Spanish in Central America, were, with one exception, at ILR 1+ in speaking after their initial training. All participants progressed to ACTFL Advanced (seven participants) or Superior (two participants), or the ILR 2–3 range. Guntermann concludes from these results that the integration of a homestay experience with formal instruction lay the groundwork for supporting language gains through the work abroad experience. Many of the Peace Corps practices that were laid out by Guntermann were subsequently integrated into the Flagship overseas model:

- Continual assessment of results and improvement of practices.
- Proficiency assessment and minimum proficiency entrance goals.
- Integration of formal instruction, homestay and work tasks.
- Use of authentic materials to increase skills in all four modalities.
- Self-reflective practices to improve and measure learner progress.

Brecht *et al.* (1995) proposed the research agenda that would be the springboard for the model of overseas Flagship programs. While incorporating knowledge gained from established elements of the Peace Corps and Foreign Service Institute training, this research agenda focused on the adaptation of these professional models in a higher education setting that articulates domestic classroom preparation with continuing overseas interventions designed to maximize language gains in study abroad. In a large-scale study, Brecht *et al.* (1995) showed proficiency and other language gain results across modalities (speaking, reading and listening). More broadly, they posed the questions which would inform further research on overseas language acquisition, setting the stage for comprehensive examination of the gains in proficiency across the four modalities, the effectiveness of interventions in overseas immersion, the minimal duration for gains and the background preparation needed for significant language gain at higher proficiency levels. The development of the Language Utilization Report (LUR; Davidson & Lekic, 2010) facilitated this extensive research.

The LUR is an online system for overseas immersion student reporting and self-reflection, in which students report weekly on how they use their time in academic and free-time activities. Thus, the LUR tracks the overall immersion experience, providing both quantitative data on the time spent on various activities and qualitative student self-reflection, primarily in English, on progress and challenges in language acquisition and cultural adaptation. Davidson and Lekic (2010, 2012) presented results from studies of Russian Flagship students at ILR 2 to ILR 3 who were enrolled in the Russian Flagship overseas capstone program. Their findings include descriptions of which specific overseas activities (such as participation in homestay family activities, homework, reading for pleasure, watching media and time with friends) promoted language gains most effectively in the ILR 2–4 ranges, as well as differences between heritage and non-heritage learners. Davidson and Lekic (2012: 73) found that well-prepared heritage learners rated the internship component of their study abroad program of 'great value' in their 'linguistic and intellectual growth'. These studies provide a promising start to further research that attempts to understand the specific impacts of the internship component as one aspect of an overseas program of study for students with high levels of proficiency in the language.

In order to pursue the research agenda that Lafford (2013) lays out for experiential language learning overseas, we will examine the experience of Flagship students as they progress to professional levels of proficiency. Lafford (2013: 80) notes the importance of 'active and reflective' learning as a basis for experiential learning. The categories she outlines as specific to the English language learner experience in terms of the characteristics of setting, participants and interactions largely correspond to the key experiences that Flagship students reflect on in their LURs with respect to their internship experiences (NSEP, 2014). In particular, Lafford suggests frameworks for examining:

- Formal and informal registers at the workplace.
- Potential for extended discourse (presentations).
- Power relations in the workplace and appropriate discourse based on hierarchy.
- Mix of languages in the workplace (use of target language, English, and other local or international languages commonly used in the field). (Lafford, 2013: 84–88)

Lafford advocates developing assessment instruments and specific studies of all aspects of these interactions, from discourse analysis to learner outcomes and assessment to pedagogy and social aspects. Lafford has laid out an ambitious agenda to which the data and reflections now being generated within the Flagship can make a significant contribution.

The Language Flagship Overseas Internship Model

There are currently 10 overseas Flagship centers that include internship experiences conducted in 10 overseas centers in 8 countries. The internship experience is an integrated component of overseas programs across a wide range of languages (Arabic, Chinese, Hindi-Urdu, Korean, Persian, Portuguese, Russian, Swahili and Turkish) where students are consistently reaching ILR 3 level and above across modalities (particularly in Russian where heritage students have registered ILR 4 and 4+ scores) (Davidson, 2015; NSEP, 2014). Davidson and Lekic note that the internship is among the interventions associated with gains in professional proficiency (Davidson & Lekic, 2010). Internship programs in Arabic, Chinese, Russian, Turkish and Swahili are managed by the American Councils for International Education. Two overseas program models are administered in China: the model at Tianjin National University includes part-time internships in the target language intertwined with year-long language support and direct-enrollment classes at the university (a model similar to those for Arabic and Russian) and the Nanjing University model, administered jointly with BYU, that includes a dedicated semester for full-time internship opportunities in cities throughout China. The University of Hawai'i at Mānoa administers the Korean Flagship internships in partnership with the Korea University in Seoul. The University of Texas partners with the American Institute of Indian Studies (AIIS) in Lucknow and Jaipur, India, for its Hindi-Urdu program. The University of Georgia is starting a new overseas program in Brazil in São João del Rei. The expectation across all internships in overseas Flagship programs is immersion in the target language at a fully professional level. To meet this expectation, several programs have taken steps to address challenges in finding appropriate professional placements where English or French, rather than the target language, are the dominant language in some professional fields (e.g. in India, Tanzania and Morocco).

The development of the Flagship capstone overseas programs, and especially the design and administration of the internship components, evolved as the program grew and higher education partners entered the program with preexisting overseas programs, in particular the American Councils programs developed in Russia and the existing university-administered Chinese programs in Qingdao and Nanjing. Over time, through program monitoring by NSEP and peer reviewers and collaboration with Flagship project directors from the domestic institutions, the varied approaches are merging in many aspects, although different models and practices still exist among the 10 overseas study locations. All of the larger Flagship overseas internship programs offer a wide range of internship options across many sectors: business and finance, law, health, environment, sciences, non-governmental organizations, media, education, arts and culture and other areas. Internships may engage students in discourse with a wide range of language speakers such as educated professionals, agricultural workers, craftspeople, teachers in an environment with children, and immigrants who are non-native speakers of the target language. In some internships, Flagship students operate in a diglossic or triglossic environment, in which they have to negotiate knowing only one or two of the languages in use. In most cases, successful and engaging internships lead to exposure to unfamiliar (from their previous overseas study or classroom learning) modes of discourse and expand the student's linguistic and sociocultural knowledge.

Internships in the Russian Overseas Flagship Program

One prominent overseas program model that incorporates the professional internship experience was developed by the American Councils for International Education for the Overseas Russian Flagship Program (Davidson & Frank, 2012). The design of the overseas program explicitly draws on previous SLA research on overseas environments (Davidson, 2012; Freed, 1995; Kinginger, 2009) to promote language and culture learning. The main characteristics of the model, outlined by Davidson and Frank (2012: 10–13), include the following:

- Specialized curricular materials for intensive language acquisition to the ACTFL Superior/ILR 3–3+level.
- Professional development for overseas faculty.
- Direct enrollment in courses at the overseas partner university.
- Immersive living environments.
- Professional internships.
- Language partners and tutors.
- Student self-reflection in LURs.
- Systematic proficiency assessment.

The American Councils' model for overseas Flagship program design is distinctive in that the professional internships are with local organizations, in the target language and tightly integrated with the program of language instruction, university courses, homestays and cultural co-curricular programs. The internships are a substantial component of the program: students participate in internships 8–10 hours per week for at least one semester. Students fill out LURs that include extensive material on the internship experiences for self-reflection and review by the academic program manager. This model is currently in place in the overseas Arabic, Russian, Swahili and Turkish Flagship capstone programs and in the new Chinese Flagship Program at Tianjin Normal University in China.

Internships in the Chinese Overseas Flagship Program

The other major internship model in overseas Flagship programs, originally situated in Qingdao, China, was largely for graduate students, who were required to find their own independent overseas internships. This requirement was based on the hypothesis that full immersion and independent responsibility for all aspects of life in China would lead to the greatest linguistic, cultural and professional growth. A broad study of Chinese language immersion programs in China and Taiwan at the time found the Flagship program in Qingdao to be the model with the most extensive internship program (Kubler, 2004). Kubler, however, argued that immersion alone is insufficient for gains in language proficiency at higher proficiency levels, and that a combination of ongoing language training and immersion is necessary. In his conclusion on internship components, Kubler suggested that the programs would be improved with the opportunity for continued formal language instruction and language support during the internship period.

When the national Language Flagship Program moved to support only undergraduate programs (Nugent & Slater, this volume), responsibility for the capstone in China shifted to BYU, a US university with a Chinese Flagship Program and Nanjing University in China. Eventually, administration of the internship component of the program was shifted to the American Councils, in collaboration with those two universities. In the Chinese Overseas Flagship Program, the internship takes place in the second half of the academic year following a first semester of intensive Chinese language study and direct enrollment in courses in students' major fields at Nanjing University. The internships are with local organizations or with local branches of international organizations in a number of cities and locations throughout China. The students are responsible for obtaining their own internship placements with guidance from a resident adviser; they live for four to six months independently in cities throughout China near their internship site. The internship objectives include:

(1) The ability to apply professional Chinese language in a broad range of communicative functions and in a wide variety of work-related tasks.
(2) Demonstration of a firm grasp of Chinese social interactions, behavioral norms and perspectives, as well as an understanding of administrative, commercial and political processes in China.
(3) The ability to interact appropriately and function efficiently in a professional Chinese setting.
(4) Demonstrated professionalism and independence in a language immersion environment. (Chinese Flagship Internship Program, 2014b: 3)

One drawback to this approach to the internship was that some participants experienced attrition in their Chinese language proficiency during the internship period. This issue was addressed by the program in recent years, however, by the addition of language tutoring and support designed to assist students in continuing to make language proficiency gains during the internship period. This additional support included 12 mandatory one-on-one Skype sessions with Nanjing University teaching staff to reinforce language acquisition, as well as an optional online Chinese language support program to assist with ongoing or emerging language difficulties and to help students to prepare for proficiency testing (Chinese Overseas Flagship Internship Program, 2014b).

The Chinese Flagship Program at Arizona State University developed language support for students in the internship phase overseas in the early years, before the development of current overseas interventions outlined above (Spring, 2012). Spring (2012) notes the structure of the four- to six-month internship program that places students in an internship related to their specialization:

> The range of internships held by students in China is extensive. For example, a student of media worked at a television station; a student majoring in finance interned in a bank; pre-law students have worked at law firms; business and communications majors have worked at export companies that focus on international trade; other internships involved working at a Chinese medical university hospital, assisting in the production of a journal on architectural design, and being a member of a team that conceptualized and designed museum exhibitions on ethnic culture. (Spring, 2012: 151–152)

In part to compensate for some of the language support elements that had been missing in the early program design, Arizona State University introduced a three-credit online capstone course to supplement the internship semester (Spring, 2012). The areas covered by the Arizona State University capstone course largely correspond to the key areas for development outlined by Lafford (2013). Spring (2012) outlines course objectives to include:

- Reflection on cultural practices.
- Increased understanding of Chinese workplace relationships.
- Practice of information-gathering skills needed in the field of work.
- Continued language learning focusing on specialized vocabulary and presentation style.
- Extended professional and community networks beyond those at the internship site. (Spring, 2012: 152)

With these additional interventions, the independent internship experience provides students the chance to process linguistic, social and cultural information gained in the workplace both for language gains and professional growth.

Internships in the Korean Overseas Flagship Program

The Korean Flagship Program at the University of Hawai'i at Mānoa administers its own capstone in Seoul, Korea, in partnership with Korea University. The internship component is understood to be a part of a larger mission of the Korean Flagship Program to partner with the business sector and government:

> As the three diamonds in the Flagship logo symbolize, creating a solid partnership among education, government and business to advance language education in the United States is a foundational mission of the Language Flagship. The basic idea is that the government and business function as supporters of Flagship education and, at the same time, beneficiaries to receive well-trained global professionals with superior language proficiency. (Sohn, 2012: 16)

Sohn further notes that the Korean Flagship not only established partnerships with businesses and other organizations to provide internships to students, but also broadened its outreach mission by soliciting business and international partners to help in funding the program by providing student scholarships. Kong (2012) links the program design and the internship to an overall approach of task-based language instruction. In the Korea program, the students conduct their internship search remotely while participating in the domestic component in Hawai'i. Kong (2012) writes:

> Internships provide students real-life tasks while the other components of the program can provide pedagogic tasks. They learn how to build relationships with colleagues and how to function in a professional setting performing various target tasks. Through the internship experience as well as content/language study in Korea, students acquire deeper understanding of Korean society and culture and eventually become ready to be a Korea specialist. (Kong, 2012: 41)

Flagship Student Overseas Internship Experience: Reflections

Qualitative data from student self-reporting during the capstone, as provided in LURs, provide a growing body of documentation of the professional and linguistic benefits of the professional internship experience undertaken by students at the ILR 2 to ILR 3 or higher language proficiency levels. Student self-reporting through the LURs documents a range of training and experience that shows the specific linguistic benefits of the professional internship aligned to language acquisition needs at this level. As students progress from Advanced High through Superior and toward distinguished levels of proficiency, they move from compensatory strategies to cognitive and metacognitive strategies, and they decrease emphasis on developing informal linguistic competence and begin to concentrate on emotional, social and sociocultural and formal linguistic registers and discourse strategies (Leaver & Shekhtman, 2002). The types of gains reflected in student LURs are outlined in the 2014 National Security Education Program annual report. Concentration on formal linguistic registers is seen frequently in student reflection on general workplace culture and 'appropriate language register for different cultural situations within the workplace hierarchy (e.g. how to behave with a director, when to use informal language)' (NSEP, 2014: 39). Students present examples of the acquisition of professional discourse levels through descriptions of encounters with specialized vocabulary, and culturally specific professional phone and email etiquette. Students reflect on the acquisition of more specialized discourse and symbol sets in the target language through knowledge of foreign lab protocols and scientific symbols, website terms and web search strategy, abbreviations specific to their professional setting and higher-level issues in professional writing, vocabulary and punctuation. Social and emotional intelligence in professional settings are exemplified through reflections on managing conflict and negotiations and conveying constructive criticism in an acceptable manner within the culture (NSEP, 2014).

Student reflections publicly available through a variety of program newsletters mirror the types of statements and observations commonly made in the LUR reporting. Some of the most telling accounts are those in which students share mistakes or failures in the internship with prospective or future students on the capstone. The following account of a poor internship interview performance by a Flagship student on the capstone in China illustrates how the student perceived moving from using compensatory strategies for getting through an interview to a cognitive strategy involving both preparation and integration of personality in the target language and authentic situation:

For your interview, make sure you thoroughly research what the company is all about and any press they've had. A big mistake I made was writing a script and trying to follow it too closely. When I received a question I wasn't prepared for, I wasn't able to gracefully pick up the pieces and answer the question effectively. Research is important, but be yourself as well. Don't be intimidated and let your personality shine through in the interview. (Chinese Flagship Internship Program, 2014a: 6)

This student reflection explicitly demonstrates the move from a compensatory strategy (writing a script) to a cognitive strategy to overcome inhibition and center on personality rather than rehearsed speech.

Likewise, another Chinese Flagship intern, completing an assignment to write a restaurant review for a local magazine, reflected on his failure to be granted an interview by the restaurant manager. The manager responded to the interview request with suspicious questions about the magazine and its audience. The student reflects:

Fair questions indeed, but her tone was not one of curiosity, she was looking for a weakness. As she spoke, tensions rose, and my Chinese ability began to steadily decline. Our 'negotiation' went on for another 10 or 15 minutes, until, in a bit of a huff, I left, exasperated, frustrated, and with no return appointment set for an interview. I had failed... One of the things that frustrated me the most about the encounter above was that it exposed my weakness as a negotiator, a journalist, and a Chinese speaker in general...I wondered, though, if I had just spent more time learning about my company, if I could have more clearly explained what my plan was with the article, if I could have just controlled my emotions, if I would have dressed a little nicer. (Chinese Flagship Internship Program, 2014a: 9)

The student concludes that he needs to take more responsibility for his own learning at this stage. In this instance, we observe a strategic cognitive approach to taking responsibility for emotions and for improving professional interaction in the target language. Both of these examples demonstrate the progression to cognitive and emotional awareness needed to attain the Superior level of language proficiency.

Students in the Flagship who are majoring in biological and physical sciences have pointed out the value of formal linguistic development in pursuing research in their fields and in successfully completing their professional internships. One student in a Chinese biology laboratory reported:

My internship experience enhanced my professional Chinese skills in practical ways through discussing experimental procedures, analyzing results and planning future experiments. It required me to quickly master a wide range of scientific vocabulary to be able to communicate effectively. (The Language Flagship, 2013: 1)

A student who interned in a Russian biology lab noted the importance of the preparation he received on campus at the University of Wisconsin-Madison before entering the internship experience: 'Similar to what I am currently doing with researchers [during my lab internship in Russia], each week my tutor and I would read, critically analyze, and discuss a selected scientific article, noting the differences between Russian and English scientific writing styles' (The Language Flagship, 2014: 2). Elsewhere he describes his lab internship activities:

> I shadow colleagues when they carry out laboratory research, provide on-the-spot translation to Russian of results produced in English, and proofread scientific articles for publication in English....To expand my Russian scientific vocabulary, my colleagues and I discuss experiment design and technique as well as scientific articles written in Russian. (The Language Flagship, 2014: 4)

Likewise, LURs document gains in areas such as professional presentation skills; acquisition of specialized vocabulary in a variety of fields; editing, translating and writing skills; specific reading skills in the target language (proofreading marks, chemical formulas, abbreviations); correct punctuation and email correspondence in formal settings. These activities illustrate Leaver and Shekhtman's (2002: 29) contention that, 'In working with authentic materials and texts, Superior-level students have to understand genre. Government protocols, for example, are prepared differently from business contracts'.

Flagship students also report gains in their internship in dealing with increasingly sophisticated levels of discourse and unfamiliar discourse types. One Flagship student reported on her experiences with a filmmaker in Alexandria, Egypt, in which she did screenwriting and interviews with actors in Arabic: 'Film courses, internships with local organizations, and comprehensive conversation sessions with language mentors greatly improved my listening and speaking skills, specifically in understanding cultural references and colloquialisms' (The Language Flagship, 2013: 2). Many students comment on the need to shift registers depending on whether the manager is in the room, and the difficulty of negotiating the subtle and sometimes inconsistent use of informal and formal modes of address (NSEP, 2014).

Professional norms in the target culture are also a common topic of student self-reporting and reflection. Observations of differences in US and foreign work culture environments permeate student self-reporting. Differences in work culture, such as punctuality and time management, are often noted. One Flagship student interning in a Chinese industrial design firm was surprised on her first day by the company lunchtime routine:

While some people in my office took advantage of the lunchtime exercise classes, others choose to take a siesta. On my first day in the office I was pleasantly surprised when everybody started taking out reclining lawn chairs, fuzzy blankets and eye masks around 1:30 pm. It seems to be an unspoken rule that 12 pm to 2 pm is a time for eating, resting and enjoying each other's company. (Chinese Flagship Internship Program, 2013: 9)

The same student also noted more specific work differences in how Chinese architects design projects, and added that one of her challenges was accepting the criticism of her own designs. Similarly, Flagship students in various internships have noticed differences in workplace culture. A Flagship student pursuing a cultural internship with a Chinese symphony orchestra observed:

I was also able to experience the dynamics of professional life in a primarily government-funded ensemble. The opportunity to see the Chinese orchestra model in action and understand the attitudes of musicians born and raised in the Chinese educational system was truly invaluable. (Chinese Flagship Internship Program, 2013: 2)

The same student observes that 'my cultural understanding of and my ability to function socially with China both experienced substantial growth' through the internship experience (Chinese Flagship Internship Program, 2013: 2).

The internship offers the opportunity for students to negotiate complex interactions in institutions that may function very differently in the host culture than in the student's home culture. One example is from a Flagship student interning in a Chinese law firm that specializes in defending Chinese clients in courts abroad. The student describes the need to move on to the level of translation of cultural norms and practices: 'The difficulty of this area lies in translation, not the translation of language, but rather the translation of legal traditions, legal thinking and legal strategy' (Chinese Flagship Internship Program, 2013: 3).

Students also note the importance in the internship of accurate language and appropriate behavior in professional contexts, such as in conferences and on the phone. Students are also thrust into authentic, sometimes high-stakes, situations in which their language skills are stretched in difficult or specific tasks. Such tasks include managing conflict situations, negotiating, requesting resources or payment, conveying constructive criticism, expressing opinions in a culturally appropriate manner and participating in role-play exercises for professional training. Cultural norms in negotiation and conflict (tone of voice, level of assertiveness) may vary greatly across cultures. Students must negotiate such elements as the differences in the cultural semiotics of smiling. Students must also be cognizant of gender differences in addressing work colleagues. Developing the cultural competence to effectively negotiate each of these authentic situations plays an integral part in developing higher-level professional language proficiency across modalities.

The Flagship experience also helps students to be aware of the steps in developing professional language proficiency: the proficiency-based assessments and the process of self-reflection give Flagship students the framework to monitor linguistic strengths and weaknesses across all four modalities. This undergraduate science student interning in the Chinese biology lab was, in fact, able to articulate the gains from her internship in all four modalities:

> From a professional standpoint, I had ample opportunity to improve all four basic language skills. In terms of listening, I improved by participating in weekly lab meetings, wherein I listened to presentations given by lab members over the status of their current research projects; attending occasional lectures given by students and scientists from the Institute; working with my two mentors on experiments in the lab; and listening to casual conversations among my colleagues, from whom I picked up a good amount of slang terms. My speaking skills were improved by giving occasional presentations in lab meeting, ordering supplies and reagents over the phone, and communicating with colleagues and mentors on a day-to-day basis. I practiced reading by following protocols written in Chinese and translating a review article that the lab hopes to publish soon from Chinese to English. While writing opportunities were not quite as abundant, especially when compared to the amount of writing I did last semester, I still found ways to improve by keeping a lab notebook in Chinese and taking notes during lab meeting. (Chinese Flagship Internship Program, 2013: 4)

This student has developed a framework for linking the internship experience to specific areas of language proficiency, and also to linking her proficiency to areas of professional growth and appreciation of culture. She concludes that she has 'gained a deeper understanding of the Chinese culture and how science is conducted in China: this will be instrumental in helping me to achieve my goals of collaborating with Chinese scientists on future research endeavors' (Chinese Flagship Internship Program, 2013: 4).

Flagship students also frequently report on the development of social relationships and networking through the internship experience. A student interning with a small Chinese startup company developed a close working relationship with the chief executive officer (CEO) and was able to play a variety of roles in the company during her internship. She reported appreciation for the social relationships she developed at the company: 'I am also very grateful for my coworkers, who immediately treated me like family and assisted me whenever I needed help. They have become like a second family to me' (Chinese Flagship Internship Program, 2013: 8). Some students note the opportunity to gain historical perspective by learning from the life experience shared by senior colleagues (NSEP, 2014). Forming work relationships in overseas settings may push the boundaries of what is currently considered acceptable in most areas of US corporate culture. For example, alcohol consumption in overseas work cultures can be an issue: a student in the Korean Flagship Program discussed her anxiety over participation in a corporate dinner expected during an internship with a Korean company. Having survived the first dinner, the student reported on much closer relationships with work colleagues and her insight that the communication and relationships formed at these dinners may help Korean companies function more effectively (Korean Language Flagship Center, 2012).

As the practice of using the LURs is disseminated across all overseas capstone programs within the Flagship, a wealth of information and cross-linguistic and cross-cultural comparisons of language acquisition experiences and strategies will be available for more in-depth analysis. For now, we may conclude that although it is difficult to evaluate separately the impact of the professional overseas internship from other aspects of the overall program leading to unprecedented undergraduate language gains, the internships are providing authentic professional experiences in the language precisely in the areas shown to enhance language proficiency gain at the ILR 2+ through ILR 4 levels. This qualitative experience illustrates the benefits of professional activity in expanding cultural understanding through active participation in the workplace. By combining higher-level language and cultural learning with overseas professional experience, the Flagship is piloting an integrated approach to higher-level language study, culture and professional education across fields and disciplines, and in doing so is fulfilling the mandates of its authorizing legislation and the needs of the nation. The program graduates will bring valuable perspectives and cross-cultural communication skills into international relations through their future careers in the government, academic and private sectors.

Disclaimer: The views expressed in this chapter are solely the views of the author and do not necessarily reflect the views or policy of the Department of Defense.

References

American Council on the Teaching of Foreign Languages (ACTFL) (2012) Proficiency guidelines. See http://www.actfl.org/publications/guidelines-and-manuals/actfl-proficiency-guidelines-2012 (accessed 7 July 2015).
Belnap, R.K. and Abuamsha, K. (2015) Taking on the 'ceiling effect' in Arabic. In T. Brown and J. Brown (eds) *To Advanced Proficiency and Beyond: Theory and*

Methods for Developing Superior Second Language Ability (pp. 105–116). Washington, DC: Georgetown University Press.

Berka, S. and Grandin, J. (2014) The University of Rhode Island International Engineering Program: Merging technology with the humanities. *Russian Language Journal* 64, 24–51.

Brecht, R.D., Davidson, D.E. and Ginsberg, R.B. (1995) Predictors of foreign language gain during study abroad. In B.F. Freed (ed.) *Second Language Acquisition in a Study Abroad Context* (pp. 37–66). Amsterdam/Philadelphia, PA: John Benjamins. Originally appeared in *NFLC Occasional Papers*, June 1993, 1–30.

Brown, N.A. (2014) Unlocking professional opportunities through foreign language study. *Russian Language Journal* 64, 71–81.

Burke, B.M. (2013) Looking into a crystal ball: Is requiring high-stakes proficiency tests really going to improve world language education? *Modern Language Journal* 97 (2), 531–534.

Chinese Flagship Internship Program (2013) Chinese Flagship Internship Bulletin, Summer 2013. See http://flagship.americancouncils.org/chinese/sites/flagship.americancouncils.org.chinese/files/Summer%202013%20Newletter.pdf (accessed 3 October 2014).

Chinese Flagship Internship Program (2014a) *The Internship Bulletin, Summer/Fall 2014*. See http://flagship.americancouncils.org/chinese/?q=content/nanjing-internship-newsletter (accessed 12 June 2015).

Chinese Flagship Internship Program (2014b) Chinese overseas flagship internship manual. See http://flagship.americancouncils.org/chinese/sites/flagship.americancouncils.org.chinese/files/COF%20Internship%20Handbook.pdf (accessed 3 October 2014).

Coleman, J.A. (1998) Language learning and study abroad: The European perspective. *Frontiers* 4, 167–203.

David L. Boren National Security Education Act of 1991. P.L. 102–183. See http://www.intelligence.senate.gov/laws/david-l-boren-national-security-education-act-1991 (accessed 20 July 2015).

Davidson, D.E. (2012) Meeting the need for high-level language professionals: NSEP, the Language Flagship Model and lessons and challenges for language acquisition and assessment at the advanced and superior levels (ILR 2–3). Presentation at the Interagency Language Roundtable, February 10, 2012. Foreign Service Institute, Arlington, VA. See http://www.govtilr.org/Calendars/2011-12ILRCalendarPublic.htm

Davidson, D.E. (2015) The development of L2 proficiency and literacy within the context of the federally supported overseas language training programs for Americans. In T. Brown and J. Brown (eds) *To Advanced Proficiency and Beyond: Theory and Methods for Developing Superior Second Language Ability* (pp. 117–150). Washington, DC: Georgetown University Press.

Davidson, D.E. and Lekic, M.D. (2010) The overseas immersion setting as contextual variable in adult SLA: Learner behaviors with language gain to level-3 proficiency in Russian. *Russian Language Journal* 60, 53–76.

Davidson, D.E. and Frank, V. (2012) The overseas component of the Language Flagship: Addressing learner needs within an acquisition-rich environment. *Journal of Chinese Teaching and Research in the U.S.: Special Issue for The Language Flagship* 4, 8–15.

Davidson, D.E. and Lekic, M.D. (2012) Comparing heritage and non-heritage learning outcomes and target-language utilization in the overseas immersion context: A preliminary study of the Russian Flagship. *Russian Language Journal* 62, 47–78.

Ehrman, M. (2002) Understanding the learner at the Superior-Distinguished threshold. In B.L. Leaver and B. Shekhtman (eds) *Developing Professional-Level Language Proficiency* (pp. 245–259). Cambridge: Cambridge University Press.

Eisen, S. (2014) The Language Flagship Model and the humanities. *Russian Language Journal* 64, 5–23.

Franklin, K. (2010) Long-term career impact and professional applicability of the study abroad experience. *Frontiers* 19, 169–190.

Freed, B.F. (1995) Language learning and study abroad. In B.F. Freed (ed.) *Second Language Acquisition in a Study Abroad Context* (pp. 3–33). Amsterdam/Philadelphia, PA: John Benjamins.

Guntermann, G. (1995) The Peace Corps experience: Language learning and training in the field. In B.F. Freed (ed.) *Second Language Acquisition in a Study Abroad Context* (pp. 149–169). Amsterdam/Philadelphia, PA: John Benjamins.

Hannigan, T.P. (2001) The effect of work abroad experiences on career development for U.S. undergraduates. *Frontiers* 7, 1–23.

Harpham, G.G. (2011) *The Humanities and the Dream of America*. Chicago, IL: The University of Chicago Press.

Humanities +: Bridging the humanities and the world of work (2015) Brigham Young University. See http://humanitiesplus.byu.edu/ (accessed 7 July 2015).

Interagency Language Roundtable (ILR) (2014) ILR Skill Level Descriptions. See www.govtilr.org (accessed 7 July 2015).

International Engineering Program (2015) The University of Rhode Island. See http://web.uri.edu/iep/ (accessed 7 July 2015).

Jackson, F.H. (2015) Expanded understandings and programmatic approaches for achieving advanced language ability. In T. Brown and J. Brown (eds) *To Advanced Proficiency and Beyond: Theory and Methods for Developing Superior Second Language Ability* (pp. 185–204). Washington, DC: Georgetown University Press.

Kinginger, C. (2009) *Language Learning and Study Abroad: A Critical Reading of Research*. Houndmills: Palgrave Macmillan.

Kong, D.K. (2012) Task-based language teaching in an advanced Korean language learning program. *The Korean Language in America: Journal of the American Association of Teachers of Korean* 17, 32–45.

Korean Language Flagship Center (2012) *Korea Flagship Times*. See http://koreanflagship.manoa.hawaii.edu/newsletter/index.html (accessed 3 October 2014).

Kubler, C. (2004) Learning Chinese in China: Programs for developing Superior-to Distinguished-level Chinese language proficiency in China and Taiwan. In B.L. Leaver and B. Shekhtman (eds) *Developing Professional-Level Language Proficiency* (pp. 96–118). Cambridge: Cambridge University Press.

Lafford, B.A. (2013) The next frontier: A research agenda for exploring experiential language learning in international and domestic contexts. In J.C. Amaro, G. Lord, A. de Prada Pérez and J.E. Aaron (eds) *Selected Proceedings of the 16th Hispanic Linguistic Symposium* (pp. 80–102). Somerville, MA: Cascadilla Proceedings Project.

Leaver, B.L. and Shekhtman, B. (2002) Principles and practices in teaching Superior-level language skills: Not just more of the same. In B.L. Leaver and B. Shekhtman (eds) *Developing Professional-Level Language Proficiency* (pp. 1–33). Cambridge: Cambridge University Press.

Leaver, B.L. and Campbell, C. (2015) Experience with higher levels of proficiency. In T. Brown and J. Brown (eds) *To Advanced Proficiency and Beyond: Theory and Methods for Developing Superior Second Language Ability* (pp. 3–21). Washington, DC: Georgetown University Press.

Modern Language Association (MLA) Ad Hoc Committee on Foreign Language (2007) Foreign languages and higher education: New structures for a changed world. See http://www.mla.org/pdf/forlang_news_pdf.pdf (accessed 7 July 2015).

National Security Education Program (NSEP) (2014) National security education 2014 annual report. See http://www.nsep.gov/content/reports-and-publications (accessed 7 July 2015).

Small, H. (2013) *The Value of the Humanities.* Oxford: Oxford University Press.

Sohn, H. (2012) Korean Flagship: A new frontier for advanced language study. *The Korean Language in America: Journal of the American Association of Teachers of Korean* 17, 3–17.

Spring, M.K. (2012) Languages for specific purposes curriculum in the context of Chinese-Language Flagship Programs. *Modern Language Journal* 96 (Focus Issue), 140–157.

The Language Flagship (2013) *Discourse: Newsletter of the Language Flagship, Fall 2013.* See http://www.thelanguageflagship.org/media/docs/discourse/fall_2013.pdf (accessed 3 October 2014).

The Language Flagship (2014) *Discourse: Newsletter of the Language Flagship, Spring 2014.* See http://www.thelanguageflagship.org/sites/default/files/Discourse_Spring%20 2014.pdf (accessed 3 October 2014).

Tonkin, H. and Quiroga, D. (2004) A qualitative approach to the assessment of international service-learning. *Frontiers* 10, 131–149.

U.S. Department of Education (2014) For public feedback: A college ratings framework. See http://www.ed.gov/news/press-releases/public-feedback-college-ratings-framework (accessed 11 July 2014).

Vande Berg, M., Connor-Linton, J. and Paige, R.M. (2009) The Georgetown consortium project: Interventions for student learning abroad. *Frontiers* 18, 1–75.

10 Beyond Proficiency Gains: Assessing the Academic, Cultural and Professional Impact of the Flagship Experience on Alumni

Mahmoud Al-Batal and Christian Glakas

Introduction

Those of us who have learned a second language know that learning languages is a personal investment that reaps remarkable dividends for those willing to put in the effort. A large body of literature exists that discusses – with ample evidence – the numerous benefits of studying other languages and cultures (Armstrong & Rogers, 1997; CAL, 2010; The College Board, 2004; Curtain & Dahlberg, 2010; Diaz, 1983; Grosse, 2004; Horn & Kojaku, 2001; O'Connell & Norwood, 2007; Timpe, 1979; Weatherford, 1986). These studies demonstrate that learning languages can have a remarkable impact on an individual's cognitive abilities, academic success, understanding of his or her own language and culture, and career trajectories. In today's increasingly interconnected world, language and intercultural skills provide a path to remarkable academic, cultural and professional opportunities.

Yet despite these documented benefits of language learning, the United States still lags behind much of the rest of the world in the number of citizens who have achieved even minimum levels of proficiency in more than one language. US Secretary of Education Arne Duncan pointed out in 2012 that only 18% of Americans reported speaking a language other than English compared to 53% of Europeans who are capable of conversing in a second language (Skorton & Altschuler, 2012). While the US educational agenda has recently placed more emphasis on enhancing the capabilities of high school and college graduates in science, technology, engineering and math (STEM) through multiple STEM initiatives, language education has not received the same level of national attention as these fields. As a result, the US educational system continues to struggle, with varying levels of success, against a multitude of factors both financial and cultural to keep language education among the top national priorities for education.

The magnitude of the language problem in the United States is reflected in data on the number of schools that provide language instruction: the number of public and private elementary schools offering foreign language instruction decreased from 31% to 25% from 1997 to 2008, and the number of middle schools offering foreign language instruction decreased from 75% to 58% (Rhodes & Pufahl, 2009). In addition, about 25% of elementary schools and 30% of middle schools in the United States report a shortage of qualified foreign language teachers. This downward trend in language education in schools was also reflected in higher education, where we find that only 50.7% of colleges and universities required foreign language study in 2009–2010, down from 67.5% in 1994–1995 (Skorton & Altschuler, 2012). Recent severe cutbacks to language education programs in the US have caused the situation to deteriorate further, triggering alarms about a 'language crisis' in the United States (Berman, 2011) and further exacerbating concerns about the future and the economic competitiveness of the United States in the world economy (CED, 2006; O'Connell & Norwood, 2007; Wiley et al., 2012).

To address the national deficit in language education in the United States, the Language Flagship program was established in 2002, one of the national initiatives that emerged in the post–9/11 era. The program's motto of 'creating global professionals' reflects its interest in reversing the prevailing trend in the United States and in training cadres of Americans to achieve an American Council on the Teaching of Foreign Languages (ACTFL) Superior level of proficiency (ILR 3; Appendix A) in 1 of 10 languages: Arabic, Chinese, Hindi, Urdu, Korean, Persian, Portuguese, Russian, Swahili or Turkish. The program combines intensive language study in the United States with a year-long, immersive study abroad experience that includes direct enrollment in a national university and a target language-based internship in a corporation or non-governmental organization (NGO). Since its inception, the Flagship has graduated 384 undergraduate students, 225 of whom have been certified by the Flagship as having achieved ACTFL Superior or ILR 3 proficiency in speaking and at least one other modality (reading, listening or writing). The Flagship pedagogical model continues to evolve in order to further serve students' needs and to reflect the latest innovations in language education. Many Flagship alumni are now working in various spheres, including government, NGOs, academia, education, business and law, while others are continuing their education at graduate level.

Objectives and Research Questions

The present study aims to assess the academic, cultural and career impact of the Flagship experience on the Flagship alumni who have completed the program and are now working or pursuing graduate education. It also aims to investigate the extent to which these alumni utilize their language skills in their current jobs or academic programs. Thus far, assessment of the impact of the Flagship experience on its alumni has focused mainly on their language proficiency gains via standardized tests in speaking, listening and reading. But do alumni go on to use those language skills after they graduate? And what other skills and abilities do they feel that they developed through the course of their advanced language studies? Although numerous studies have examined the cognitive and academic benefits of learning a second language (Armstrong & Rogers, 1997; Curtain & Dahlberg, 2004; Dumas, 1999), no studies, to our knowledge, have previously been conducted with the aim of answering these questions for advanced-level language study programs that incorporate study abroad components, either within the Flagship or in the broader field of second language acquisition.

The present study will pursue this line of inquiry, guided by the following research questions:

(1) To what extent do alumni of Flagship programs feel that their Flagship language learning experience enhanced the academic skills they need for their careers or future study?
(2) To what extent do the alumni feel that their Flagship language learning experience enriched their perspectives of the target cultures and the world?
(3) To what extent do the alumni feel that the Flagship language learning experience prepared them for the careers they have chosen?
(4) In which professional and academic fields are the highest number of Flagship alumni pursuing careers and utilizing their language skills?
(5) In which professional and academic fields are Flagship alumni using their language skills most frequently?
(6) Is there a difference in the frequency of language use in professional or academic activities between Flagship alumni who achieve Superior-level proficiency before graduation and those who did not achieve Superior-level proficiency?

While our study is based on the Flagship and its alumni, our ultimate goal in this research is to contribute to a better understanding of the benefits of language study in general, and at higher levels of proficiency in particular, in areas that go beyond utilizing the language for communication.

Methods and Participants

Survey

This study is based on the Flagship Alumni Survey, which was administered to alumni of Flagship programs. The survey was originally designed to gather feedback from Flagship alumni and to evaluate the accomplishments of the Flagship between 2002 and 2012. To meet these broad goals, we developed a questionnaire consisting of 65 items: 63 multiple-choice items (including 5 binary-response items, 9 categorical-response items and 49 ordinal-response items) and two open-ended response items. The survey included items on a variety of topics, including alumni views on the quality of their Flagship programs, the benefits that they felt that they gained from participating in their programs and their careers since completing their undergraduate studies. Survey items were grouped as follows:

(1) Background knowledge of target language and culture before joining the Flagship (4 items).
(2) Language and program information (language of study, university, etc.; 5 items).
(3) Satisfaction with the domestic Flagship program (6 items).
(4) Satisfaction with the overseas Flagship program (6 items).
(5) Influence of the Flagship capstone overseas program on the development of language skills, understanding and knowledge of different cultures, and the ability to work internationally (10 items)[1].
(6) Influence of the Flagship on academic and professional skills (12 items).
(7) Influence of the Flagship on global awareness and personal growth (3 items).
(8) Influence of the Flagship on professional careers (for alumni who entered employment after graduation; 8 items).
(9) Influence of the Flagship on graduate studies (for alumni who pursued graduate degrees; 4 items).
(10) Demographic information, including field of employment or graduate study (5 items).
(11) Comments and suggestions (2 items).

A pilot survey was administered online to three Flagship alumni in February 2012. After reviewing the pilot survey responses, the researchers eliminated one survey question and revised another question, but made no additional changes. The final version of the survey was administered online between April 2012 and June 2014. Permission to administer the survey was obtained from the Institutional Review Board of our own institution as well as from all other institutions involved. A copy of the full survey and the results are available at http://utarabicflagship.org/about/the-afp/.

This chapter will focus on an analysis of the survey items in item groups 5–10 listed above. The researchers created items in groups 5–7 to help answer research questions 1–3 by collecting information on the types of knowledge and abilities gained by Flagship alumni through their advanced language studies that would prepare them for careers as global professionals. Such abilities included:

- Intellectual and academic abilities and understanding of oneself and others.
- Understanding of different cultures and global perspectives.
- Specialized knowledge of the target country and/or region.
- Ability to conduct research and work in groups.
- Ability to work in a professional environment and interact with professionals in one's field.
- Presentations and public speaking.
- Preparation for entering the job market or graduate study.

The researchers created the items in groups 8–10 to learn what professional and academic fields Flagship alumni have entered since graduating from their programs and how frequently alumni use their language skills in their professional and academic careers. Response data for these items will be used to answer research questions 4–6.

Participants

One hundred and forty-nine alumni of US Language Flagship programs participated in the survey. The researchers sent the link to the online survey to Flagship coordinators and directors at 24 Flagship programs at 20 universities. Flagship alumni were invited to take the survey through their Flagship programs; participation in the survey was voluntary.[2] As with any survey, the responses provide a great deal of information about the individuals who responded to the survey, but their greater value lies in the fact that they allow us infer from the survey sample to the larger population in question. Thus, we hope to draw inference from the analysis of our sample data (Flagship alumni who responded to this survey) to inform our understanding about the larger population (all Flagship alumni). To that end, it is necessary to describe our survey respondents in order to illustrate the sample's similarity to the full population of Flagship alumni.

Table 10.1 offers a snapshot of the Flagship languages studied by the 149 alumni who responded to this survey.

We can see that the Chinese and Arabic Flagship Programs saw the highest levels of participation in this study. This matches our expectations, as these two languages have traditionally seen the highest number of students participating in and graduating from their programs among all Flagship languages. We also see that the alumni of Flagship programs in Russian, Korean, Hindi/Urdu, Portuguese, Swahili and Persian also participated in this study, albeit in predictably smaller numbers, given the smaller sizes of those programs.[4]

Table 10.1 Survey respondents, by language of study

Survey respondents, by language	Total	%
Chinese	62	41.6
Arabic	56	37.6
Russian	12	8.1
Korean	11	7.4
Hindi/Urdu[3]	3	2.0
Portuguese	2	1.3
Swahili	2	1.3
Persian	1	0.7
Total	149	100

Table 10.2 Self-reported OPI ratings of respondents, by level

Most recent self-reported ACTFL OPI score	Total	%
Superior	51	34.2
Advanced High	53	35.6
Advanced Mid	22	14.8
Advanced Low	9	6.0
Intermediate High	5	3.4
Intermediate Mid	2	1.3
Intermediate Low	1	0.7
Don't know	6	4.0
Total	149	100

Regarding the language proficiency of our respondents, Table 10.2 presents information on the self-reported oral proficiency score for each survey respondent from their most recent ACTFL Oral Proficiency Interviews (OPIs).

We see that over one third of respondents (34.2%) reported achieving Superior proficiency on their most recent OPI, while over half (56%) reported achieving Advanced proficiency (Advanced High, Advanced Mid and Advanced Low, collectively). Less than 6% of respondents reported an OPI score below Advanced. This distribution of OPI scores resembles the distribution of all Flagship graduate OPI scores, as tracked by the Flagship.[5] When compared to the general data gathered from the Language Flagship Program, the data submitted by our respondents indicate that our sample constitutes a good representation of the larger population of Flagship graduates.

Data analysis procedures

To answer research questions 1–5, we tallied frequency counts and calculated percentages for relevant items on the survey. Not every respondent answered every question, so the total number of respondents that answered each individual question will be reported for each table ($'n=X'$). To answer research question 6, we performed a Pearson's chi-squared test of independence to determine how likely it is that the higher proportion of superior-proficiency respondents who reported using their language skills every day in their professional careers (compared to respondents who did not achieve Superior proficiency) is due to chance.

We will now present the results of our survey in order to illustrate the impact of the Flagship experience on alumni.

Results and Discussion

Non-linguistic benefits of advanced critical language study

The mission of the Flagship is for students to graduate with Superior proficiency in 1 of 10 languages critical to global understanding and to US national security and economic competitiveness. Flagship students achieve high proficiency in their languages, as shown by regular Flagship OPI testing upon graduation. However, the program, as expressed in its mission statement, also strives to produce well-rounded graduates 'who will take their place among the next generation of global professionals' (The Language Flagship, 2013). In this section, we present the individual survey questions and accompanying response data in three broad categories: intellectual benefits and academic skills, cultural knowledge and regional expertise and professional development.

Intellectual benefits and academic skills (research question 1)

As indicated in the introduction of this chapter, language learning can provide a rich intellectual experience for learners and help promote better understanding of self and others. Nearly all Flagship alumni who participated in this study (over 90%) felt that the program provided an intellectually stimulating environment and that it helped them to be aware of different perspectives from around the world, while also allowing them to better understand their own country and culture. Complementing these intellectual benefits, alumni also indicated that the program, through intensive language study and the various activities connected with it, helped them to develop tangible academic skills, including conducting research and working in groups. Table 10.3 shows the responses to these questions as they relate to the Flagship as a whole, while Table 10.4 focuses on the study abroad component of the Flagship.

These results provide remarkable evidence that Flagship programs, which offer intensive and focused language study, coupled with a rich overseas experience, can help language learners develop a range of perceived benefits related to their intellectual growth, their insights into other cultures and their understanding of different perspectives. Additionally, the fact that over

Table 10.3 Learning environment and global awareness

To what extent do you agree with the following statements:	Strongly agree (%)	Agree (%)	Disagree (%)	Strongly disagree (%)
The Flagship program provided me with an intellectually stimulating learning environment (n=138)	60	36	4	0
Participating in the Flagship program contributed to my awareness of different points of view from around the world (n=137)	74	24	1	0

Table 10.4 Understanding of the US and perspective on own culture

To what extent has your study abroad experience influenced your:	Strongly (%)	Moderately (%)	Minimally (%)	Not at all (%)
Understanding of the United States and its place in world affairs (n=141)	52	42	5	1
Perspective on your own culture (n=141)	74	23	3	1

90% of participants selected either 'strongly' or 'moderately' in response to the statements in Table 10.4 suggests that study abroad can play a beneficial role in shaping students' understanding of their own country and culture.

In regard to the development of specific academic skills, nearly all respondents stated that the Flagship contributed to enhancing their abilities in conducting research and improving their confidence working in groups. Table 10.5 shows that over 25% of respondents felt that the Flagship 'strongly' contributed to their skills in these areas, with over 45% of respondents stating that the program 'moderately' contributed to their development of these skills.

The results presented in Table 10.5 lend support to the claim that foreign language study can have academic and career benefits (Armstrong & Rogers, 1997; Carreira & Armengol, 2001; Grosse, 2004; Saunders, 1998) by showing that alumni perceive that their participation in the Flagship contributed to abilities that are valued in both academic settings and in the workplace. The fact that nearly one third of the respondents indicated that participation in the Flagship played a strong role in building their research and group-work

Table 10.5 Group work and research

How did your participation in your Flagship program contribute to your:	Strongly (%)	Moderately (%)	Minimally (%)	Not at all (%)
Confidence working in groups (*n*=134)	28	47	20	5
Conducting research (*n*=134)	29	46	20	6

skills, while close to half of them indicated that it played a moderate role in building these skills, should serve as an incentive for language programs to think of ways that task-based and project-based teaching, which can serve to enhance those skills, could be further integrated within language programs to enhance the research and group-dynamic benefits of language study.

Cultural knowledge and regional expertise (research question 2)

Flagship graduates are expected to possess advanced cultural skills and intercultural insights for careers in federal government, global business, NGOs and other fields of employment. To that end, Flagship language courses, both in the United States and overseas, aim to present a wide range of culturally relevant subject matter through which students study the language. Additionally, the study abroad component offers a unique opportunity for students to develop regional knowledge and cultural expertise: in addition to taking a full academic load of courses in the target language, each student participates in a professional internship during the capstone. The internship is meant to help students develop their professional skills while also providing an opportunity to work in their host country, using the target language in a professional setting with their native-speaker colleagues.

Survey respondents stated in overwhelming numbers that they felt that they had indeed gained cultural knowledge and regional expertise. Table 10.6 shows the extent to which the participants believed that the

Table 10.6 Understanding of country/region of target language

To what extent do you agree with the following statement:	Strongly agree (%)	Agree (%)	Disagree (%)	Strongly disagree (%)
The Flagship program provided me with knowledge and understanding of the country/region in which my target language is spoken (*n*=138)	74	25	1	0

Table 10.7 Specialized knowledge of region of target language

	Strongly (%)	Moderately (%)	Minimally (%)	Not at all (%)
To what degree did participation in the Flagship contribute to developing specialized knowledge of your region of study? (*n*=134)	62	30	6	2

program provided them with knowledge and understanding of the region in which their Flagship language is spoken, and Table 10.7 examines the extent to which students felt that they developed more specialized knowledge of that region.

Tables 10.6 and 10.7 show that Flagship alumni feel strongly that the program helped them to develop knowledge and understanding of their region of study. Table 10.6 shows that 99% of respondents indicated that they believed that the program provided them with knowledge and understanding of the region in which their Flagship language is spoken (74% 'strongly agree' and 25% 'agree'). Table 10.7 shows that 62% of respondents felt that the Flagship contributed 'strongly' to their developing specialized knowledge of their region of study.

Focusing on the overseas internship, Table 10.8 looks at the role of the internship in shaping participants' understanding of life in their host country.

Over two thirds of respondents described their internships as either 'very beneficial' (36%) or 'beneficial' (38%) in influencing their understanding of life in their host country. For those alumni who reported that they found the internship slightly or not beneficial at all, this might be a reflection of the quality of the internship in which they were involved. The quality of internships varies widely depending on the country, the organization

Table 10.8 Overseas internship

	Very beneficial (%)	Beneficial (%)	Slightly beneficial (%)	Not at all (%)
How beneficial was your internship in influencing your understanding of life in your host country? (*n*=138)	36	38	13	12

offering the internship and the tasks connected with the internship. Internships that offer limited cultural or linguistic exposure will not be beneficial to alumni.

These results underscore the importance of the year-long, full-immersion study abroad component of the Flagship. They also demonstrate the importance of building an active, culturally and linguistically rich internship component within the program. This is crucial in helping students develop domain-specific expertise alongside the linguistic and cultural knowledge and the regional expertise that they develop through their language program.

Professional development (research question 3)

Since its establishment in 2002, the Flagship has designed and implemented new models for advanced language learning. These models include research-based pedagogies that utilize group work, content-based instruction, in-language research projects and presentations, completion of an in-language internship and direct enrollment in universities abroad. In addition, Flagship programs aim to provide students with invaluable professional development opportunities while on the path to superior language proficiency. The following tables reflect the impact of these professional development opportunities on Flagship alumni and how they have prepared alumni for life after graduation. Table 10.9 conveys the respondents' views on how the Flagship experience helped them to network with professionals in their field of interest, operate in a professional environment and develop their public speaking and presentation skills.

For each question in Table 10.9, over 60% of respondents said that the Flagship contributed 'strongly' or 'moderately' to their abilities in the specified area. Most notably, nearly half of the respondents (48%) stated that the Flagship contributed 'strongly' to their public speaking and

Table 10.9 Development of professional skills

How did your participation in your Flagship program contribute to your abilities in the following areas:	Strongly (%)	Moderately (%)	Minimally (%)	Not at all (%)
Networking with professionals in your field of interest (n=134)	22	39	29	10
Operating in a professional working environment (n=134)	27	37	27	9
Public speaking and presentation (n=133)	48	40	10	2

Table 10.10 Preparation for professional career

To what extent do you think the Flagship...	Strongly (%)	Moderately (%)	Minimally (%)	Not at all (%)
...helped you to focus your career trajectory? (n=138)	44	33	18	5
...contributed to your preparation for entering the job market? (n=138)	42	36	20	2
...increased your competitiveness within your professional field? (n=138)	55	32	12	1

presentation skills, with an additional 40% indicating that the program contributed 'moderately' to their development of these skills. Given that students are routinely required to deliver presentations in the target language in their Flagship courses, it is not surprising that so many alumni feel that the program helped them to improve their presentation skills and build their confidence in public speaking, and that those skills would transfer to public speaking or presentations that they might need to give in English or other languages.

The alumni who participated in this study also indicated that the Flagship helped them to focus their career trajectories, to prepare for entering the job market and to be competitive within their professional field. Table 10.10 shows the graduates' responses to questions on these topics.

For each question listed in Table 10.10, over 75% of the respondents indicated that the Flagship helped them 'strongly' or 'moderately' in the specified area, with 55% of graduates saying that the program 'strongly' increased their competitiveness within their professional field.

In addition to preparing students for professional careers, survey data indicate that the Flagship is also helping prepare students for postgraduate academic careers. Of the respondents who pursued a graduate or professional degree after completing their bachelor's degree, most feel that the program helped prepare them for their graduate studies (Table 10.11).

Table 10.11 Preparation for graduate school

	Strongly (%)	Moderately (%)	Minimally (%)	Not at all (%)
To what extent do you think the Flagship program contributed to your preparation for graduate school? (n=60)	43	32	22	3

The data show that 75% of respondents who pursued advanced degrees feel that the Flagship contributed 'strongly' or 'moderately' to their preparation for graduate school. Flagship alumni clearly feel that they gain valuable professional development through their participation in the program, and that the Flagship helped them to prepare for and succeed in their future professional and academic careers.

These results provide further evidence for the benefits of advanced language study and immersion experience overseas. The work that students do as part of their language study, whether collaborating in groups, making presentations or presenting opinions and supporting them, has transferred into life skills that have helped students prepare for and embark on their professional and academic careers.

The real world: Alumni language use in employment and graduate school (research questions 4–6)

In order to illustrate how the Flagship has benefitted alumni in their professional and academic careers after completing their bachelor's degree, our survey also collected information on how often alumni report using their Flagship language skills in their jobs and graduate studies since graduation. Over half of the alumni who completed the survey reported using their Flagship language skills in a job since graduating from the program; a quarter of them reported using their language skills in graduate school. Table 10.12 shows the different ways in which alumni have used their language skills since completing their Flagship studies.

Table 10.12 Language use since graduation[5]

	In a job (%)	In graduate school (%)	Informal use (%)	Not at all (%)
Since graduation, how have you used your language skills? (n=138)	53	25	90	4

These data help to show how effective the Flagship has been in training students who go on to apply their linguistic skills in a job or in graduate school. However, Table 10.12 presents data from all respondents, some of whom had not yet entered the workforce and many of whom had not pursued graduate studies. To gain a better understanding of how alumni are using the target language after graduation, we will look at the responses from only those respondents who have entered the workforce, and then from only those who have pursued graduate degrees. Table 10.13 presents data on the frequency with which working alumni reported using their language skills in their positions.

Table 10.13 Language use in professional employment, days per month

	Every day (%)	16+ days (%)	5–15 days (%)	1–5 days (%)	Don't use (%)
If you are currently employed, how many days per month do you use your language skills in your work? (n=114)	33	10	4	17	36

Limiting our view to those alumni who were working at the time of the survey (n=114), we see that nearly two thirds of all employed respondents reported using their Flagship language skills in their jobs. Perhaps most impressively, one third of those individuals reported using their Flagship language skills in their jobs every day. An additional 10% of respondents reported using their language skills at least 16 days per month, and over 20% of respondents reported using their Flagship language between 1 and 15 days per month. Taken together, we see that 64% of all respondents who were working at the time of the survey reported that they used their Flagship language skills in their jobs.

Similarly, when we limit our view to those respondents who had pursued a graduate degree (n=60), we see that over 80% of them reported using their language skills at some point in their graduate studies.

As shown in Table 10.14, the vast majority of respondents who have pursued a graduate degree reported using their language skills in their graduate careers, with nearly one third (32%) reporting that they used their language skills 'often' in their graduate studies.

With so many alumni using their language skills in their professional and academic careers, it is worth taking a closer look at the data to see what factors are associated with higher language use among alumni. Data analysis reveals two interesting trends relevant to research questions 4, 5 and 6:

(1) Alumni in certain *fields of employment* reported using their language skills more frequently than alumni in other fields.

Table 10.14 Language use in graduate school

	Often (%)	Sometimes (%)	Rarely (%)	Never (%)
If you have pursued a graduate degree, how often did you use your language in your graduate studies? (n=60)	32	27	25	16

(2) Alumni who achieved *higher proficiency levels* reported using their language skills more frequently in their jobs and in their graduate studies than those who achieved lower proficiency levels.

Considering first the issue of association between fields of employment or graduate study and reported language use, we will present data on the types of jobs and graduate programs that Flagship alumni have entered since graduation. We will also show how many alumni within each field reported using their language skills in their professional or academic careers, and the frequency with which they use those skills.

Flagship students possess a wide variety of academic and professional interests, and they follow those interests into many different professional and academic fields after graduation. Not surprisingly, alumni who enter certain professional fields reported using their Flagship language skills in their jobs more often than alumni in other fields. Table 10.15 presents the various fields in which respondents reported working, along with the number of respondents working in each field and the number (and percentage) of alumni within each field who use their Flagship language skills in their jobs.[6]

Table 10.15 presents information that helps answer research questions 4 and 5. It shows that the most common field of employment for Flagship graduates to enter was education and educational services, with over a quarter of all employed respondents (33/112) working in this field. The next most common field for respondents to have entered was business (15), followed by government (14), linguist/translator (12) and non-profit

Table 10.15 Professional use of Flagship language skills, by field of employment

Field of employment* (n=112)	Total no. of respondents working in field (n=132)	Use Flagship language skills in job	
		No.	%
Education and educational services	33	28	85
Business	15	6	40
Government	14	11	79
Linguist/translator	12	10	83
Non-profit	11	9	82
Finance, insurance and real estate	8	6	75
Communications and media	6	4	67
Marketing, advertising and sales	5	2	40

* Fields in which fewer than five respondents reported working, including creative, development, engineering, healthcare, hospitality, IT, legal, logistics, retail and scientific, were omitted from both Table 10.15 and Table 10.16.

(11). Of the alumni who entered each of those fields of employment, those who entered education and educational services were the most likely to use their language skills in their jobs (85%), followed by those in the linguist/translator category (83%), non-profit (82%), government (79%) and business (40%). Among the fields that were omitted from Table 10.15 due to the low number of respondents reporting in those fields, the most interesting results were found in the field of development, in which 75% of respondents reported using their language skills (three quarters). This provides evidence that Flagship alumni are not only using their language skills as translators, but are also applying those skills in a variety of fields for different types of public, private and non-profit organizations. The lower rate of language usage among alumni who reported working in business held across languages, although the data do show that alumni who graduated before 2010 and described working in business reported higher language use in their jobs than those who graduated in 2010 or afterward. This suggests that it may take several years before alumni working in business have the opportunity to use their language skills in their careers. Whether this is due to the extensive training programs that many private sector organizations have for new employees or due to other factors is an interesting question for future study.

Focusing on the frequency with which respondents use their Flagship language in their jobs, Table 10.16 presents information on how many alumni in each field reported using their language skills every day in their jobs.

Table 10.16 shows that over half (55%) of the respondents working in education – the most popular field of employment for Flagship alumni – are using their language skills every day. This is the second highest rate of

Table 10.16 Daily professional use of Flagship language skills, by field of employment

Field of employment* (n=112)	Total no. of respondents working in field	Use Flagship language skill *every day* in job	
		No.	%
Education and educational services	33	18	55
Linguist/translator	12	7	58
Government	14	5	36
Non-profit	11	5	46
Business	15	4	27
Finance, insurance and real estate	8	2	25
Communications and media	6	2	33

daily language use in any field, second only to linguist/translator (58%). Smaller numbers of alumni also reported using their language skills 'every day' in their careers in the fields of development (two out of four alumni, or 50%) and logistics (one out of three alumni, or 33%). Taken together, Tables 10.15 and 10.16 show that Flagship alumni have been able to obtain employment in a variety of professional fields and use their language skills in their jobs. Considering the number of alumni working in different fields of employment, as well as the frequency with which they use their language skills in their positions, it is clear that the fields of education, translation, government service and non-profit organizations see the highest number of Flagship alumni obtaining employment and putting their Flagship language skills to use. More broadly, the information in Tables 10.15 and 10.16 shows that foreign language skills can be professionally useful to language learners who embark on a wide variety of career paths after completing their undergraduate studies.

Turning to alumni graduate studies, the data reveal different trends regarding the numbers of alumni who use their language skills in different academic fields. The data show variation in the numbers of alumni entering different academic fields, but the respondents' reported language use does not vary widely between disciplines. Table 10.17 presents the various academic fields in which respondents reported pursuing advanced degrees, along with information on the number of respondents in each field, and the number (and percentage) of respondents within each discipline who use their Flagship language skills in their studies.

Table 10.17 Alumni use of Flagship language skills in graduate school, by field of study

Field of graduate or professional degree* (n=53)	Total no. of respondents working in field	Use Flagship language skills in studies	
		No.	%
International/public affairs	20	17	85
Business	7	6	86
Linguistics and language teaching	6	6	100
Cultural and regional studies	6	5	83
Law	6	4	67
History	5	5	100
Government	5	5	100

* Fields of study in which fewer than five respondents reported pursuing graduate degrees, including art, classics, economics, education, healthcare, medicine and science, information studies, international development, literature, philosophy, sociology and urban planning, were omitted from both Table 10.17 and Table 10.18.

Table 10.18 Frequency of alumni use of Flagship language skills in graduate school, by field of study

Field of graduate or professional degree* (n=53)	Total no. of respondents studying in field	Use Flagship language skills 'often' in studies	
		No.	%
International/public affairs	20	6	30
Cultural and regional studies	6	5	83
History	5	4	80
Linguistics and language teaching	6	3	50
Government	5	3	60
Business	7	1	14

Of the 53 respondents who pursued advanced degrees and provided a description of the type of graduate program in which they were enrolled, over a third of them (20) described their program as international/public affairs. Significantly fewer alumni reported entering graduate programs in any other field, with no more than seven respondents reporting in any one of the remaining subject areas. Respondents reported high language use in all fields, with at least 67% of alumni in each field appearing in Table 10.17 reporting using their language skills in their graduate programs.

Focusing on the frequency of language use reported by alumni pursuing advanced degrees (with the response options of 'often', 'sometimes', 'rarely' and 'never'), the results are somewhat surprising. Table 10.18 shows the number of respondents who reported using their Flagship language skills 'often' in their studies.

Unlike in employment, where the most popular field (education) also saw a very high frequency of language use (55% 'everyday' language use), the most popular field of graduate study (international/public affairs) actually shows a relatively low percentage of alumni using their skills 'often' in their studies (30%). While 85% of alumni in international/public affairs graduate programs reported using their language skills at some point during their studies (Table 10.17), the low rate of students reporting using those skills 'often' in their studies may be due to the high number of core classes required by many international/public affairs graduate programs, many of which may not require research conducted in foreign languages.

Turning to research question 6, the data show that alumni who achieve higher levels of proficiency report higher language use in their jobs and also in their graduate studies than do alumni with lower proficiency levels. We will explore this issue first in the employment data and then turn to

Table 10.19 Professional use of Flagship language skills, by field of employment

Proficiency (n=107)	Total no. of respondents with this proficiency	Use Flagship language skills in job	
		No.	%
Superior	39	29	74.4
Advanced High or below	68	39	57.4

the graduate studies data. In terms of language use in employment, the data reveal a noticeable difference between alumni who reach Superior proficiency and those who do not. Table 10.19 illustrates this difference, showing the number (and percentage) of Superior-level alumni who use their language skills regularly in their jobs compared with the number (and percentage) of alumni with proficiency below Superior.

We see that, among employed respondents, 74.4% of the Superior-level alumni reported using their language skills in their jobs, compared with 57.4% of alumni whose proficiency was Advanced High or below. The difference widens when we examine the percentages of alumni who use their language skills every day in their jobs, as shown in Table 10.20.

We can see that the percentage of employed, Superior-level alumni who reported using their language skills every day (46.2%) was nearly twice as high as the percentage for those with proficiency of Advanced High or lower (26.5%). A Pearson's chi-squared test of independence revealed the differences between these two percentages to be statistically significant ($p < 0.05$). The test showed that the alumni of Flagship programs who achieved Superior proficiency in the target language before graduation were more likely to report using their language skills on a daily basis in their jobs than the alumni with proficiency scores of Advanced High or below.

Alumni language use in graduate school follows a similar trend, albeit at a lower proficiency threshold. The data do not reveal a significant difference in reported language use between alumni who achieved Superior proficiency and those who achieved Advanced High proficiency or lower.

Table 10.20 Daily professional use of Flagship language skills, by field of employment

Proficiency (n=107)	Total no. of respondents with this proficiency	Use Flagship language skills every day in job	
		No.	%
Superior	39	18	46.2
Advanced High or below	68	18	26.5

Table 10.21 Alumni use of Flagship language skills in graduate school, by field of study

Proficiency (n=59)	Total no. of respondents with this proficiency	Use Flagship language skills in graduate studies	
		No.	%
Superior	29	25	86.2
Advanced High	18	17	94.4
Advanced Mid or below	12	7	58.3

However, the data do show a substantial difference in reported language use between alumni who achieved Advanced High or above (including Superior), and those with proficiency below Advanced High. Table 10.21 presents data on the use of Flagship language skills by alumni with various proficiency levels in their graduate studies.

Over 85% of alumni who achieved either Advanced High or Superior proficiency (42/47) reported using their Flagship language skills in their graduate studies, while only 58.3% of alumni who achieved Advanced Mid proficiency or lower reported using their language skills in their graduate studies. This difference – between graduate school language use among those alumni who achieved Advanced High proficiency (or above) and those who did not – becomes even more pronounced when one considers the frequency with which alumni reported using those skills (see Table 10.22).

Of the alumni who achieved Advanced High or Superior proficiency (47), 18 (38.3%) reported using their language skills 'often' in their graduate studies. Of the 12 students who pursued graduate degrees and achieved Advanced Mid proficiency or lower, none reported using their language skills 'often' in their graduate studies.

Table 10.22 Frequency of alumni use of Flagship language skills in graduate school, by field of study

Proficiency (n=59)	Total no. of respondents with this proficiency	Use Flagship language skills **often** in grad studies	
		No.	%
Superior	29	11	37.9
Advanced High	18	7	38.9
Advanced Mid or below	12	0	0

Conclusion

Our study of the academic, cultural and professional impact of the Flagship experience demonstrates that most alumni surveyed believe that their Flagship language and culture learning experience has been largely positive. More specifically, our results indicate that, in addition to the language proficiency gains they made through the program, the alumni believe that their language learning experience:

- Enhanced the academic skills they need for their careers or future graduate study.
- Enriched their perspectives of the target cultures and the world.
- Prepared them for the careers they have chosen.

In terms of language use by Flagship alumni, our results indicate that:

- Over half of the alumni surveyed reported using their Flagship language skills in a job since graduating from the program.
- A quarter of them reported using their language skills in graduate school.
- Alumni working in fields such as education, government and NGOs reported using their language skills more frequently than alumni in fields such as business and finance.
- Alumni who achieved higher proficiency levels reported using their language skills more frequently in their jobs and in their graduate studies than those who achieved lower proficiency levels.

Going beyond the Flagship, our findings suggest that language learning can and does have a salutary impact on those students who pursue advanced levels of study and who engage in a significant overseas immersion program. Just as education in STEM subjects can prepare young people for success in the increasingly interconnected 21st-century workforce, so too can the study of world languages and cultures. Excluding language and culture from the national STEM-oriented educational agenda does a great disservice to our students and will deprive them of a crucial tool for success in their future professional careers.

While the results of this study should lend encouragement to all advocates of foreign language education, we must now ask how we as educators can enhance the quality of our own programs to increase the benefits of language study for our students. We need to consider how best to reconfigure our existing language programs in order to provide students with the skills that they need to obtain employment and succeed in their careers. To that end, dialogue with various public and private sector organizations can help us to identify the types of additional language and culture skills that businesses and government agencies seek in candidates for positions that demand such skills.

Additionally, we must encourage our foreign language colleagues throughout higher education to follow up with their alumni in order to gain a better understanding of the specific needs of these alumni in the job market and how our language programs could better help fulfill these needs. This information can help language programs attract the best prospective students while also protecting the programs themselves from the types of programmatic and budgetary cuts that have occurred throughout US institutions of higher learning over the last few decades.

We hope that this study provides support to the idea that the study of world languages and cultures is not a luxury to be engaged in only by those students who wish to 'see the world', but rather a viable avenue for developing professional skills that can help students follow their passions into exciting and rewarding careers. Further efforts to demonstrate the utility of language learning will be necessary to broaden support for this idea and put language learning in its appropriate place alongside STEM subjects as a pathway to professional success in the 21st century.

Acknowledgments

The authors would like to thank University of Texas at Austin Arabic Flagship student Stephen Nelson Clarke for his help analyzing data for this chapter.

Notes

(1) The Flagship capstone overseas program is a year-long study abroad immersion experience that Flagship students undertake after they achieve Advanced proficiency. Students take advanced language courses, content-based courses in the target language and direct enrollment courses in the target language at a nearby university. They also complete a one-semester internship with a local organization in which all communication is conducted in the target language. Students have the option to live with host families or in a dorm or apartment. For more on the Flagship overseas experience, see: http://thelanguageflagship.org/content/overseas-0.

(2) It is not possible to report a response rate for our survey because we did not send the survey to alumni directly; the coordinators and/or directors of each program sent the survey link to their alumni.

(3) Hindi and Urdu are taught jointly in the Hindi/Urdu Flagship Program.

(4) Flagship students who completed the capstone year between 2006 and 2014 were distributed by language as follows: Chinese (44.1%), Arabic (26.1%), Russian (19%), Korean (5.2%), Swahili (2.4%), Hindi/Urdu (1.4%), Turkish (0.9%), Persian (0.5%), Portuguese (0.5%).

(5) Flagship data for the entire time range were unavailable at the time of this writing, although data for all alumni who completed the capstone between 2012 and 2014 indicate the following distribution:

- Superior – 48.6%
- Advanced High – 36.0%
- Advanced Mid – 12.1%

- Advanced Low – 1.9%
- Intermediate High – 1.4%
- (no scores below Intermediate High)

The fact that the proficiency scores presented in Table 10.2 were self-reported, combined with the fact that 4% of respondents indicated that they did not know their most recent proficiency score, may explain the variation that we see between the figures in Table 10.2 and the data presented here.

(6) For the question presented in Table 10.12, respondents were allowed to select all of the options that applied to them, which explains why the percentages total more than 100%.

(7) The Flagship Alumni Survey provided respondents with the option to use multiple categories to describe their jobs and their graduate fields of study. Many respondents utilized this option, and in Tables 10.15 and 10.16, each job is reported in each category used to describe it. So, if one respondent described her position as government and also translator/linguist, that single job would be counted in both categories. Similarly for Tables 10.17 and 10.18, if a respondent described a graduate program as international/public affairs and government, that program would be counted in both categories. However, the *n* reported in all tables refers to the number of individuals who submitted a response to that question.

References

Armstrong, P. and Rogers, J. (1997) Basic skills revisited: The effects of foreign language instruction on reading, math and language arts. *Learning Languages* 2 (3), 20–31.

Berman, R.A. (2011) The real language crisis. *Academe* 97 (5), 30–34.

Carreira, M.C. and Armengol, R. (2001) Professional opportunities for heritage language speakers. In J.K. Peyton, D.A. Ranard and S. McGinnis (eds) *Heritage Languages in America: Preserving a National Resource* (pp. 109–142). McHenry, IL/Washington, DC: Delta Systems and Center for Applied Linguistics.

Center for Applied Linguistics (CAL) (2004) Why, how and when should my child learn a second language? See http://www.hcpss.org/f/academics/worldlanguages/whyhowwhen_brochure.pdf (accessed 29 July 2015).

The College Board (2004) College-bound seniors: A profile of SAT program test-takers. See http://www.collegeboard.com/prod_downloads/about/news_info/cbsenior/yr2004/2004_CBSNR_total_group.pdf (accessed 27 March 2015).

Committee for Economic Development (CED) (2006) Education for global leadership: The importance of international studies and foreign language education for U.S. economic and national security. See https://www.ced.org/pdf/Education-for-Global-Leadership.pdf (accessed 4 July 2015).

Curtain, H.A. and Dahlberg, C.A. (2010) *Languages and Children: Making the Match: New Languages for Young Learners, Grades K-8* (4th edn) Boston, MA: Pearson.

Diaz, R.M. (1983) The impact of second-language learning on the development of verbal and spatial abilities. PhD dissertation, Yale University.

Dumas, L.S. (1999) Learning a second language: Exposing your child to a new world of words boosts her brainpower, vocabulary and self-esteem. *Child* 72 (74), 76–77.

Grosse, C. (2004) The competitive advantage of foreign languages and cultural knowledge. *Modern Language Journal* 88, 351–373.

Horn, L.J. and Kojaku, L.K. (2001) High school academic curriculum and the persistence path through college: Persistence and transfer behavior of undergraduates 3 years after entering 4-year institutions. *Education Statistics Quarterly* 3 (3), 65–72.

Interagency Language Roundtable (ILR) *Interagency Language Roundtable Skill Level Descriptions*. See http://www.govtilr.org (accessed 16 June 2015).

The Language Flagship (2013) About Us. See http://www.thelanguageflagship.org (accessed 8 September 2015).

O'Connell, M.E. and Norwood, J. (eds) (2007) *International Education and Foreign Languages: Keys to Securing America's Future*. Washington, DC: National Academies Press.

Rhodes, N. and Pufhal, I. (2009) Foreign language teaching in U.S. schools: Results of a national survey, executive summary. Center for Applied Linguistics. See http://www.cal.org/what-we-do/projects/national-k-12-foreign-language-survey (accessed 27 March 2015).

Saunders, C.M. (1998) *The Effect of the Study of a Foreign Language in the Elementary School on Scores on the Iowa Test of Basic Skills and an Analysis of Student-participant Attitudes and Abilities*. PhD dissertation, University of Georgia.

Skorton, D. and Altschuler, G. (2012) America's foreign language deficit. *Forbes Online Magazine*. See http://www.forbes.com/sites/collegeprose/2012/08/27/americas-foreign-language-deficit/ (accessed 1 October 2014).

Timpe, E. (1979) The effect of foreign language study on ACT scores. *ADFL Bulletin* 11, 10–11.

Weatherford, H.J. (1986) Personal benefits from foreign language study. Washington, DC: ERIC Clearinghouse on Languages and Linguistics. Retrieved from ERIC Database (ED276305).

Wiley, T.G., Moore, S.C. and Fee, M.S. (2012) A 'languages for jobs' initiative: Policy innovation memorandum No. 24. Council on Foreign Relations. See http://www.cfr.org/united-states/languages-jobs-initiative/p28396 (accessed 1 October 2014).

11 Raise the Flag(ship)! Creating Hybrid Language Programs on the Flagship Model

Thomas J. Garza

A Pedagogy of Economics

For any university-level language program striving to attain standards-based[1] goals, a variety of factors, including time, audience, goals and environment, is brought to bear on curriculum design and pedagogical practices. Occasionally, however, extenuating circumstances create the need to innovate and reimagine the classroom experience and learning outcomes of courses. Such was the case for virtually all educational programs nationally at the post-secondary level, including foreign languages, following the global economic crisis of 2008. The sweeping reductions in funding available to sustain secondary and post-secondary educational programs in the US prompted many administrators to target language programs among others whose costs did not seem to be justified by their outcomes (Berman, 2011; Hu, 2009; Koebler, 2012). And yet, as Malone *et al.* (2005: 1) pointed out, prior to the downturn in the economy, 'The need for individuals who can speak and understand languages other than English is acute in many sectors in the United States, from business and social services to national security and diplomacy'. Thus, precisely at the time of growing national need for specialists with professional competence (American Council on the Teaching of Foreign Languages [ACTFL] Superior/Interagency Language Roundtable [ILR] 3; Appendix A) in a number of critical languages,[2] economic circumstances were forcing a reduction in the numbers of programs and resources needed to train such students (Beale, 2010; Jaschik, 2010; Zehr, 2011).

At the University of Texas at Austin (UT Austin), after considering and rejecting a number of cost-saving proposals, including the elimination of the requirement of two years of language study before graduation, the College of Liberal Arts turned to its Language Policy Advisory Committee (LPAC) for recommendations on further action. The LPAC, comprising faculty from each language department in the college, turned to the report of the Modern Language Association (MLA) on the restructuring of language programs for a globalized environment (MLA, 2007). LPAC focused especially on the MLA (2007: 9) report's recommendation to 'develop intensive courses and, whenever possible, language-intensive or immersion semesters during which students take multiple courses in the major simultaneously'. Under the leadership of senior associate dean Richard Flores of the College of Liberal Arts, the LPAC drafted a description of a two-semester, six-hour-per-week sequence of two intensive courses designed to replace the existing four-semester sequence of first- and second-year language courses. This year-long sequence was dubbed 'Intensive (name of language)'; successful completion of the sequence would fulfill the college's two-year foreign language requirement.

Earlier that year, the LPAC had already been occupied with reviewing the establishment of a new service-oriented language center, one oriented toward providing faculty with pedagogical and curricular support for their language courses, based on another recommendation from the MLA (2007: 9) report: 'Through a language center or other structure, develop a forum for the exchange of ideas and expertise among language instructors from all departments. Such structures prove invaluable in boosting the morale of teachers and improving the quality of professional and intellectual life'. Subsequently, in 2009, the Texas Language Center (TLC) began an operation to address the professional development needs of language teaching faculty, and to help facilitate the transition of language programs from the previous model of instruction of 18 total hours/credits (five hours per week for two first-year semesters, and four hours per week for two second-year semesters) to a model of 12 total hours/credits (six hours per week for two semesters) – without negatively affecting proficiency outcomes. Lively debate among faculty and administrators ensued as to how ambitious proficiency goals could be met with fewer total contact hours in the classroom. In devising a set of practical pedagogical and curricular recommendations for language programs that elected to change to the new format, the TLC turned to its existing Language Flagship programs in Arabic and Hindi/Urdu for curricular models and classroom practices. Founded in 2008 and 2007, respectively, these two Flagship programs quickly distinguished themselves within and outside UT Austin for innovative curricula and energetic classroom practices. Both programs collaborated with the TLC in identifying best practices and components of their curricula that might be transferable to non-Flagship language programs in the College of Liberal Arts.

By 2010, eight of the 31 modern and classical languages regularly taught at UT Austin had converted their four-semester sequences to the academic year-long 6/6 Intensive model: Arabic, French, Hebrew, Italian, Latin, Persian, Russian and Turkish. Each of these language courses completely revised existing curricula and materials to conform to the six-hour format and the particular demands of Intensive instruction. The TLC conducted workshops from 2009 through 2011 specifically designed to address issues such as revising and reshaping curricula, creating new materials for in-class and online use and restructuring the format of classroom interaction and extracurricular activities. The TLC was also proactive in promoting the new Intensive courses to students and student academic advisers in an attempt to demonstrate the efficacy of the two-semester sequence that would not only fulfill the student's language requirement, but also bring the learner to a level of functional proficiency (ACTFL Intermediate/ILR 1) after one year of instruction (TLC, 2010).

From *intense* to *Intense*

By choosing to call its new sequence of language courses 'Intensive', UT Austin had – consciously or unconsciously – entered into a long-established pedagogical conversation on the content of such a course and its mode of delivery in and outside the classroom. While the term 'intensive' is attached to a wide variety of language courses, its meaning varies greatly in both theory and practice (Schulz, 1979). A number of models use the term interchangeably with 'accelerated', meaning only that material is covered in a shorter time frame, usually with an increase in contact hours, but with little attention paid specifically to what goes on in and out of class (Demuth & Smith, 1987). The model of instruction that emerged at UT Austin, both for its Flagship courses and subsequent 'Intensive' courses, is distinguished from accelerated models in that, in addition to fewer total contact hours, curriculum and classroom practices are completely changed for such courses in order to attain the same or higher proficiency goals than in traditional courses. Thus, these Flagship-like language courses are described as 'Intensive', rather than 'intensive'; the more generic label is used for related courses and methods, a distinction in nomenclature first made in Garza (2013).

The Intensive language courses developed at UT Austin from 2009 draw heavily from established notions of instruction and course design described extensively in the literature of Soviet foreign-language pedagogy and methodology from the 1970s and 1980s. While language teaching in the Soviet Union was frequently described as based on rote memorization of grammatical and lexical material, with emphasis placed on the 'priority of conscious understanding of the rule-governed characteristics of the language' (McLaughlin, 1986: 44), the innovative pedagogy of the intensive methodology in many ways echoed the basic tenets of communicative language instruction that was developing concurrently in other parts of the world. Soviet intensive courses focused on the development of functional abilities in speaking the language, making extensive use of role play and situational language use (Zakharova, 2014: 43).

Kitaigorodskaia developed an entire school of practice based heavily on Stanislavsky theatre and performance theory, which encourages actors to transform themselves into the characters in roles they play, around her particular brand of intensive language instruction. Especially characteristic of her method was the orientation of the entire course toward communication and, like Lozanov before her, realizing the students' full potential by tapping into their 'psychological reserves of personality' (Kitaigorodskaia, 1992: 8) primarily by freeing the students from their personal identities and having them instead take on those of pre-established characters for the duration of the course. Kitaigorodskaia (1986) establishes the underpinnings of her method thus:

> Intensive instruction of a foreign language is understood to mean instruction that is focused on mastering communication in the language, primarily based on the student's psychological reserves of personality and activity not realized in regular instruction, in particular the management of the socio-psychological processes in a group and the management of communication between the instructor and students, and between the students themselves, and usually carried out in a short period of time. (Kitaigorodskaia, 1986: 4–5)[3]

The particular feature of focusing instruction on active communication between and among the participants in the classroom – rather than on the more passive reception of information via teacher-centered grammar explanations, decontextualized drills or other forms of 'practice' common to non-communicative forms of instruction – is central to the Soviet intensive model, and features prominently in the Intensive courses developed at UT Austin.

Other contributors to the pedagogy surrounding intensive instruction included Passov, who also challenged common beliefs and classroom practices in Soviet-era language teaching. Among his many contributions to the literature on intensive instruction, Passov (1977: 17) was among the first to articulate the imperative to consider the psycho-cognitive side of language learning: 'one must study not the language, but how to think in a given language. And since thinking is based on concepts, the concepts should be interpreted'.[4] He also contributed significantly to the now generally accepted practice of using materials from the target culture in the classroom to increase understanding and cultural competence in the learner:

> The idea is that language-based visual materials should be *in the fore* [of instruction]. As visual aids one can use: 1) narrative paintings or series; 2) objects and their use; 3) models; 4) static films and motion pictures. These are what is meant by *illustrative visual materials*. (Passov, 1997: 109)[5]

Passov's contentions regarding the use of authentic materials, especially visual materials, remain to this day a major tenet of proficiency-oriented instruction in general and intensive instruction in particular.

Even in the early 1990s, after the collapse of the Soviet Union, the intensive methodology made its way into a variety of post-Soviet materials produced for foreign students studying Russian language and culture in Russia. Textbooks such as *A Month in Moscow: An Intensive Course of Russian* (Alekseev *et al.*, 1993) demonstrated major shifts in traditional curricular models of, for example, the presentation of grammatical, phonetic and lexical material. The bulk of these subjects were relegated to home assignments left for the student to cover before the following class, a characteristic of Kitaigorodskaia's method as well. However, much of the 'intensive' quality of Alekseev's volume relies on the fact that it is designed for use in-country, that is, in a Russian-speaking immersion environment, and as the single subject of instruction. Students in such a class would be taking no other concurrent courses.

Such a format of instruction was characteristic of a number Soviet and post-Soviet intensive models (Zakharova, 2014), relying heavily on an immersion environment in order to create the environment for accelerated, or intensive, learning. In an attempt to reimagine such *intensive* courses as *Intensive* ones in the UT Austin model, however, the immersion experience needed to be translated into a semi-immersion experience, using considerable realia and authentic materials and experiences to give the students in Texas a virtual in-country experience without leaving Austin. Once again, the combined practices of the existing Flagship programs at UT Austin provided exemplary practices in using such materials in their courses. In addition, in-class and at-home applications of networked technologies, from internet to digital media, facilitated this transformation of the courses into semi-immersion experiences. The use of technology in Intensive instruction is discussed in greater detail below.

Still, it is not accidental that the intensive methods of the late Soviet period continue to inform the current movement to 'intensify' instruction, in a variety of languages, not only at UT Austin, but also at other institutions such as Arizona State University, Portland State University and Middlebury College. These institutions have all implemented intensive language courses that utilize methods and practices that began as part of the Soviet model. As early as 1970, pedagogical recommendations for intensifying, i.e. increasing the effectiveness and efficiency of, the process of language learning began to appear in the Soviet academic press. Among these, Lapidus (1970) was prescient in his vision for restructuring the language classroom to optimize the acquisition of oral production skills. A number of his recommendations are at the core of new Intensive courses being adopted at institutions like the University of Texas. Specifically, Lapidus (1970: 3)[6] emphasizes, 'Intensifying the learning process means to increase its effectiveness, its "productivity" *without* an increase in contact hours allotted for a given subject [emphasis mine TJG]', which became one of the foundational tenets of the new Intensive courses. He goes on to identify the characteristics of the 'intensive' classroom, which remain at the heart of the current Intensive model in use at UT Austin: (1) the creation and use of the most effective communicative exercises to make the language material active; (2) the design of an 'intensive' classroom, i.e. one packed with a variety of ever-changing modalities and types of activities; and (3) a significant increase in the quantity and efficacy of the students' extracurricular contact and work with the language and culture. Forty years ahead of his time, Lapidus could have written these mandates in regard to language teaching pedagogy in wide use today.

Lessons from the Flagship Model

As the first student cohorts were completing the initial Flagship experience in the United States in 2006, significant shifts in the pedagogy underlying the refashioned curricula, materials and classrooms inherent in the Flagship model began to be identified. In describing the experience of the first Russian Flagship programs, Davidson (2006) commented:

> The domestic Flagship Centers ensure that [Flagship] Program participants maximize exposure to authentic language through study in courses reflecting the best current thinking on adult second language acquisition, the relative contributions of implicit and explicit learning, form-focused, task-oriented models, discourse and speech genre development. (Davidson, 2006: 5)

To this directive concerning second language acquisition and pedagogy, Nugent (2007: 2), the first director of the Language Flagship program in the National Security Education Program of the US Department of Defense, commented, 'As the name "Flagship" connotes, our purpose is to remain at the vanguard of language learning by fostering innovation and setting clear entry and exit standards for comprehensive, professional language education' (Murphy et al., this volume). To those ends, Flagship programs nationally created innovative and effective standards-based language programs that focused their efforts on student progress toward established proficiency and professional goals. Those creating Flagship-like programs within the constraints, both institutional and budgetary, of most typical language programs within US academic institutions can adapt three fundamental characteristics of the federally funded programs, which can be adapted at little or no additional cost: (1) transforming curricula to reflect 'flipped' or high-interaction classrooms and a blended/hybrid approach to instruction with the incorporation of instructional technology; (2) creating student-centered programs through individualized instruction and portfolios; and (3) creating short-term or summer study abroad opportunities for students to reinforce and advance their proficiency gains from the Intensive experience.

Flipped, blended/hybrid classes and technology

The UT Austin Flagship-like Intensive model draws heavily on the successful experiences and results of the Flagship model in general, and the specific case of its own Arabic Flagship Program in particular. One of the hallmarks of the Arabic Flagship and, indeed, increasingly part of many proficiency-based classrooms, is the use of a blended, or hybrid, approach to delivering instruction. Gleason (2013: 323) offers a concise and useful definition: 'Blended (or hybrid) foreign language (FL) courses, commonly defined as those that include both a face-to-face (f2f) and a technology-enhanced component, continue to change the ways that students experience language learning'. For the Arabic Flagship, the blended orientation begins typically with the use of textbook, computer-accessed audio and video and online resources, such as *Al-Kitaab* and the UT Austin-produced listening comprehension website 'Aswaat Arabiyya' in the course of a single class session. These different types of 'texts' occur in various modalities and address various types of language processing. In between the diverse delivery of texts, students interact with them through rapid and continuous production, sometimes with the instructor, sometimes with another student, but always focusing on meaningful, i.e. contextualized and result-oriented, communication.

As blended or hybrid courses modeled on the curriculum of the Arabic Flagship, all Intensive courses at UT Austin make extensive use of technology, especially internet resources, both in class and for assignments out of class. The heavy reliance on online assignments to compensate for the number of contact hours necessary to enable students to reach appropriate proficiency levels raises questions about the efficacy of the technology in language teaching and learning. Crucial to the use of relevant technologies in Intensive courses is the fundamental refashioning of how we view the entire language classroom and the delivery and reception of course materials. In this connection, Noblitt (2005) makes a strong case for the shift to more technological interfaces in language instruction:

> The familiar skill methodologies that have been worked out in the language classroom – speaking, listening, reading and writing – must be reassessed for online implementation. The traditional learning environment has provided for the processes of reception learning (primarily through lectures and books), tutoring, and learning by doing; while primary and secondary sources, reference materials, and tools for learning have defined content. Information technology has not

only increased access to primary materials, it has also greatly increased capabilities for peer-to-peer communication. (Noblitt, 2005: 140)

Implicit in Noblitt's commentary is the suggestion that integrating instructional technology into foreign language curricula and classrooms requires not simply a transfer of existing materials onto electronic platforms or formats; rather, it involves a sea change in how both learners and instructors regard the entire language and culture learning process, from a reliance on the reception of material to its production. Moreover, he sees a shift in the opportunities for communication to occur in a variety of settings, both in and out of class.

The most significant departure of the Intensive model from a traditional language course is the implementation of the reversed, or flipped, classroom model for instruction. This model has recently gained increasing familiarity, if not popularity, thanks in large part to a *New York Times* article in 2012 (Fitzpatrick, 2012) and a more extended discussion of the flipped classroom in *The Chronicle of Higher Education* that same year (Berrett, 2012). These writers described innovative experiments in education in which lectures and ancillary materials for a given course were given to the student to listen to and review at home in advance of a rigorous and highly participatory discussion in the following class. Alvarez (2012: 18) summed up the flipped classrooms as 'Homework in class, lessons at home'. For the language classroom, the flipped model means that the bulk of overt instruction of grammar, phonetics and lexicon is relegated to outside of class time, requiring students to make extensive use of the commentaries and explanations in their textbook, digital recordings of faculty or other online presentations of relevant material, ancillary material for practicing and explaining the material individually in advance of the class meeting. Class time, then, is spent almost entirely in actively engaging the students, individually and in groups, with the material covered prior to entering the classroom.

For some language instructors, the idea of relegating the introduction of the lion's share of new linguistic and lexical material to the student outside of class is anathema to what is familiar to them. But Talbert (2014), who has grappled with the flipped classroom movement and documented it in a series of articles, neatly identifies the underlying pedagogical goal of the flipped classroom:

A misconception about the flipped classroom itself, that it is a pedagogy of abandonment, where students are loaded up with books and videos but then left to fend for themselves. This is not the intent of flipped learning at all! The idea in the flipped classroom is to leverage human and electronic resources to teach students how to learn for themselves. (Talbert, 2014: 3)

In terms of language instruction in the classroom, this focus on self-directed learning is an essential part of the students' training in language and culture acquisition. Moreover, the dramatic increase in face-to-face time with students in class that results from minimizing grammar explication or vocabulary drills is at the core of the Intensive classes' objective to bring the student to functional proficiency in two semesters. As Fitzpatrick (2012: 1) commented, 'the argument is that teachers do not need to be present in person when a group listens to a lecture passively – thereby saving physical classroom time for individual or small groups'.

Because the Intensive Russian program also makes extensive use of online materials, including some homework exercises and portfolio activities (see discussion of the portfolio), students in the course receive specialized instruction in Russian-language computer literacy through a self-paced online course, 'Café Russia: Get Ready, Get Set, Go!' produced in the Department of Slavic and Eurasian Studies (Garza & Cotey, 2010). The aim of this training, in addition to providing a tutorial on using the Cyrillic keyboard, is to help learners feel comfortable undertaking the kinds of online tasks that they do on a daily basis – but in Russian.

Alemán *et al.* (2009) contend that US university students spend on average 26 hours per week on social networking sites such as Facebook and Twitter. Intensive courses attempt to redirect their students' attention from the English-language sites and appropriate additional contact hours by introducing them to similar – in content and form – social networking sites, such as the Russian sites *Odnoklassniki, V kontakte* and *Chik-chirik*. By mastering basic skills in Russian computer literacy, the students in the Intensive courses are able navigate with relative ease and confidence entirely Russophone websites and virtual environments, providing them with access to culturally rich, authentic, contextualized materials, which they can access in or out of class at their convenience. Students are also introduced to Russian websites that parallel popular sites they use regularly, such as kniga.ru for searching books and DVDs instead of amazon.com, or yandex.ru instead of google.com for basic web information searches. Students in Intensive Russian are given focused, goal-oriented, task-based projects throughout the course that require the use of sites such as these to help learners gain confidence and facility in using the Russian-language sites instead of their English-language counterparts.

Each of the above resources is an integral part of one of the Intensive language courses at UT Austin, incorporating instructional technologies that are aligned with the objectives and proficiency goals of each course. Such online materials, characteristic of hybrid classes, make it possible to execute the flipped design of the course: facilitating meaningful and contextualized use of the language and culture outside of class and providing students with opportunities both to understand new material and to practice and review material already covered. All of these out-of-class contact hours with the language are part of the Intensive courses' objective of creating independent, autonomous learners who are not only unafraid, but eager to explore the language on their own, well beyond the parameters of the course syllabus.

Focus on the learner: Student-centered instruction and portfolios

Among the best practices that emerged from the early years of the proficiency movement in the late 1980s was the creation of communicative activities for use in the classroom, activities designed to elicit what Rivers (1983: 55) called 'autonomous interaction', or spontaneous expression in the language. Decades later, as the Flagship created programs dedicated to bringing learners to the superior level of proficiency, autonomous interaction became a critical goal on the way to the attainment of global professional proficiency, or the ability to function professionally in the linguistic, cultural and social environment of an in-country workplace. Successful programs within the Flagship cohort understood the importance of creating student-centered activities and opportunities to individualize the content and mode of communication to fit the varied professional objectives in the class. Such instruction is also a key factor in the Intensive courses, which attract students from a wide variety of disciplines, majors and backgrounds.

As part of the student-centered orientation of the Intensive Russian course, for example, individual student portfolios are compiled throughout the semester. To encourage students to understand the value and importance of the portfolio assignment as part of the larger integrated course curriculum, the final project is weighted as 20% of the final course grade. Over the years that the Intensive Russian course has been offered at UT Austin, the portfolios themselves have undergone significant transformation as students have become more familiar with constructing a portfolio as part of their instruction and assessment. In the first year of the course, portfolios took the form of a physical notebook or folder with individual print items reflecting the various activities that the students had performed. In subsequent years, portfolios frequently became digital presentations of much more varied collections of materials, including student-produced audio and video clips, web materials and weblogs of interactions with e-pals in Russia. Such materials might be turned in on thumb drives, or more often as URLs for student-built websites of the portfolio project.

The portfolio projects begin with a series of instructor-produced prompts that are organized to complement the grammatical, lexical and thematic subject matter of the basic textbooks used in the course, *Russian Stage One: Live from Russia!* (Lekic *et al.*, 2009), and *Russian Stage Two:*

Welcome Back! (Martin & Dolgova, 2010). These prompts are posted on the class Canvas[7] website as the group moves through the syllabus. Each prompt directs the student to a live Russian website, provides instructions on what specifically to do within the site and then a level-appropriate task to complete based on the material contained on the site. For example, early in the first semester, while discussing the theme of living spaces in Russia (apartments, furniture, rooms, etc.), the student might be directed to a Russian website for a furniture store. The overall appearance may be daunting to the student, with the bulk of the language on the screen being unknown, but the accompanying task is doable: 'Furnish your ideal dorm room or apartment with furniture from the site. Make a list of what pieces go into each room, its color and price'. Since the task is focused on material lexically and thematically familiar to the learners, they are comfortable scanning the site for the items needed; they simultaneously become acquainted with the layout of Russian websites and develop the confidence to explore on their own.

Students in the course must produce at least 12 entries in their portfolios by the end of the first semester. Six of these entries must come from the portfolio assignments on the Canvas website; the remaining six entries are to demonstrate other instances of Russian language and culture exposure outside of class. They may include a short synopsis of a Russian film or television program they viewed, a summary of an informal conversation with a native speaker of Russian over coffee, a printout of an email correspondence with a Russian student in Moscow, etc. Such entries allow learners to direct their efforts toward topics and tasks that reflect their individual interests and strengths in the language, emphasizing the student-centered focus of the course and, like earlier Soviet iterations of intensive methods, attempting to keep language-learning anxiety to a minimum.

Integrated study abroad programs

One of the most lauded parts of the Flagship student's experience is the Flagship capstone overseas program. Past participants of the capstone are eager to praise the overseas program and the contribution it made to their overall acquisition of the language. One past participant remarked:

> My experiences in the overseas program immensely improved my target language and helped me to grow as a person. I encountered many language and living challenges that truly helped me to become a more mature, stronger, and diversified person. The overseas Flagship program offers a truly unique opportunity that is second to none. (thelanguageflagship.org)

Comments like this are typical: students see their time abroad as a confirmation of their intensive study of the language and culture. While an academic year-long overseas program may be out of reach and unfeasible for many institutions and for many students, the creation of integrated short-term or summer programs presents a productive alternative within a Flagship-like Intensive program.

At UT Austin, several of the Intensive language programs have organized and conducted summer abroad programs designed to continue the two-semester Intensive experience through the end of the academic year. Though these programs are open to all students at the university, their content and structure are specifically designed to articulate with the year-long Intensive courses that precede them. While such short-term programs cannot boast the acculturation and proficiency gains of the academic-year overseas experience, even these shorter programs have become essential parts of the Intensive courses at UT Austin. They have also produced a number of results that reflect the overall success of the students in the Intensive courses.

The Intensive French program invites its students to continue their study of the language and culture at their French summer program in the city of Lyon. This intensive language and culture program is directed by the Department of French and Italian in cooperation with the Université Jean Moulin. The program provides students the opportunity to live and study in France for seven weeks; two UT Austin French faculty members accompany the group. This Lyon program has become a popular 'third semester' for its Intensive course students, who want to reinforce their language skills and cultural literacy before continuing with third-year French the following fall.

The Department of French and Italian also directs the Rome study program, an intensive Italian language and culture program open to all undergraduate and graduate students of UT Austin. The Rome study program gives students of all majors the opportunity to study six weeks in the Italian capital during the summer, while visiting other historic Italian sites on weekends. Italian families host students and provide a first-hand cultural experience of Italian daily life and the language in use. Like the Lyon program, the Rome program has become popular with students who have completed the two-semester Intensive Italian course.

For students of Russian, the Moscow Plus program offers students five weeks of study at Moscow International University. This program provides a 'bridge course' designed to reinforce and enhance skills acquired in prior coursework in order to ensure a smooth transition into the next level of instruction for students who have completed either the Intensive Russian course or two years of Russian in another format. The course, entitled 'Walking through Moscow' ['Ia shagaiu po Moskve'], uses the physical city and sites of everyday interaction as the classroom for students at the end of each week. After learning and practicing appropriate speech and cultural patterns in class for interactions in specific settings in the city, such as ordering a meal or making a purchase, the students go out to the site with the instructor and practice their Russian. Sites from past summers have included a restaurant, a department store, a theatre, the metro, a chocolate factory, a radio station, a newspaper publisher and a police station.

Preparing Instructors for Intensive Instructors

Without question, key to the success of Intensive language courses is the preparation of instructors to create, lead and conduct assessment in such courses. The rapid pace of both conducting the class and moving through material is daunting, even to the most seasoned language professional, as much of the traditional wisdom of classroom presentation and practice of material does not transfer entirely to the Intensive learning environment. Thus, whether in-service or pre-service, appropriate professional development for instructors of Intensive language courses is essential.

Even as Soviet iterations of intensive instruction began to spread in the 1990s, the necessity for special teacher preparation was critical. As Kitaigorodskaia (1992: 229) remarks, 'Recently, the need for special training of teachers to implement the system of intensive foreign language instruction is felt acutely'.[8] In a similar vein, at the Texas Language Summit at University of Texas,[9] one of the final recommendations of the Language Roadmap for the 21st Century: Texas (2007) emphasized the need to refashion traditional teacher preparation into a program that takes into consideration the much more integrated and content-driven curriculum required for proficiency outcomes for today's language courses:

> The [current state and national] standards themselves will be used to reframe the teacher education curriculum to better inculcate best practices that are effective for implementing early language learning programs and extended sequences. A focus on content-based instruction, a contextualized, input-rich learning environment, and the integration of culture throughout the curriculum will be required to create a setting in which learners can attain the desired advanced linguistic and cultural proficiency levels. (Language Roadmap for the 21st Century: Texas, 2007: 16)

Teacher education and professional development programs that focus on the kind of instruction and environment that the Flagship and, in turn, Intensive language courses strive to create must thus be considered in tandem with curriculum and materials development.

As the courses of Intensive Russian were expanded to all five sections in fall 2012 and graduate student assistant instructors (AIs) assumed teaching responsibilities for the course, the imperative to redesign and administer an extensive program of teacher preparation quickly became apparent. While all five AIs were experienced in teaching the 'traditional' four-semester sequence of Russian, none had taught the Intensive curriculum in the new, two-semester, six-hour-per-week format. Teacher training sessions were therefore conducted in the summer prior to the start of the fall Intensive Russian courses. These sessions began with detailed explanations of the differences between Intensive and non-Intensive instruction, and how the syllabus must reflect this essential characteristic of the course. Veteran instructors of the Intensive Russian course also conducted model classes with actual students to demonstrate the very high level of interaction that must occur in every class session, and how to facilitate communication between and among students in a variety of activities. Time was also devoted to demonstrating how best to work with the textbook and how not to resort to using it as the sole impetus for interaction in the class. Finally, a large part of the training sessions involved demonstrations of the use of various technologies and media to model speech and behavior, provoke commentary and stimulate further discussion of the material. In this connection, new instructors were also shown how to allow the learners to take control of the presentation of material through technology, to encourage them to become more responsible for the content and its use in class.

Efforts such as this are crucial first steps to preparing instructors to take over Intensive courses. Periodic two-way observation of classes once in session, with experienced teachers observing novices and novice teachers observing their more-experienced colleagues, are essential to the ongoing health and success of the course. Each of the observations should be followed by a face-to-face meeting to go over the observation and to discuss both what was particularly successful in the session and where some improvement is needed. Finally, it is helpful to create opportunities to team teach occasionally during the semester, pairing an experienced instructor with a novice. Such direct interaction is especially helpful to establish modeling of successful techniques and methods in the practices of the newer instructor.

Positive Outcomes: Preliminary Results

Since the creation of the 6/6 Intensive language model in 2009, the Office of the Dean of Liberal Arts at UT Austin has collected and assembled data from individual language departments and other administrative units that demonstrate the success of the new courses, at least in the initial years of operation. These data directly addressed some of the concerns expressed by some faculty and department chairs about the shift to a two-semester introductory sequence of languages instead of the long-established four-semester sequence. One of the first issues that emerged was the concern that a six-hour sequence was too demanding for many students' schedules, especially those in the sciences and engineering, which required blocks of time each week for laboratory sessions. But as shown in Table 11.1, a survey of the decade 2003–2013 of student credit hours (SCHs) in all courses in the College of Liberal Arts and the corresponding percentage of those hours taken in introductory language courses indicates that the change in the overall percentage of SCHs remained virtually unchanged from the years before 2009, the implementation of the Intensive courses and in the years since.

After an initial 1.55% drop in total SCHs for language classes in the first year of the new Intensive courses, the change in the number of SCHs for language courses has remained stable over the past decade. Students appear to be unaffected by the change in the number of classroom hours that the Intensive courses require, adjusting their schedules accordingly to accommodate the daily meetings of their language classes.

As other language programs at UT Austin began to consider whether or not to change their curricula to the 6/6 model, data from the first years of Intensive language courses began to emerge that revealed an unexpected positive consequence: greater retention of students into the advanced-level language courses (third year). Table 11.2 shows the rate of retention for all students over four academic years from fall 2009 to spring 2013; from the end of the 'traditional', or four-semester, sequences and intensive, or two-semester sequences, into third-year advanced language classes.

These results show that overwhelmingly more students from the Intensive courses elected to continue with the study of their respective language (53%) than did students who had completed a traditional four-semester sequence (26%). Given the imperative of the Flagship

Table 11.1 SCHs produced by introductory language sequences

Years	Total undergrad SCHs	Total for lang intro sequence	% of SCHs for intro languages	% change
2003–2004	386,142	61,629	15.96	N/A
2004–2005	375,093	59,630	15.90	−0.06
2005–2006	361.031	56,639	15.69	−0.21
2006–2007	358,975	58,394	16.27	0.58
2007–2008	361,734	59,383	16.42	0.15
2008–2009	347,721	59,000	16.97	0.55
2009–2010	344,404	53,108	15.42	−1.55
2010–2011	335,548	52,050	15.51	0.09
2011–2012	328,162	52,688	16.06	0.54
2012–2013	331,452	52,537	15.85	−0.20

Table 11.2 Comparison of retention rates into advanced courses after standard and Intensive course sequences

Language	'Traditional' 4th-sem. retention rate (%)	Intensive 2nd-sem. retention rate (%)	+/- differential
Arabic	52	78	+26
French	40	81	+41
Hebrew	35	72	+37
Italian	25	71	+46
Persian	28	81	+53
Russian	36	77	+41
Turkish	36	73	+37

programs and the Intensive programs to bring students not only to functional proficiency, but also to professional proficiency, this finding is particularly salient. If, for example, students completed an Intensive language course in their first year in college, and then continued to study that language in a standard four-year undergraduate program, they could expect to have enough advanced courses and study abroad experience to attain these levels.

Next Steps: Flagship-Like Programs and Accreditation

Outcomes of the Intensive language programs implemented at the University of Texas, from proficiency gains to student retention, demonstrate the positive effects of adapting the methods and practices of the Flagship model to other programs. The documented success of more than a decade of Flagship programs nationwide across languages in bringing an overwhelming majority of its students to a level of professional proficiency in a variety of commonly and less commonly taught languages has provided the language teaching profession with a host of classroom and extracurricular practices, curricular innovations and assessment tools to reimagine and refashion language programs nationally (Fodel, 2012; Spellings & Oldham, 2008). But beyond the invaluable best practices that Flagship programs have provided, they have also demonstrated the inherent benefits of language programs that adhere to common yardsticks by which programs set goals and measure and assess progress: among these yardsticks are standards for determining student proficiency gains, assessing the success of curricular models and materials and evaluating faculty development.

In October 2013, faculty and administrative representatives from Flagship and non-Flagship language programs throughout the United States met for two days at UT Austin to discuss learning objectives common to these and other language programs. Participants decided to establish a national organization that would promote the kind of standards-based language programs that the Flagship supported for more than a decade. In May 2014, Partners for Languages in the United States (PLUS) was established at the Texas Language Center at UT Austin. PLUS is a not-for-profit, membership-based organization designed to take language education at US institutions to a new level of effectiveness, relevance and responsiveness. The goal of PLUS is to build a coalition of established and aspiring language programs into a nationwide system of successful programs unified by a common set of professional standards and rigorous accountability. These standards were prepared by language professionals from across the United States, representing a variety of institutions and programs, including Flagship programs. Through peer review and accreditation of national language programs, PLUS seeks to recognize the highest standards in teaching and learning to advance the use of languages in all domains and at all levels, including the highest professional usage.

Such a move to establish a national membership organization of institutions that seek to provide first-rate language education to prepare global professionals is the first step toward creating a permanent legacy of the Flagship programs. The Flagship paved the way for university language programs to innovate and create rigorous and demanding courses of domestic and overseas study to meet the need for multilingual global professionals. New iterations of Flagship-like Intensive courses, such as those at UT Austin, give non-Flagship programs the ability to address and meet this need within the institutional and fiscal constraints of contemporary academia. Together they provide students and programs alike with the opportunity to raise a symbolic flag over professional proficiency, once commonly thought to be a goal attainable only by a small number of learners (Leaver & Shekhtman, 2002), and to keep that flag flying for generations to come.

Notes

(1) 'Standards based' refers to types of instruction, assessment and outcomes that are based on the learner's ability to demonstrate measurable knowledge and skills related to the language being studied. For most language programs, both US and international, a set of accepted guidelines, such as the ACTFL Proficiency Guidelines or the Common European Framework of Reference (CEFR), are utilized to inform the assessment of student outcomes.

(2) US federal agencies determine certain non-Western European languages as 'critical' to US national security, such as Arabic, Chinese, Hindi and Russian.

(3) Под интенсивным обучением иностранному языку мы понимаем обучение, направленное на не используемые в обычном обучении психологические резервы личности и деятельности учащихся, в особенности – на управление

социально-психологическими процессами в группе и управление общением преподавателя с учащимися и учащихся между собой, и обычно осуществляемое в сжатые сроки.

(4)   […] надо обучать не языку, а мышлению на данном языке. А поскольку мышление основано на понятиях, то следует толковать понятия.

(5)   Речь идёт о том, что *на первом плане* должна быть языковая наглядность. В качестве же вспомогательных сресвт могут использоваться: (1) сюжетные картины и их серии; (2) предметы и действия с ними; (3) макеты; (4) диафильмы и кинофильмы.

(6)   Интенсифицировать учебный процесс – значит добиться повышения его 'производительности' без повышения количества часов, отводимых на данный учебный предмет.

(7)   Canvas is the name of the cloud-hosted learning management system, much like Blackboard, used at UT Austin and a number of other US universities.

(8)   Необходимость в специальной организации подготовки преподавателей к внедрению системы интенсивного обучения иностранным языкам ощущается особо остро в последнее время.

(9)   UT Austin was selected as one of three US institutions to participate in the federally funded 2007 US Language Summits project. The goal of this project was to address the economic, social and cultural imperatives for language skills and to develop a set of state and local 'roadmaps' toward the effective incorporation of language education into the US education system at all levels.

References

Alekseev, V.A., Alekseeva, N.I. and Rumiantseva, N.M. (1993) *Mesiats v Moskve: Intensivnyi kurs russkogo iazyka* [*A Month in Moscow: An Intensive course of Russian*]. Moscow: Izdatel'stvo Rossiiskogo universiteta druzhby narodov.

Alemán, A.M. and Wartman, K. (2009) *Online Social Networking on Campus: Understanding What Matters in Student Culture*. London: Routledge.

Alvarez, B. (2012) Flipping the classroom: Homework in class, lessons at home. *Education Digest* 77 (8), 18–21.

Beale, L. (2010) U.S. students hurting in foreign languages. *Pacific Standard*. See http://www.psmag.com/books-and-culture/u-s-students-hurting-in-foreign-languages-13529 (accessed 5 May 2015).

Berman, R.A. (2011) The real language crisis. *Academe: Bulletin of the American Association of University Professors* 97 (5), 30–34.

Berrett, D. (2012) How 'flipping' the classroom can improve the traditional lecture. *The Chronicle of Higher Education*, 19 February 2012. See http://chronicle.com/article/How-Flipping-the-Classroom/130857/ (accessed 20 May 2014).

Davidson, D.E. (2006) The national Flagship program in Russian: Preparing Americans for level 3 proficiency and beyond. *NewsNet: News of the American Association for the Advancement of Slavic Studies* 45 (3), 1–5.

Demuth, K.A. and Smith, N.B. (1987) The foreign language requirement: An alternative program. *Foreign Language Annals* 20 (1), 67–77.

Fitzpatrick, M. (2012) Classroom lectures go digital. *The New York Times*, 24 June 2012. See http://www.nytimes.com/2012/06/25/us/25iht-educside25.html?_r=0 (accessed 20 May 2014).

Fodel, K. (2012) Breaking down language barriers. *Military Advanced Education* 7 (9), 8–10. See http://www.kmimediagroup.com/military-advanced-education/articles/447-military-advanced-education/mae-2012-volume-7-issue-9-november/6097-breaking-down-language-barriers-sp-143 (accessed 2 May 2015).

Garza, T.J. (2013) Keeping it real: Intensive instruction and the future of Russian language and culture in the US. *Russian Language Journal* 63, 7–24.

Garza, T.J. and Cotey, Y. (2010) Café Russia: Get ready, get set, go. University of Texas at Austin, Austin, TX. See http://laits.utexas.edu/cafe-russia/ (accessed 2 May 2015).

Gleason, J. (2013) Dilemmas of blended language learning: Learner and teacher experiences. *CALICO Journal* 30 (3), 323–341.

Hu, W. (2009) Foreign languages fall as schools look for cuts. *The New York Times Education.* See http://www.nytimes.com/2009/09/13/education/13language.html?_ r=0 (accessed 12 May 2015).

Interagency Language Roundtable (ILR) *Interagency Language Roundtable Skill Level Descriptions.* See http://www.govtilr.org (accessed 16 June 2015).

Jaschik, S. (2010) Disappearing languages at Albany. *Inside Higher Ed.* See https://www. insidehighered.com/news/2010/10/04/albany (accessed 1 May 2010).

Kitaigorodskaia, G.A. (1986) *Metodika intensivnogoobucheniia inostrannym iazykam* [*A Method of Intensive Instruction of Foreign Languages*]. Moscow: Vysshaia shkola.

Kitaigorodskaia, G.A. (1992) *Intensivnoe obuchenie inostrannym iazykam: Teoriia i praktika* [*Intensive Instruction in Foreign Languages: Theory and Practice*]. Moscow: Russkii iazyk.

Koebler, J. (2012) Education funding for foreign languages cut. *U.S. News & World Report Education.* See http://www.usnews.com/education/blogs/high-schoolnotes/2012/01/16/education-funding-for-foreign-languages-cut (accessed 12 May 2015).

The Language Flagship (2014) Overseas model: Quotes from students at Flagship overseas centers. See http://www.thelanguageflagship.org/content/overseas (accessed May 19, 2014).

Language Roadmap for the 21st Century: Texas. Report of the Texas Language Summit at the University of Texas at Austin (2007) University of Texas at Austin.

Lapidus, B.A. (1970) *Intensifikatsiia protsessa obucheniia inoiazychnoi ustnoi rechi: Puti i priemy* [*Intensifying the Teaching of Foreign Language Oral Speech: Ways and Means*]. Moscow: Vysshaia shkola.

Leaver, B.L. and Shekhtman, B. (2002) *Developing Professional-Level Language Proficiency.* New York: Cambridge University Press.

Lekic, M.D., Davidson, D.E. and Gor, K. (2008 and 2009) *Russian Stage One: Live from Russia! Vols. 1 and 2.* Dubuque, IA: Kendall Hunt Publishing.

Malone, M.E., Rifkin, B., Christina, D. and Johnson, D.E. (2005) Attaining high levels of proficiency: Challenges for foreign language education in the United States. *CAL Digest* Washington, DC: Center for Applied Linguistics.

Martin, C.I. and Dolgova, I.A. (2010) *Russian Stage Two: Welcome Back!* Dubuque, IA: Kendall Hunt Publishing.

McLaughlin, B. (1986) Multilingual education: Theory East and West. In B. Spolsky (ed.) *Language and Education in Multilingual Settings* (pp. 32–52). Clevedon: Multilingual Matters.

MLA Ad Hoc Committee on Foreign Languages (2007) Foreign languages and higher education: New structures for a changed world. See https://www.mla.org/flreport (accessed 28 May 2015).

Noblitt, J.S. (2005) The online language learning environment: New roles for the humanist. *Russian Language Journal* 55 (180–182), 129–142.

Nugent, M. (2007) Word from Flagship. *Discourse: Newsletter of the Language Flagship,* Fall 2007, 2.

Partners for Languages in the U.S., The University of Texas at Austin. See http://www. utexas.edu/cola/orgs/plus/ (accessed 2 May 2015).

Passov, E.I. (1977) *Osnovy metodiki obucheniia inostrannym iazykam* [*Fundamentals of Foreign Language Teaching Methodology*]. Moscow: Russkii iazyk.

Rivers, W.M. (1983) *Communicating Naturally in a Second Language: Theory and Practice in Language Teaching*. Cambridge: Cambridge University Press.

Schulz, R.A. (1979) Intensive language instruction: How and where it works. *ADFL Bulletin* 11 (2), 37–41.

Spellings, M. and Oldham, C.A. (2008) *Enhancing Foreign Language Proficiency in the United States: Preliminary Results of the National Security Language Initiative*. Washington, DC: U.S. Department of Education, Office of Postsecondary Education.

Talbert, R. (2014) Flipped learning skepticism: Can students really learn on their own? *The Chronicle of Higher Education*. 20 April 2014. See http://chronicle.com/blognetwork/castingoutnines/2014/04/30/flipped-learning-skepticism-can-students-really-learn-on-their-own/ (accessed 11 June 2014).

Texas Language Center (TLC) (2010) *Intensive Languages: High Voltage Learning*. Austin, TX: University of Texas.

Zakharova, E.V. (2014) *Soviet, Russian and American Developments in Intensive Instruction: A Movement towards Practical Application*. PhD dissertation, University of Texas at Austin.

Zehr, M.A. (2011) Foreign language programs stung by federal budget cuts. *Education Week* 30 (33), 19.

Conclusion

Karen Evans-Romaine and Dianna Murphy

The Language Flagship represents a major innovation in foreign language education at the post-secondary level in the United States. Contributors to this volume have explored many different aspects of this innovation: the rationale and history of the federal program (Chapter 1); models for Flagship program design (Chapter 2); curricular strategies to promote interdisciplinary learning (Chapter 3) and learner independence (Chapter 4); co-curricular enhancements such as telecollaboration (Chapter 5), online language cafés (Chapter 6) and professional overseas internships (Chapter 9). Contributors also shared findings from research studies that investigated diverse topics such as heritage language learners in Language Flagship programs (Chapter 7), oral proficiency development in telecollaborative learning (Chapter 5), the development of intercultural competence in an overseas immersion setting (Chapter 8) and alumni perceptions of the impact of the Language Flagship program (Chapter 10). Application of Language Flagship design principles to non-Flagship language programs is the subject of the final chapter (Chapter 11).

Authors of these chapters met in person at two annual Language Flagship national meetings to discuss the goals of the volume and to provide input and feedback on each other's work. The collegiality with which authors approached this undertaking is, in our experience as directors of one Flagship program at one university, emblematic of the initiative more broadly: faculty and staff involved in Language Flagship programs are passionate about undergraduate language teaching and learning, and they are eager both to share ideas and to learn from others. It is in the spirit of sharing that we decided to conclude this collection with a brief discussion of some of the challenges that we have collectively faced in designing, implementing and sustaining Flagship programs at our universities.

The most obvious challenges are curricular. All Flagship programs must develop new advanced-level courses and co-curricular enhancements for students at higher levels of proficiency, far beyond what had been offered in the past. Many programs have also had to redesign the curriculum at lower levels of instruction. Determining the focus of new courses, and the sequencing and articulation of new and existing courses, is an undertaking that requires a tremendous amount of time, expertise and goodwill on the part of a team willing to dedicate sustained effort to the project. A related challenge is the need to develop new materials. For many of the languages that we teach, there is a dearth of textbooks or other instructional materials for students beyond Interagency Language Roundtable (ILR) 1: many Flagship programs have developed their own curricular materials and even written and published new textbooks. All programs have developed strategies for promoting interdisciplinary language learning, described in Chapter 3 of this volume. Other forms of curricular enhancements – on campus, during study abroad and in collaboration with partner institutions abroad – are discussed in Chapters 2, 6, 7, 9 and 11.

At many of our universities, Flagship programs coexist alongside more traditionally designed language majors, minors and the courses that support them. Flagship instructors often face the challenge of needing to differentiate instruction, as one language class might include Flagship students, students majoring or minoring in the second language (L2) and students pursuing language study but not a degree in the L2. As separate Flagship classes are not always possible, the traditional third- or fourth-year foreign language course in particular can become even more challenging than usual, with students with no study abroad experience (and perhaps no interest in or no possibility of studying abroad) together with students who have studied the language overseas for a summer or longer. Providing differentiated instruction to diverse groups of students requires careful curricular planning, flexible classroom tasks and homework assignments and skilled use of paired and small-group instruction in order to take advantage of the greater mix of language abilities and cultural knowledge. Faculty teaching in overseas institutions face similar issues in accommodating diverse groups of US students who may have similar levels of proficiency in the L2 at the beginning of the capstone overseas program, but, coming from different US universities, have had very different curricular experiences.

Finally, there are time constraints for students, faculty and staff alike. In order for students to achieve ILR 2 proficiency by the time of application to Flagship capstone overseas programs, they must have access to, and be able to enroll in, far more instructional contact hours than are typical even for most US undergraduate majors. It can be extremely difficult for US undergraduates, especially those majoring in coursework-intensive fields such as engineering, or who work many hours in addition to going to school, to dedicate the time required by Flagship programs for intensive language study, during both the academic year and summer, on their home US campus and overseas, for the four to five years – and occasionally longer – that it takes for students to complete the program.

The challenge most frequently cited by Flagship directors is often linked to curricular challenges, but is not as immediately obvious: the need for strong and sustained local institutional support for the program. This support begins in the academic department in which the program is housed: as Chapters 1 and 11 imply, there can be a mix of enthusiasm for and resistance to change in the way language is taught and student learning is assessed, both within one department and across foreign language departments at one university. The introduction of a program like the Language Flagship involves, at the very least, careful and tactful discussions with colleagues who may feel that a more broad interdisciplinary approach to language teaching could threaten or undermine the study of literature, in order to convey that ILR 3 proficiency includes deep knowledge of language and culture, often expressed most powerfully through literature.

Necessary institutional support must also come from faculty and instructional staff outside of the department who are open to engaging in long-term collaboration requiring the investment of time and funding, both of which can be in short supply. The Flagship goal of training professionals in a wide variety of disciplines involves collaboration with colleagues in non-language departments whose faculty, instructors or graduate teaching assistants could teach courses, units or independent studies in their area of specialization in the L2. Such innovation has its costs: not only must there be interest in the collaboration, but also an instructor's department must have the means to provide the necessary course or partial course release. For this kind of program to be successful, collaboration must extend to units responsible for undergraduate student advising, student housing, study abroad and financial aid. Directors and staff of Flagship programs report that ongoing communication with many other units is critical to maintaining these collaborative relationships. Initial negotiations with cooperating units, both curricular and administrative, are not sufficient: constant contact with these units is vital in order to convey the importance of the program for its participants, for the units involved and for alumni.

Finally, institutional support must also come from the academic leadership of the university: campus leaders such as provosts and deans must be willing to help sustain a program that enrolls relatively small numbers of students, especially in courses at the upper levels of instruction in the L2. This institutional support must include direct financial support for instruction and administration. In addition, students need access to scholarships and other forms of financial aid to enable them to devote summers (a time when many students work to earn money to pay for tuition and living expenses in the upcoming academic year) to intensive domestic or overseas L2 study, to participate in overseas programs with tuition and fees that may surpass those at the students' home university and, for many students, to devote a fifth or even sixth year to their undergraduate education. The federal Language Flagship scholarships can defray some of those costs to students, but do not completely cover them.

These challenges, related to curricular innovation, instructional materials development, institutional and budgetary constraints and the need for collegial and institutional support, not to mention those related to assessment of student learning, articulation (both between courses and between domestic and overseas programs of study), student retention and attrition, professional and pedagogical training of instructional staff, student career advising and placement and student security and safety overseas, among many other areas, could provide enough material for a separate volume. We mention in these concluding remarks just a few challenges, shared with us by authors of this volume, in part to acknowledge to readers that the process of engaging in the kind of effort required to establish and sustain Language Flagship programs has not always been smooth. While the Language Flagship has accomplished much in its short history, there is much left to be done for our future and the future of our students. Yet, the very experience of working with students who intend to reach a professional level of language proficiency, and maintaining contact with alumni who have achieved that goal and work in a variety of professional settings, is tremendously inspiring. This book came into being because of the authors' belief that many lessons learned from the Language Flagship can be applied broadly. We look forward to continuing to learn from each other and from our students, to developing new approaches to the teaching and learning of language and culture and to sharing our experiences and findings with colleagues in and outside Flagship programs in the years to come.

Appendix A

Comparison of the Proficiency Scales of the American Council on the Teaching of Foreign Languages and the US Interagency Language Roundtable

Two major scales for measuring functional language abilities are widely used in the United States today. The first is the scale developed by the Interagency Language Roundtable (ILR), an organization of federal US government agencies established to coordinate and share information related to languages (Interagency Language Roundtable, n.d.). Initially based on level descriptions and an oral interview assessment protocol developed in the 1950s by the Foreign Service Institute in the US Department of State, the ILR scale is used primarily by US government agencies to measure the language proficiency of personnel, employment applicants and participants in US government-sponsored programs. The second scale, the *ACTFL Proficiency Guidelines* (ACTFL, 1982, 1986, 2012; Breiner-Sanders *et al.*, 2000, 2002; Breiner-Sanders *et al.*, 2002), was developed by the American Council on the Teaching of Foreign Languages (ACTFL), based on the ILR scale and adapted for educational contexts. The ACTFL Proficiency Guidelines are frequently used in US educational institutions at the secondary and post-secondary level (See Table A.1 for a comparison of the two scales.)

Table A.1 Comparison of the ACTFL and ILR Scales

	ACTFL1	*ILR2*
Novice	Novice Low (NL)	0 (No Proficiency)
	Novice Mid (NM)	
	Novice High (NH)	0+ (Memorized Proficiency)
Intermediate	Intermediate Low (IL)	1 (Elementary Proficiency)
	Intermediate Mid (IM)	
	Intermediate High (IH)	1+ (Elementary Proficiency, Plus)
Advanced	Advanced Low (AL)	2 (Limited Working Proficiency)
	Advanced Mid (AM)	
	Advanced High (AH)	2+ (Limited Working Proficiency, Plus)
Superior (S)		3 (General Professional Proficiency)
3+ (General Professional Proficiency, Plus)		
Distinguished (D)		4 (Advanced Professional Proficiency)
4+ (Advanced Professional Proficiency, Plus)		
5 (Functionally Native Proficiency)		

Both scales include descriptions of levels for different skill areas (speaking, listening, reading and writing.) As Kagan and Martin (this volume) note, the ILR has also recently developed a scale to describe levels of competence in intercultural communication. The structure and protocol for administering and rating Oral Proficiency Interviews (OPIs) differs between the ILR and ACTFL scales, as does the differentiation of functional abilities, with the ACTFL scale providing greater differentiation at lower levels and the ILR at higher levels. For more detailed comparisons of the ACTFL and ILR scales, see, for example, Malone and Montee (2010).

Notes

(1) The ACTFL Proficiency Guidelines (1982, 1986, 2012) are published online by ACTFL. See www.actfl.org/publications/guidelines-and-manuals/actfl-proficiency-guidelines-2012.
(2) Detailed information about the ILR scale can be found online. See www.govtilr.org/Skills/ILRscale1.htm

References

American Council on the Teaching of Foreign Languages (ACTFL) (1982) ACTFL Provisional Proficiency Guidelines 1985. Yonkers, NY: ACTFL.
American Council on the Teaching of Foreign Languages (ACTFL) (1986) ACTFL Proficiency Guidelines 1986. Yonkers, NY: ACTFL.
American Council on the Teaching of Foreign Languages (ACTFL) (2012) ACTFL Proficiency Guidelines 2012. See http://www.actfl.org/sites/default/files/pdfs/public/ACTFLProficiencyGuidelines2012_FINAL.pdf (accessed 15 June 2015).
Breiner-Sanders, K.E., Lowe, P., Miles, J., and Swender, E. (2000) ACTFL proficiency guidelines-speaking: Revised 1999. Foreign Language Annals, 33 (1), 13–18.
Breiner-Sanders, K.E., Swender, E., and Terry, R. (2002) Preliminary proficiency guidelines–writing: Revised 2001. Foreign Language Annals, 35 (1) 9–15.
Interagency Language Roundtable (ILR) (n.d.) About the ILR. See www.govtilr.org/skills/irl scale history.htm (accessed 17 September 2015).
Malone, M. and Montee, M. (2010) Oral proficiency assessment: Current approaches and applications for post-secondary foreign language programs. Language and Linguistics Compass 4 (10), 972–986.

Appendix B

US and Overseas Universities with Language Flagship Programs[1]

Arabic
    University of Arizona
    University of Maryland, College Park
    University of Oklahoma
    University of Texas, Austin
    Arab-American Language Institute in Morocco (AALIM) in partnership with Moulay Ismail University, Morocco*

Chinese
    Arizona State University
    Brigham Young University
    Hunter College
    Indiana University
    San Francisco State University
    University of Hawai'i, Mānoa
    University of Minnesota
    University of Mississippi
    University of North Georgia†
    University of Oregon
    University of Rhode Island
    Western Kentucky University
    Nanjing University, China‡
    Tianjin Normal University, China*

Hindu and Urdu
    University of Texas, Austin
    Jaipur Hindi Center, India§
    Lucknow Urdu Center, India§

Korean
    University of Hawai'i, Mānoa
    Korea University, South Korea§

Persian
    University of Maryland, College Park

Portuguese
    University of Georgia, Athens
    Federal University of São João del Rei, Brazil§

Russian
    Bryn Mawr College
    Portland State University
    University of California, Los Angeles
    University of Wisconsin, Madison
    Al-Farabi Kazakh National University, Kazakhstan*
    St. Petersburg State University, Russia*

Swahili
    Indiana University
    Training Centre for Development Corporation, Tanzania*

Turkish
    Indiana University
    Ankara University, Turkey*

* Overseas Flagship Center managed by American Councils for International
Education
† ROTC Flagship program
‡ Overseas Flagship Center managed jointly by Brigham Young University
and American Councils for International Education
§ Overseas Flagship Center managed by Domestic Program

Note

(1)   The list of Language Flagship programs is current as of the 2015–16 academic year.

Index